Take-Home Leveled Readers

Below-level

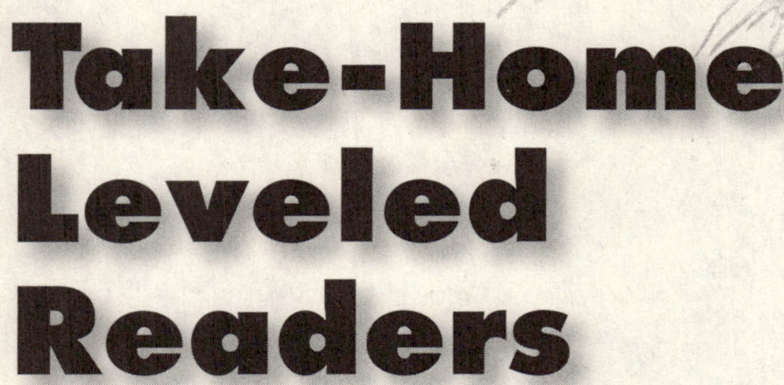

Science

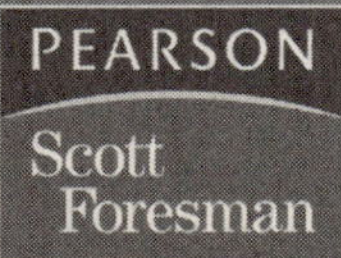

PEARSON
Scott Foresman

Editorial Offices: Glenview, Illinois • Parsippany, New Jersey • New York, New York
Sales Offices: Needham, Massachusetts • Duluth, Georgia • Glenview, Illinois
Coppell, Texas • Sacramento, California • Mesa, Arizona
sfsuccessnet.com

ISBN: 0-328-19733-5

2 3 4 5 6 7 8 9 10 V004 13 12 11 10 09 08 07 06 05

Table of Contents

To the Teacher

Scott Foresman provides three Leveled Readers for every chapter of *Scott Foresman Science*, Grades 1–6: a *Below-Level Leveled Reader*, an *On-Level Leveled Reader*, and an *Advanced Leveled Reader*.

All three readers teach the same science concepts, same vocabulary, address the same target reading skill and contain the same graphic organizer as the corresponding student edition chapter, just at three different reading levels—providing access to important science content for all students. The On-level and Advanced readers also use additional examples to enrich the chapter and extend ideas

This book contains reproducible copies of the Below-Level Leveled Readers for Grade 6. These are designed for you to reproduce and send home with your students as appropriate. Encourage students to share these books with parents or family members in order to practice reading skills and reinforce science content.

Online versions of these and other readers are also available through the Scott Foresman Leveled Reader Database.

Classification

by Erin Rogers

Genre	Comprehension Skill	Text Features	Science Content
Nonfiction	Compare and Contrast	• Captions • Chart • Diagrams • Glossary	Classifying Living Organisms

Scott Foresman Science 6.1

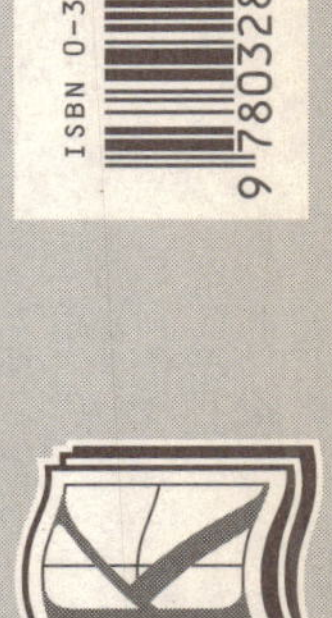

Vocabulary

adaptation

bacteria

biosphere

classification

fungus

nonvascular plant

species

vascular plant

What did you learn?

1. Explain how the adaptations of a cactus help it survive in its environment.

2. When scientists classify organisms into kingdoms, what characteristics do they look for in an organism?

3. What are two characteristics of the members of the chordate phylum?

4. **Writing** in Science Every year, scientists discover about ten thousand new organisms, but they believe that there are millions more that have not yet been discovered. Write to explain why so many living things on Earth are still unknown.

5. **Compare and Contrast** A fern and a tulip are both examples of vascular plants. But they also have differences. Compare and contrast these two plants.

2

Photographs: Every effort has been made to secure permission and provide appropriate credit for photographic material. The publisher deeply regrets any omission and pledges to correct errors called to its attention in subsequent editions. Unless otherwise acknowledged, all photographs are the property of Scott Foresman, a division of Pearson Education. Photo locators denoted as follows: Top (T), Center (C), Bottom (B), Left (L), Right (R), Background (Bkgd).
Title Page: Andreas von Einsiedel/©DK Images; 2 ©1992 John Cancalosi/DRK Photo; 3 (BL) ©David Fleetham/Getty Images, (BL) ©Eric Soder/NHPA Limited, (CC) ©George Bernard/OSF/Animals Animals/Earth Scenes; 4 (TL) ©Gerry Ellis/Minden Pictures, (CL) ©Kennan Ward/Corbis, (BL) ©Jeffrey Rotman/Photo Researchers, Inc.; 5 ©J. Eastcott/Y. Eastcott Film/NGS Image Collection; 6 (CL) Getty Images, (CL) ©George Grall/NGS Image Collection, (CL) Natural History Museum/©DK Images, (BL) Jerry Young/©DK Images, (BL) ©DK Images; 7 (BL) Jerry Young/©DK Images, (BL) ©DK Images; 9 (TL) ©Wolfgang Baumeister/Photo Researchers, Inc., (TL, CL) ©Eye of Science/Photo Researchers, Inc., (CL) ©Andrew Syred/Photo Researchers, Inc., (BL) ©DK Images, (BL) ©Martin Harvey/Peter Arnold, Inc.; 10 Getty Images; 11 ©Clouds Hill Imaging Ltd./Corbis, (B) ©SciMAT/Photo Researchers, Inc.; 12 (BR) ©Chinch Gryniewicz/Ecoscene/Corbis, (CL) ©DK Images; 13 (BL) ©DK Images, (BL) ©Mary Rhodes/Animals Animals/Earth Scenes; 14 (CR, B) ©DK Images; 15 (TL) ©Franklin Viola/Animals Animals/Earth Scenes, (TR) ©Norbert Wu/Minden Pictures, (CL, BL) ©DK Images, (BR) ©Fred Bavendam/Minden Pictures.

ISBN: 0-328-13970-X

Glossary

adaptation — a characteristic that enables an organism to live in a certain environment

bacteria — single-celled organisms that do not have a nucleus

biosphere — the region of Earth that can support life

classification — a grouping of things according to their similarities

fungus — type of many-celled organism that often grows in moist, dark places

nonvascular plant — a type of plant that passes materials directly from cell to cell

species — a group of very similar organisms, which are able to interbreed

vascular plant — a type of plant that has tubes, or vessels, for carrying water and nutrients

Classification

by Erin Rogers

Where on Earth do organisms live?

The Biosphere

Living things can be found almost everywhere. They can live deep in the oceans or high up in Earth's atmosphere. The part of Earth that supports living things is called the **biosphere.** Living things and their environments make up the biosphere. Examples of different environments in the biosphere are deserts, oceans, fields, beaches, backyards, and cities.

Scientists have already discovered and named almost two million different organisms, or living things, in Earth's biosphere. However, there may still be millions of organisms that have not been discovered yet. Each year scientists name about ten thousand new organisms.

The dry, hot desert provides an environment for many living things.

Animal Phyla

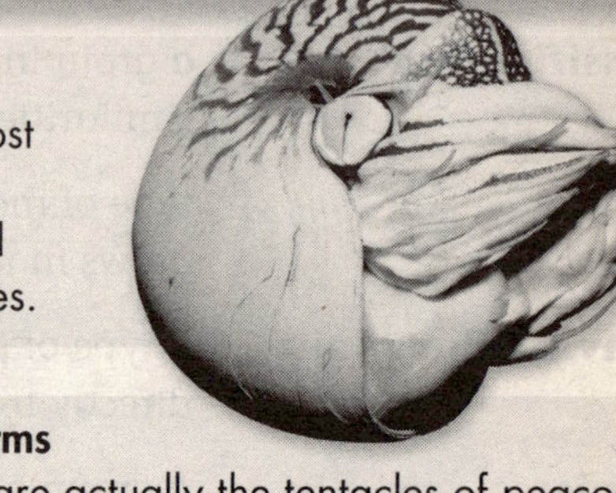

Cnidarians

Though they may look like plants, these inhabitants of the coral reef are animals. Cnidarians have a single body opening surrounded by a ring of stinging cells. Jellyfish and anemones are also in this phylum.

Mollusks

Mollusks have soft bodies, and most have hard shells. Clams, squid, octopuses, snails, and slugs are all mollusks. Mollusks are invertebrates.

Segmented worms

These feathers are actually the tentacles of peacock worms. The tentacles are used to catch food on the ocean floor, where these worms live. Leeches and earthworms are also in this phylum.

Arthropods

This tarantula is not an insect, but it belongs to the same phylum as insects—arthropods. All arthropods have segmented bodies, jointed legs, and hard skeletons on the outside of their bodies. Spiders, crabs, millipedes, and centipedes are all Arthropods.

Echinoderms

This sea star lives in the ocean and has tough, spiny skin. The bodies of echinoderms have five parts. Brittle stars, sea lilies, sea urchins, and sea cucumbers are all echinoderms.

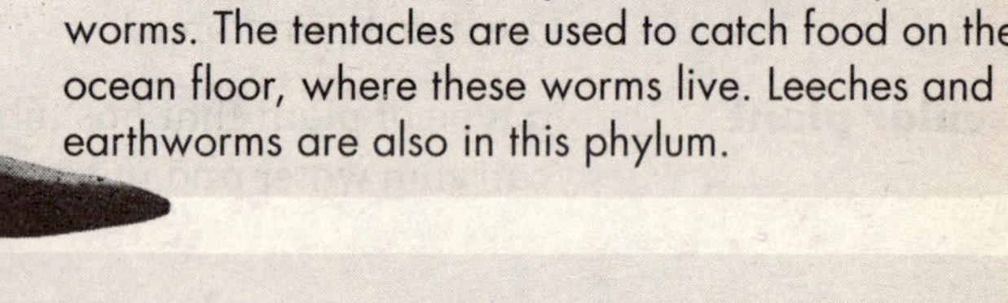

Chordates

This gorilla is a vertebrate, one kind of animal in the chordate phylum. The gorilla is warm-blooded. Its body remains at a constant temperature no matter what the temperature is outside. Other vertebrates, such as reptiles, are cold-blooded.

Animal Classification

You can probably name many different animals. However, the animal kingdom is much more diverse than you might think. The animal kingdom is divided into about 35 phyla.

Although animals can be very different from one another, they all share certain characteristics. All animals are multicellular organisms. All animals get their food by eating other organisms. All animals have cells that contain a nucleus. Unlike plant cells, the cells of animals do not contain a cell wall.

Invertebrates are animals that do not have a backbone. They make up about 95 percent of all animal species on Earth. Some invertebrates are tiny, such as the microscopic mites that cover animals' bodies. Other invertebrates can be large, such as the giant squid, which can grow to 20 meters long.

Vertebrates are animals with backbones. Fish, amphibians, reptiles, birds, and mammals are all vertebrates. All vertebrates are a part of one phylum, called chordates.

Why are there still so many living things that have not been discovered? One reason is that there are parts of Earth that are hard for scientists to study. There is still a lot to learn about Earth's deep oceans, polar areas, dense rain forests, and vast deserts. Many organisms are also very tiny and hard to find.

Each organism in the biosphere interacts with other organisms and the environment. This produces a web of interactions. All parts of the web are connected. This web is constantly changing. A small change in one part of the web can cause a large change in another part of the web. Humans play an important part in this web.

Dandelions poke through this sidewalk. Your neighborhood is part of the biosphere.

These colorful fungi grow on the damp forest floor.

This blackside hawkfish sits still among the coral. The fish and the coral are both living organisms.

Variety Among Living Things

How many living things can you name? There is an amazing variety of living things on Earth. The organisms found on Earth have many different body plans and structures. Because of these differences, organisms can live in almost every place on Earth.

All living things share some common features. They are all made of cells. They all require a source of energy. They all reproduce. However, they are different in some very important ways too.

Living things have characteristics that help them survive and reproduce in their environments. These characteristics are called **adaptations.** For example, a cactus has many adaptations that help it to survive in a dry desert

This cactus can survive in the desert with very little water.

Snails live in water and on land.

This parrot fish has a mouth designed to scrape algae off the surrounding coral.

Plants can be either vascular or nonvascular. A **vascular plant** has cells that form tubes, or vessels, to carry water and nutrients throughout the plant. They can carry materials long distances, even to the top of a redwood tree. There are at least 260,000 species of vascular plants.

Some vascular plants make seeds and some do not. Examples of plants that do not make seeds are horsetails and ferns. Tulips, grasses, maple trees, and tomato plants are all examples of seed-making plants. There are two types of plants that make seeds. Gymnosperms are seed plants that do not produce flowers. Some examples of gymnosperm plants are evergreens, such as pine or fir trees. Angiosperms are seed plants that produce flowers.

A **nonvascular plant** does not carry its materials through tubes. These plants get their nutrients by slowly passing them from one cell to another. For this reason, most nonvascular plants are small. Scientists have found about eighteen thousand species of nonvascular plants.

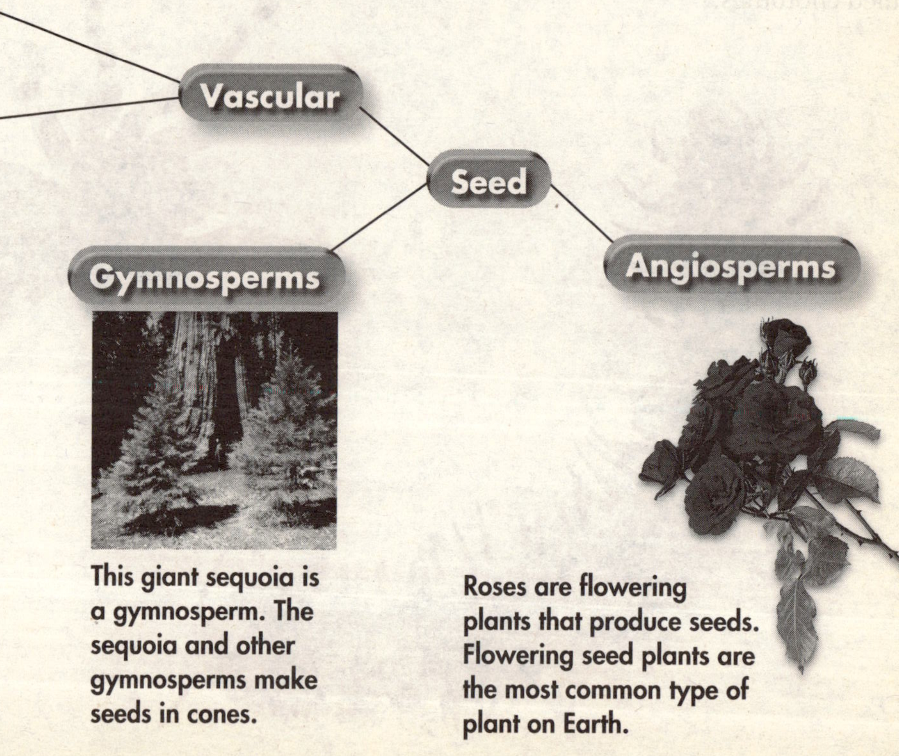

This giant sequoia is a gymnosperm. The sequoia and other gymnosperms make seeds in cones.

Roses are flowering plants that produce seeds. Flowering seed plants are the most common type of plant on Earth.

How are plants and animals classified?

Plant Classification

There is a wide variety of plants within the plant kingdom. Plants come in many different colors, sizes, and shapes. Some plants are very large, such as the coast redwoods in California. These trees can be up to 112 meters tall! Other plants are tiny. The duckweed that covers many ponds is only 0.6 millimeters tall. No matter what their size, plants are extremely important to every living thing on Earth. Most living things depend on plants for energy. Plants also help make the climate on Earth stable.

environment. The spines of the cactus are actually leaves. Their shape helps keep water from leaving the plant. The spines also protect the cactus from being eaten.

There is clearly great variety among organisms. Yet, some groups of organisms share many of the same characteristics. These organisms may be members of the same **species.** A species is a group of very similar organisms. To be in the same species, the organisms must be able to mate with one another and produce offspring that are also able to produce offspring.

Even if organisms are part of the same species, they can look very different from one another. They can be different sizes, colors, and shapes. But because they are the same species, they have similar body plans and structures, such as the horses you see here.

There are many different species within each group of organisms. Scientists believe that 99 percent of all species that have ever lived on Earth no longer exist.

Nonvascular plants, such as this moss, live in damp places where water is plentiful.

Horsetails are plants that do not produce seeds. They used to be very common, but today only thirty-five species can be found.

What characteristics do these horses share?

How do scientists group organisms?

How Organisms Are Grouped

How do scientists study so many different kinds of organisms? Have you noticed how a music store organizes the CDs it sells? You can find your favorite singer's music because the store groups the CDs by the artists' names or by the type of music they perform. A CD is usually placed in a group with other CDs that are similar to it. This is how scientists group Earth's many organisms. Organisms with similar characteristics are grouped together. The grouping of things according to their similarities is called **classification.**

Fungi are different from plants. Although many fungi look like plants and have cells that are similar to plants, they are actually quite different. Plant cells have a substance called chlorophyll. Chlorophyll helps plants make their own food. Fungi do not have chlorophyll. Instead, fungi take in nutrients from other organisms.

A fourth kingdom is called the protist kingdom. Most protists are tiny, single-celled organisms. Protists are different from bacteria because their cells have a nucleus, and bacteria do not. There are more than 200,000 species of protists.

Some protists are like animals. They get energy by eating other organisms. An example of this type of organism is the amoeba. Other protists are more like plants. These protists contain chlorophyll. They make their own food through the process of photosynthesis. An example of a plantlike protist is algae. Other protists are more like fungi. These protists grow in damp environments with a lot of nutrients. They absorb food through their cell membranes.

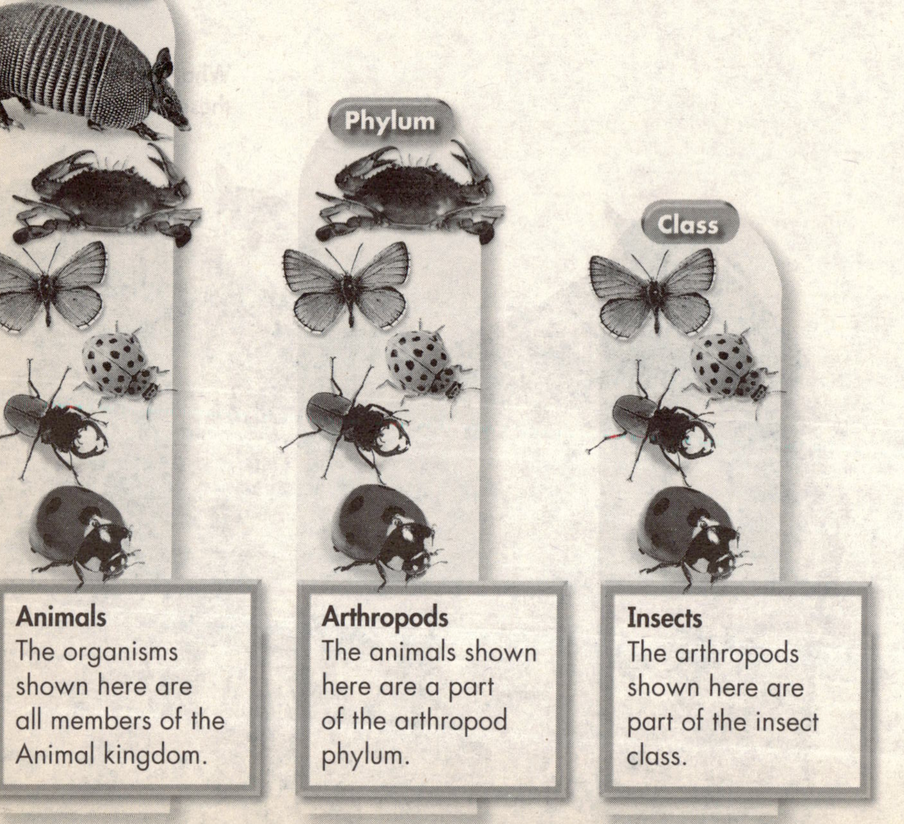

Animals
The organisms shown here are all members of the Animal kingdom.

Arthropods
The animals shown here are a part of the arthropod phylum.

Insects
The arthropods shown here are part of the insect class.

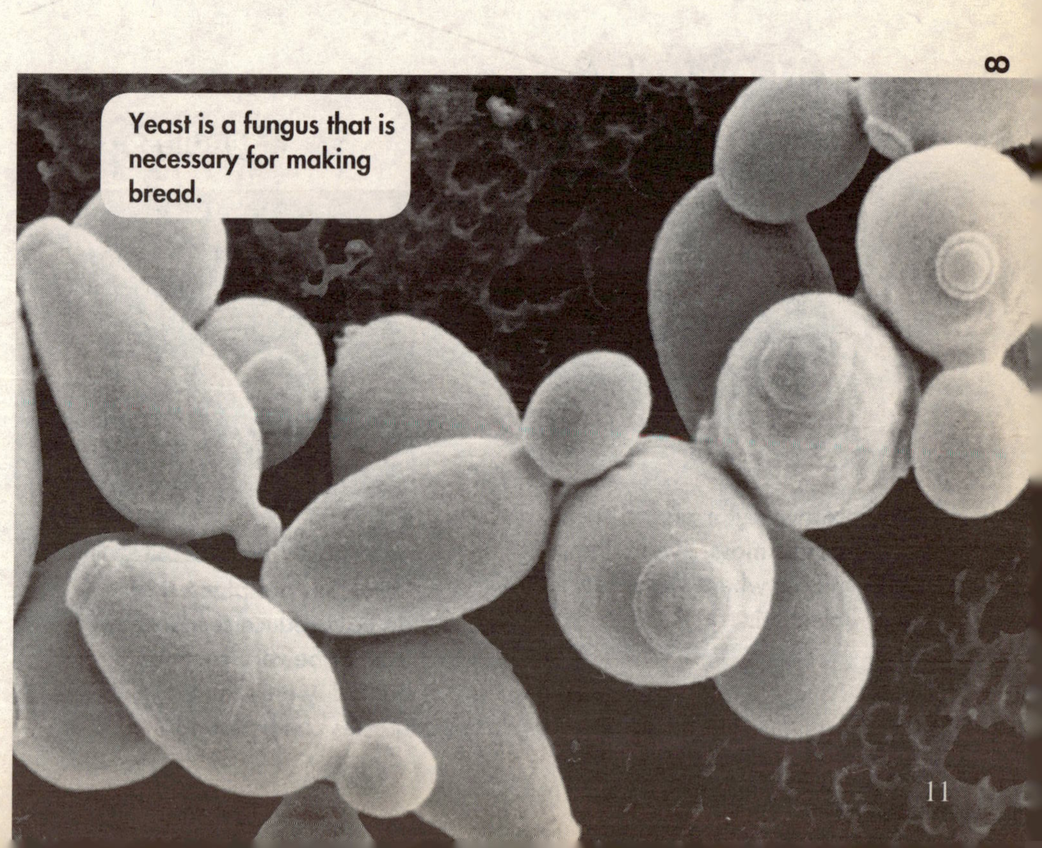

Yeast is a fungus that is necessary for making bread.

A third kingdom is called fungi. A **fungus** is an organism with more than one cell that grows in moist, dark places. They grow on top of other organisms. As the fungi grow, they give off chemicals that break down these organisms. They get the nutrients they need from this process.

Some different types of fungi are mushrooms, molds, and yeast. In mushrooms and molds, cells are connected by a system of strands called hyphae. Hyphae can form thick, large mats. For example, a single mushroom in Oregon has a web of underground hyphae that spreads across twenty-two hundred acres. That is the same size as 1,665 football fields! The hyphae take in the nutrients that the fungi need to grow. Yeast cells are different than mushrooms and molds. They are not connected by hyphae.

In the past, scientists used different systems of classification. Even today, more than one system is being used. However, most scientists use a system similar to the one that a man named Carolus Linnaeus developed in the 1700s.

Linnaeus divided all organisms into two large groups or kingdoms. One group was the plant kingdom and the other group was the animal kingdom. Then he divided these kingdoms into smaller groups based on the features of the organisms. Today most scientists use a classification system that divides all living things on Earth into six kingdoms instead of two. These kingdoms are then divided into smaller and smaller groups.

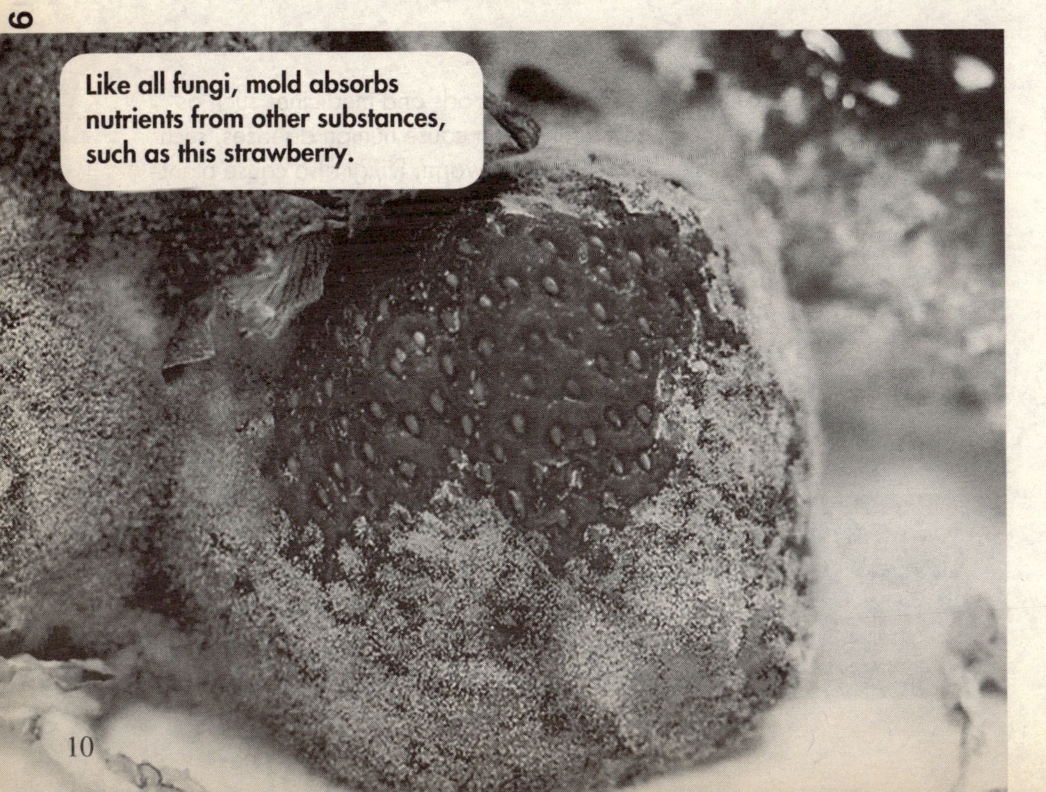

Like all fungi, mold absorbs nutrients from other substances, such as this strawberry.

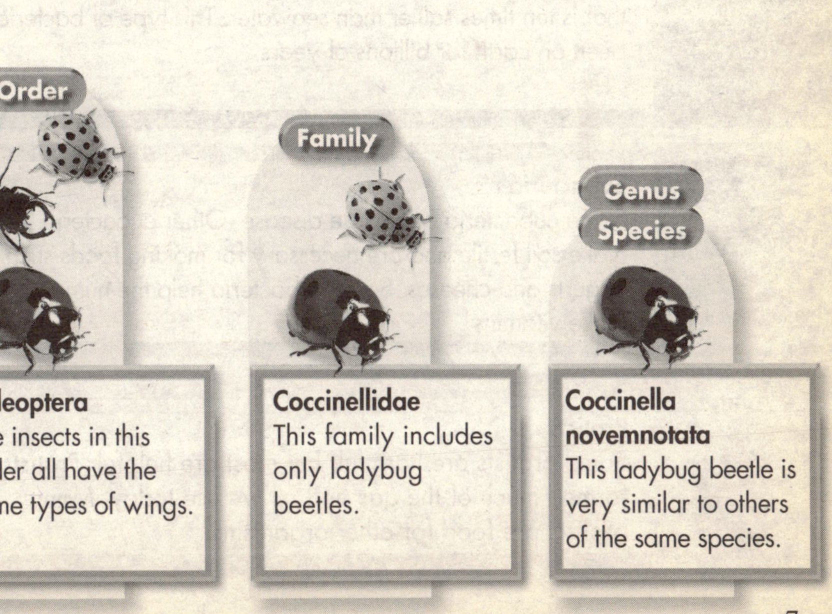

The Six Kingdoms

Linnaeus did not have the scientific tools that scientists use today. He did not have powerful microscopes that magnify the cells of an organism. With more advanced scientific tools, Linnaeus might have found that some organisms do not fit into either the plant kingdom or the animal kingdom. For example, **bacteria** are single-celled organisms that do not have a nucleus. Both plant and animal cells have a nucleus. This difference was an extremely important discovery. Many scientists believed that bacteria should be grouped separately from plants and animals. Today, most scientists group organisms based on their cell structure, how they get food, and how they reproduce.

Many scientists today group all organisms into six different kingdoms. One kingdom is called archaebacteria. This kingdom includes bacteria that live where there is no oxygen, in very salty water, or in very hot water. Most other types of organisms cannot survive in these environments.

Another kingdom, called eubacteria, is made up of all other bacteria. These bacteria are found in almost every environment. They even live in your body! There are as many bacteria in your mouth as there are people on Earth!

Archaebacteria
Archaebacteria live in water that is extremely hot or in water that is ten times saltier than seawater. This type of bacteria has been on Earth for billions of years.

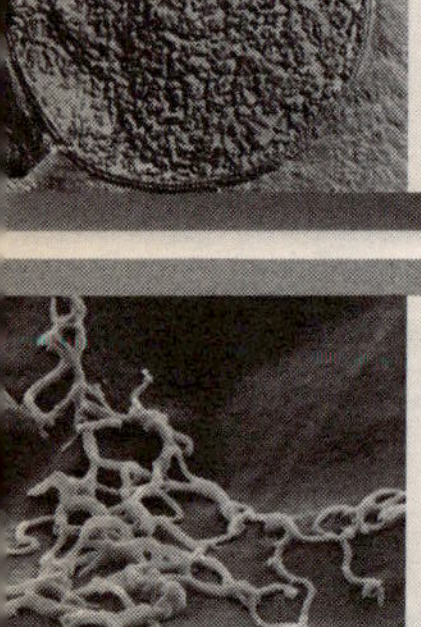

Eubacteria
Some eubacteria can cause disease. Other eubacteria help make soil fertile and are necessary for making foods such as yogurts and cheeses. Some eubacteria help the human body make vitamins.

Protists
Some protists are harmful, but most are helpful. Protists formed much of the gas and oil we use today. Many protists are food for other organisms.

Fungi
Fungi are used to make foods and medicines such as penicillin. Some fungi can cause human diseases, such as athlete's foot and ringworm. Fungi also cause plant diseases called rusts.

Plants
Plants are necessary for life on Earth. Like all plants, these trout lilies have roots, stems, and leaves. Plants trap the Sun's energy to produce sugars.

Animals
Animals get energy by eating other organisms. This topi lives in Africa. It has special adaptations that make it able to find and eat the type of food it needs.

Cells

by Marcia K. Miller

Genre	Comprehension Skill	Text Features	Science Content
Nonfiction	Make Inferences	• Captions • Charts • Diagrams • Glossary	Cells

Scott Foresman Science 6.2

PEARSON
Scott Foresman

DK

scottforesman.com

ISBN 0-328-13973-4

9 780328 139736

90000

Vocabulary

chromosome

diffusion

DNA

endoplasmic reticulum

mitochondria

mitosis

organelle

osmosis

ribosome

What did you learn?

1. How did microscopes lead to the discovery of cells?

2. What are the three parts of cell theory?

3. Why must a cell copy its DNA before it divides?

4. **Writing** in Science A new cell forms. The cell grows, but it does not divide. Write what you think will happen to this cell and why. Include details from the book to support your answer.

5. **Make Inferences** A single brain cell contains thousands of mitochondria. What can you infer from this about the brain's need for energy?

Illustration: Title Page: Robert Ulrich; 6-7, 9-10, 12 Robert Ulrich; 11 Bob Kayganich
Photographs: Every effort has been made to secure permission and provide appropriate credit for photographic material. The publisher deeply regrets any omission and pledges to correct errors called to its attention in subsequent editions. Unless otherwise acknowledged, all photographs are the property of Scott Foresman, a division of Pearson Education. Photo locators denoted as follows: Top (T), Center (C), Bottom (B), Left (L), Right (R), Background (Bkgd).
2 ©Dr. David Patterson/Photo Researchers, Inc.; 3 (L) ©Janet Foster/Masterfile Corporation, (CC) Hilda Canter-Lund/Freshwater Biological Association, (BC) ©Eric Grave/Science Photo Library/Photo Researchers, Inc.; 4 ©Dr. Jeremy Burgess/Photo Researchers, Inc.; 5 (TL) Science & Society Picture Library, (TR) Science Museum, London/DK Images, (CL) ©Bettmann/Corbis, (CR) ©DK Images, (BL) ©Oliver Meckes/Photo Researchers, Inc., (BR) Photo Researchers, Inc.; 8 ©Michael Mahovlich/Masterfile Corporation; 14 ©Bettmann/Corbis

ISBN: 0-328-13973-4

Cells

by Marcia K. Miller

Glossary

chromosome a part of a cell that carries the instructions for building all of the cell's proteins

diffusion the movement of a substance from an area of higher concentration to an area of lower concentration

DNA a material that stores information about how an organism will grow and develop

endoplasmic reticulum a set of folded membranes that work as a cell's transport system

mitochondria organelles that turn the chemical energy of food into a form a cell can use

mitosis the process in which the nucleus of a cell divides

organelle a structure that performs specific functions in a cell

osmosis the diffusion of water across a cell membrane

ribosome the organelle that starts the process of making proteins

13

What is a cell?

Jobs of Cells

The organisms shown here live in pond water. Like all living things, they are made of cells. A cell is the smallest unit that can sustain life.

Each of these organisms has just one cell. It might surprise you how different each one can look. Yet all single-celled organisms must perform the same basic tasks to stay alive. They must get energy, remove wastes, grow, and reproduce. These are the same things that all living organisms must do to stay alive.

You need to use a microscope to see most single-celled organisms. Single-celled organisms are tiny, but their many parts do many jobs. Each part in a cell does a different job. For example, green algae get energy from sunlight. They use this energy to make food. The paramecium has hair-like structures that help it swim. In any one-celled organism, each part of its single cell performs a task.

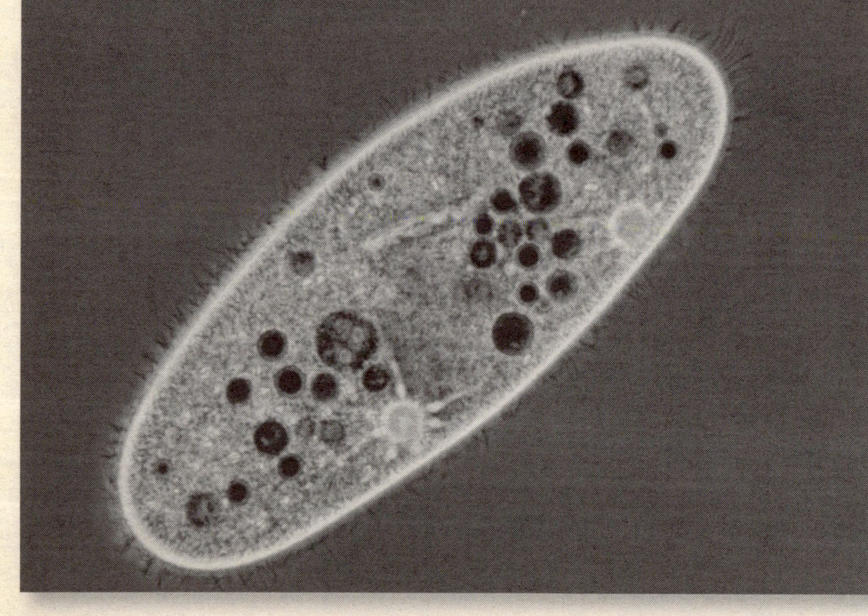

paramecium

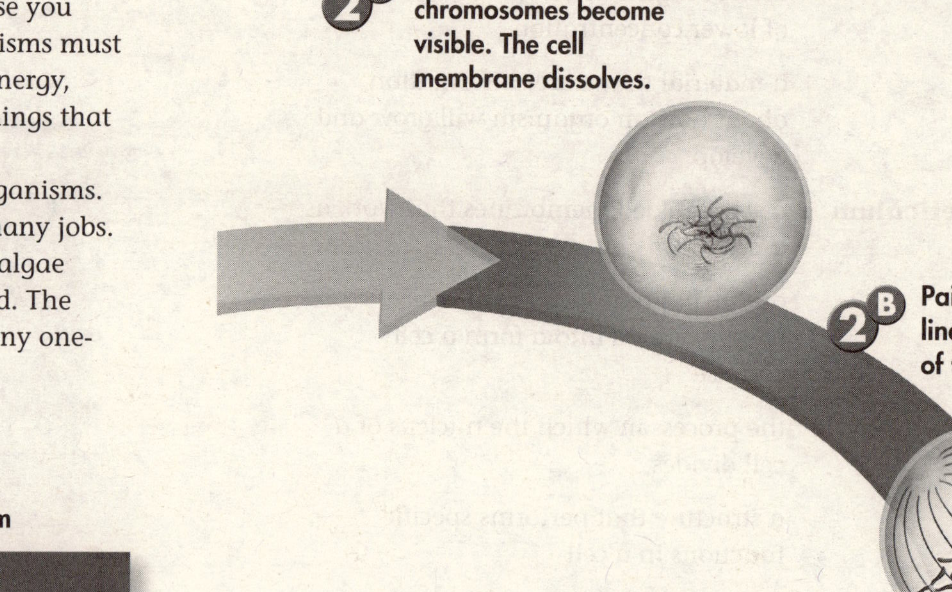

Mitosis

Every species has a fixed number of chromosomes. These chromosomes are in pairs inside the cell. They have the operating instructions for the cell. A healthy cell needs a full set of chromosomes to function correctly. Mitosis gives each new cell the right number of chromosomes. Though usually described in stages, mitosis is an ongoing process. The cell cytoplasm divides when mitosis has completed its stages.

All living things, big or small, are made of cells. Larger organisms have many cells; they are multicellular. In large organisms, different cells have adaptations to do different tasks. Think about your own body. Your muscle cells are specialized for movement. Your skin cells are specialized for protection. These specialized cells allow your body to work efficiently.

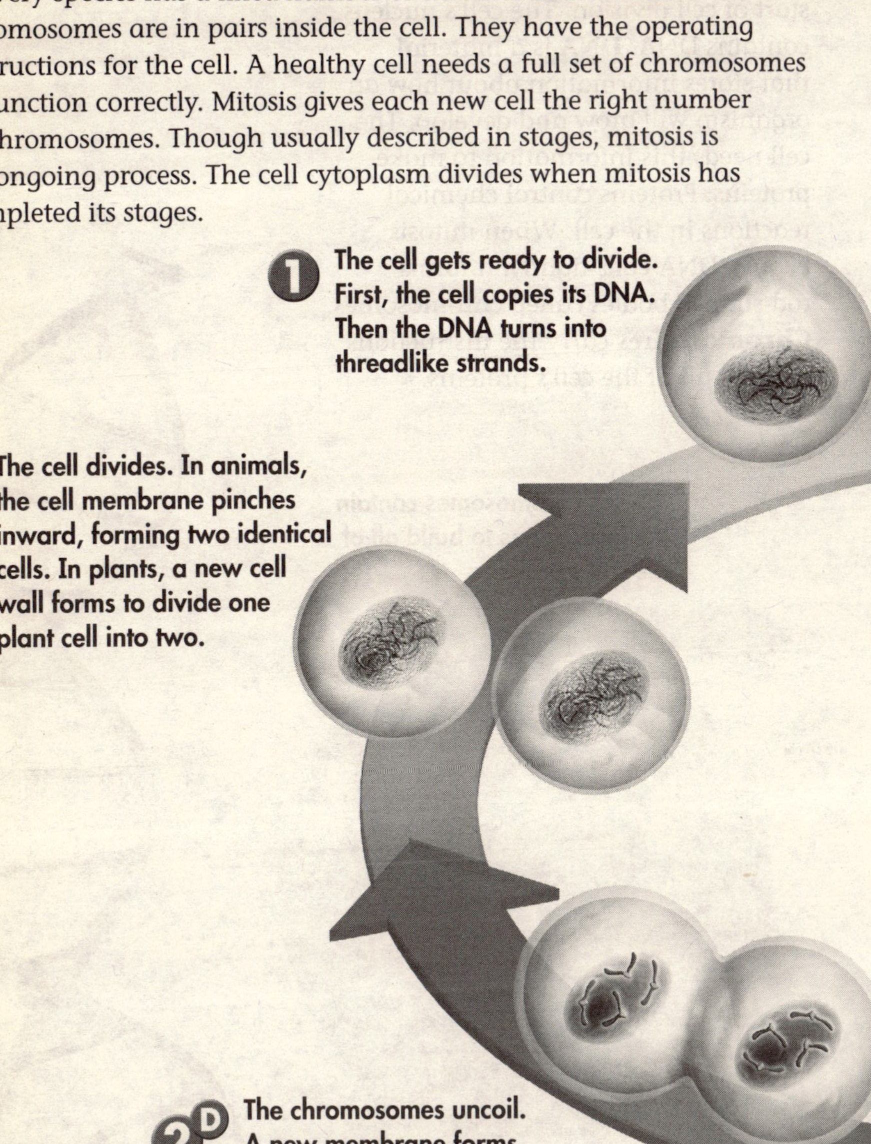

The Cell Theory

Cells were not discovered until the microscope was invented. Before then, nobody knew that cells existed because nobody could see them.

Robert Hooke was the first person to describe cells. Hooke was born in England in 1635. He made a microscope by putting lenses in a tube. He used it to look at thin layers of cork. Cork, the bark of a cork tree, is made of dead cells. Hooke thought that cork cells looked like tiny rooms. He was the first person to call such structures "cells."

Around that time, the Dutch scientist Anton van Leeuwenhoek was making microscopes too. He used them to look at single-celled organisms in pond water. His microscopes were not very powerful, but they could show blood and bacteria cells.

Over time, scientists learned more about cells. They put forth new ideas. In 1838 the German scientist Matthias Schleiden said that all plants are made of cells. The next year, another German scientist named Theodor Schwann said that all animals are made of cells. Soon scientists concluded that all living things are made of cells. In 1855 Rudolf Virchow stated that new cells could come only from existing cells. These important conclusions are the basis of cell theory.

Cell Theory
- All living things are made of one or more cells.
- Cells are the basic units of living things.
- All cells come from existing cells.

Mitosis is the process in which the nucleus of a cell divides. This is the start of cell division. The cell's nucleus contains DNA. **DNA** is a material that stores information about how an organism will grow and develop. The cell needs this information to make proteins. Proteins control chemical reactions in the cell. When mitosis begins, DNA coils tightly. It forms rod-shaped bodies called chromosomes. **Chromosomes** carry the instructions to build all of the cell's proteins.

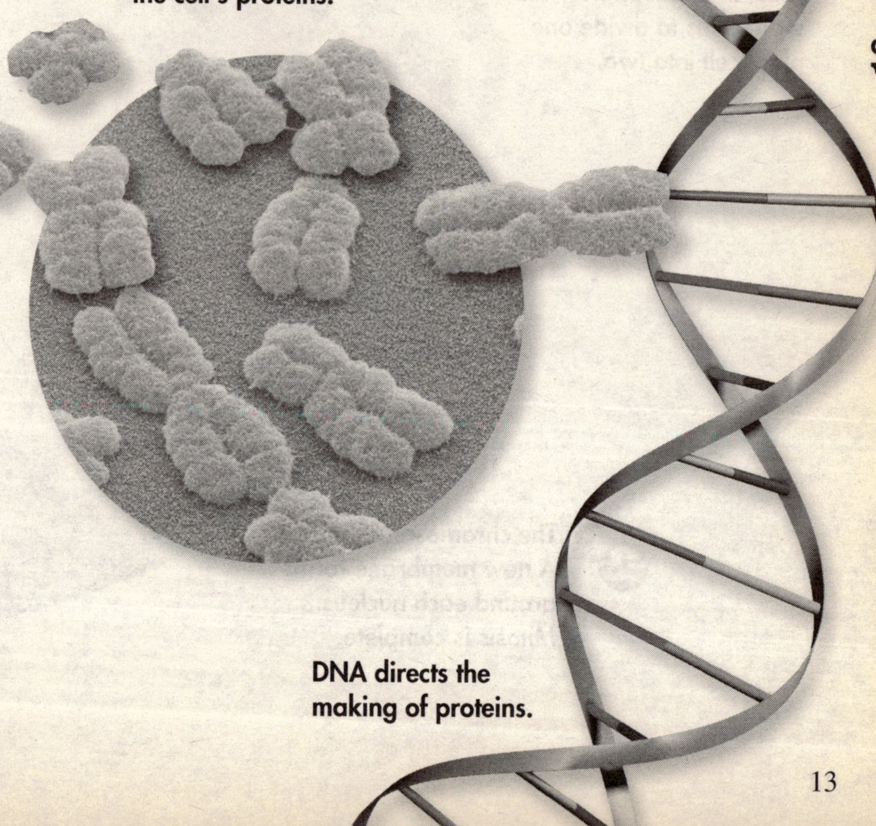

A cell's chromosomes contain the instructions to build all of the cell's proteins.

DNA directs the making of proteins.

Cell Division

Cells can only get so large. But if cells must stay small how can organisms grow? When single-celled organisms get too large, they divide into two new cells. Multicellular organisms grow by making more cells. They do this by dividing cells they already have. Each new cell will be a copy of the old cell. As new cells form, the organism gets bigger. Cell division also makes new cells to replace old cells that get damaged or worn out.

Chromosomes are rod-shaped structures that contain DNA.

Learning About Cells

1655 Robert Hooke discovers cells.

1683 Anton von Leeuwenhoek uses microscopes to look at single-celled organisms.

1828 Robert Brown discovers the cell nucleus.

1838 Matthias Schleiden and Theodor Schwann propose the cell theory.

1855 Rudolf Virchow states that cells can come only from other living cells.

1865 Julius von Sachs shows that chlorophyll is located in chloroplasts.

1875 Microscopes similar to those used today are in common use.

1931 Ernst Ruska and Max Knoll invent the electron microscope.

1953 George E. Palade describes ribosomes.

What are the functions of organelles?

Parts of a Cell

All cells must perform key functions to stay alive. For example, a cell must take in, store, and release energy. It must also make proteins, release wastes, and recycle materials. A cell must control what comes in and goes out of it. These jobs are done by organelles. **Organelles** are structures that perform different functions within the cell.

Animal Cell

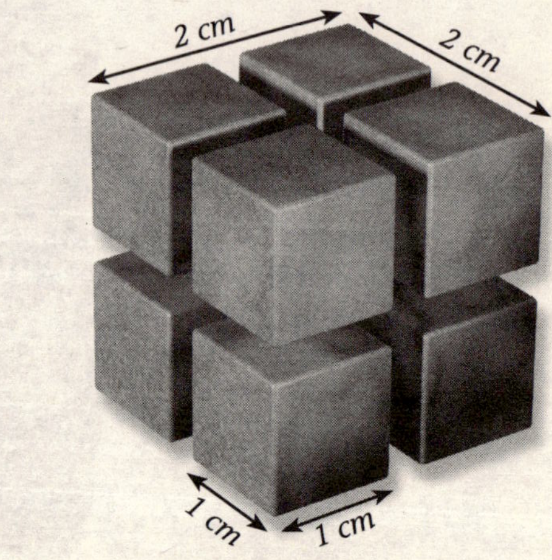

Surface Area

A cell needs more food as it grows. It also produces more wastes. The cell membrane and the organelles also become larger. But the surface area, or the area of the cell membrane, does not grow as fast as the volume of the materials inside the cell. Soon there is not enough cell membrane to let enough materials in and out of the cell.

Look at the this diagram. The eight small cells have the same amount of material inside as the large cell does. Can you tell which has more surface area?

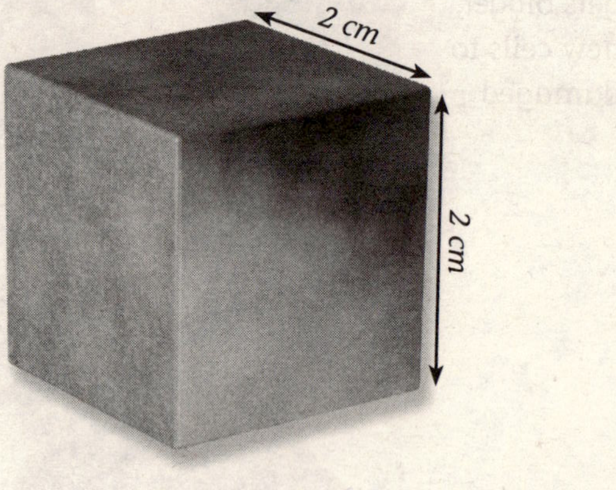

How do cells grow and divide?

Cell Size and Growth

Different types of cells have different shapes, but when it comes to size, all cells are very small.

In order to meet their needs, cells must be small. To live, a cell must take in oxygen, absorb food, and release waste. All the materials it needs must move through the cell membrane to all other parts of the cell. In a larger cell, the trip from the cell membrane to other cell parts would take longer. A bit of sugar would have to travel farther in a large cell. Waste would have to travel farther to exit a large cell. If a cell grew too big, materials couldn't reach all its parts fast enough to keep the cell alive.

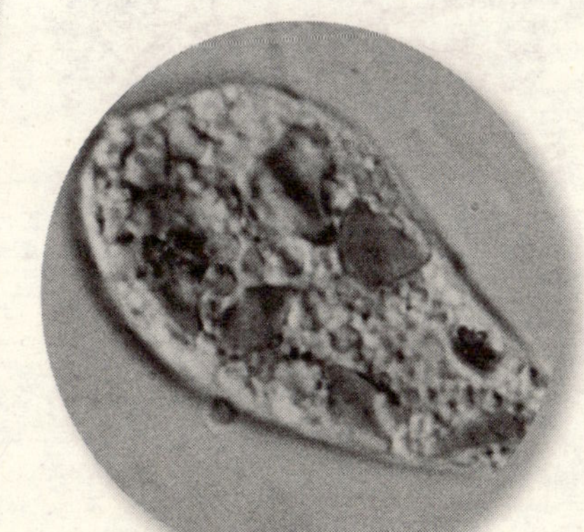

average animal cell

All cells are small, but they can have different shapes.

euglena

Different kinds of cells have different roles in multicellular organisms. Cells that perform different functions may have different organelles. Or they may have a different number of organelles. For example, your muscle cells have thousands of mitochondria. This is because muscle cells need a lot of energy to do their work. Skin cells have fewer mitochondria.

Plant and animal cells are different in some ways. Plant cells contain chloroplasts. These organelles contain chlorophyll, the chemical that makes photosynthesis possible. Most plant cells have one large vacuole, but animal cells have many smaller vacuoles. Also, plant cells have a special structure called a cell wall, which animal cells do not have.

Plant Cell

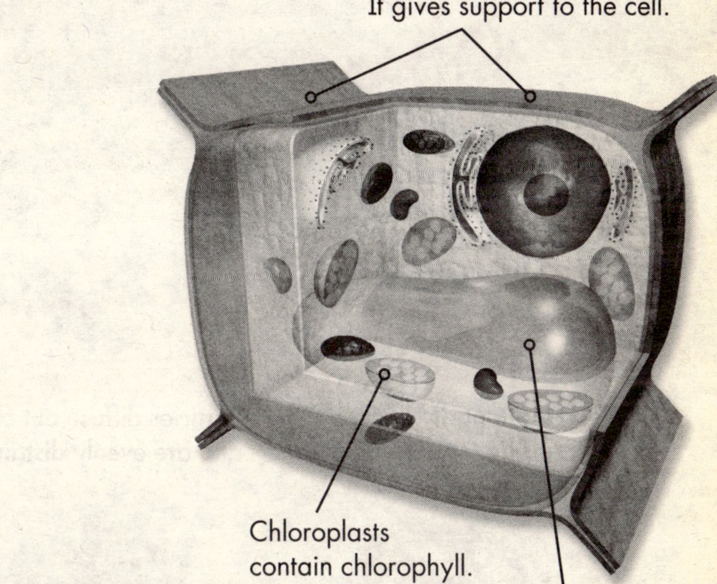

Diffusion

A cell is mostly water. No matter how many organelles it has, about two-thirds of a cell's mass is water. Substances such as nutrients or salts are dissolved in the water. How do those materials get there?

Diffusion is the movement of a substance from an area of higher concentration to an area of lower concentration. Some substances can enter and leave a cell through this process. The diagram below shows what happens during diffusion.

Diffusion takes place because the particles in matter are always moving. Over time, the particles will spread out until they evenly fill an area. Think about putting a sugar cube into a glass of iced tea. Even if you don't stir it, tiny bits of sugar slowly move away from the ones in the cube. Over time, all the sugar particles will diffuse, or spread, throughout the tea.

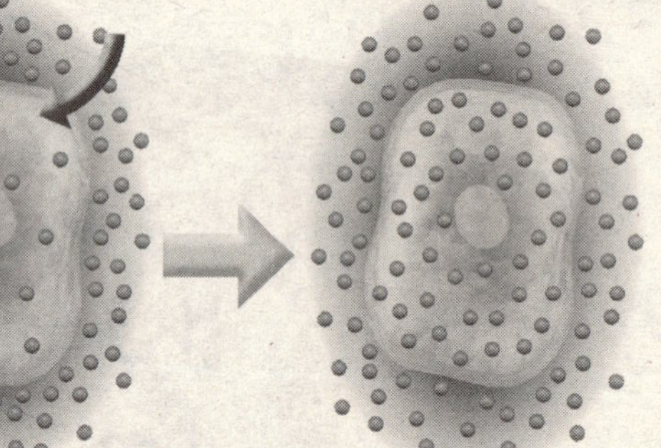

More particles are outside the cell.

Particles diffuse into the cell. Soon they are evenly distributed.

More particles are inside the cell.

Particles diffuse out of the cell and are evenly distributed.

Cells need many substances. They can get many substances through diffusion. Small particles can pass into a cell through the cell wall. For example, the water outside a cell has more oxygen particles than the water inside the cell. The cell needs oxygen. Oxygen particles move from the outside of the cell to the inside of the cell. They move from an area where there are more particles to an area where there are fewer particles.

Diffusion of Water

Cells cannot function without water, so water must move through the cell membrane. **Osmosis** is the diffusion of water across the cell membrane.

A plant will wilt if its cells do not have enough water. The cytoplasm pulls away from the cell wall. Then the cell wall is unable to support the plant. A cell with too much water can burst. The cell membrane helps keep the materials inside the cell balanced.

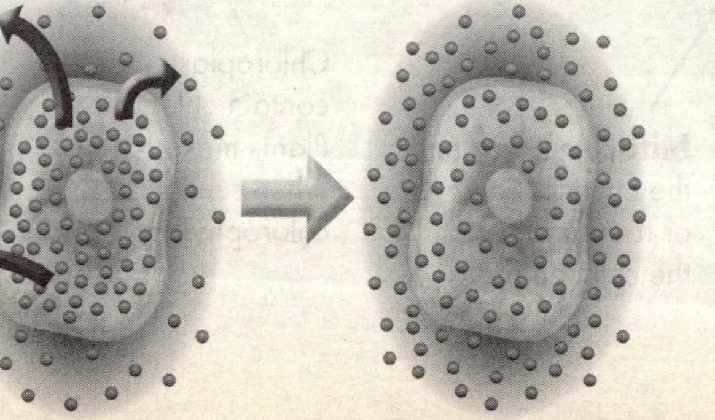

normal plant cells

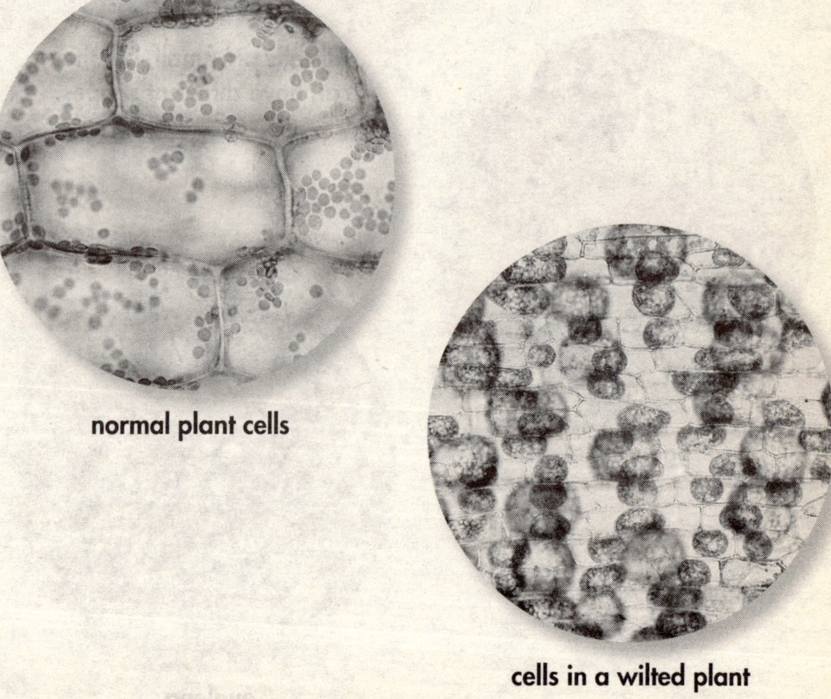

cells in a wilted plant

Reproduction

by Mary McLean-Hely

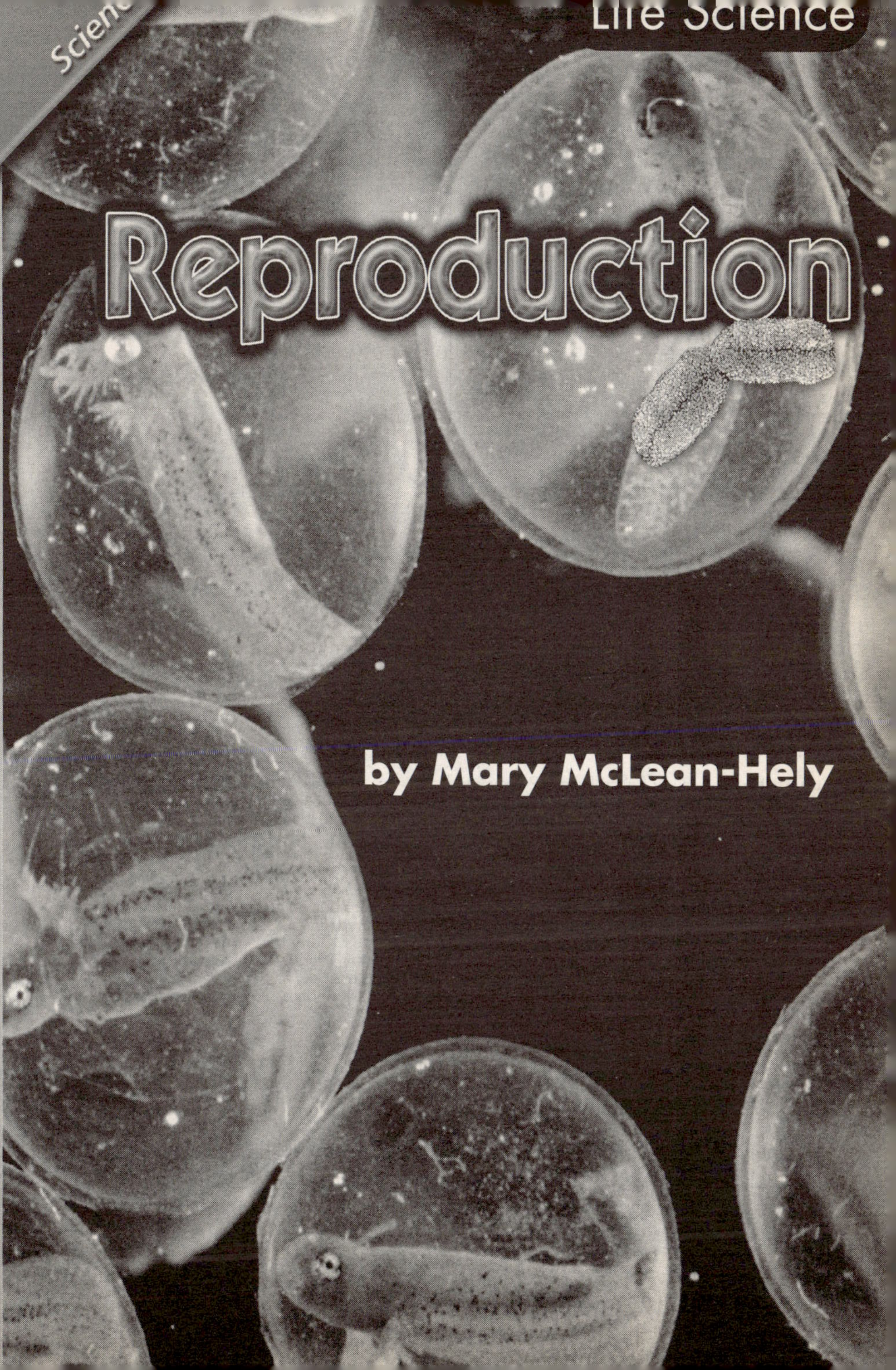

Genre	Comprehension Skill	Text Features	Science Content
Nonfiction	Sequence	• Captions • Charts • Diagrams • Glossary	Reproduction

Scott Foresman Science 6.3

PEARSON
Scott Foresman

scottforesman.com

Vocabulary

asexual reproduction

egg cells

fertilization

gene

heredity

meiosis

selective breeding

sexual reproduction

sperm cells

What did you learn?

1. What is asexual reproduction, and what are three forms of asexual reproduction?

2. How can a guinea pig with smooth fur and a pair of smooth coat genes give birth to a baby with a rough coat?

3. What happens during selective breeding?

4. **Writing** in Science   Suppose two Erminette chickens mate. Write to explain the possible feather color combinations. Use details from the book to support your answer.

5. **Sequence** Describe the process of fertilization in a flower.

Illustrations: 6, 8, 12 Robert Fenn; 19 Tony Randazzo
Photographs: Every effort has been made to secure permission and provide appropriate credit for photographic material. The publisher deeply regrets any omission and pledges to correct errors called to its attention in subsequent editions. Unless otherwise acknowledged, all photographs are the property of Scott Foresman, a division of Pearson Education. Photo locators denoted as follows: Top (T), Center (C), Bottom (B), Left (L), Right (R), Background (Bkgd).
Title Page: ©Carolina Biological Supply Company/Phototake; 2 ©Gabriel Jecan/Getty Images; 4 ©CNRI/Photo Researchers, Inc., ©Carolina Biological Supply Company/Phototake; 5 ©Andrew J. Martinez/Photo Researchers, Inc., ©DK Images; 6 ©Andrew Syred/Photo Researchers, Inc.; 7 ©Gerry Ellis/Minden Pictures, Jerry Young/©DK Images, ©DK Images; 8 ©Gerry Ellis/Minden Pictures; 9 ©James King-Holmes/Photo Researchers, Inc.; 10 ©Frans Lanting/Minden Pictures; 13 ©Fred Bavendam/Minden Pictures; 14 ©M.I. Walker/Photo Researchers, Inc., ©American Images Inc./Getty Images; 18 ©J.C. Carton/Bruce Coleman Inc.; 19 ©ThinkStock/SuperStock; 20 ©DK Images; 22 Tracy Morgan/©DK Images

ISBN: 0-328-13976-9

Glossary

asexual reproduction	when offspring come from one parent
egg cell	female sex cell
fertilization	when male and female sex cells join to form a new cell
gene	a section of DNA that controls what substances the cell makes when it makes them, determining traits of a living thing
heredity	the passing of traits from parents to offspring
meiosis	the process in which sex cells form when one cell divides into four
selective breeding	the process of selecting a few organisms with desired traits to serve as parents of offspring
sexual reproduction	when offspring come from two parents
sperm cell	male sex cell

23

Reproduction

by Mary McLean-Hely

What is asexual reproduction?

Heredity

The baby baboon below has inherited traits from both its parents. It looks like its parents because of these shared traits. It might grow to be slightly different color or size than its parents, but it will have the same basic form. The passing of traits from parents to offspring is called **heredity.**

Heredity is not just for baboons. All living things, from tigers to bacteria, inherit traits.

The Shetland sheepdog was developed in the Shetland Islands to help herd sheep. The winters there are long, and few plants grow. The farmers of the area developed the Shetland sheepdog to herd sheep and to keep the gardens safe from the flocks.

People also breed dogs that are smarter, healthier, stronger, and friendlier. Dogs come in many shapes and sizes. You can see two kinds here.

History shows that dogs and people have been friends for a very long time. In some ancient cave paintings, dogs are pictured.

But dogs have changed a lot since ancient times. Today there are almost 400 dog breeds. Most of them have been developed through selective breeding. And most breeds were developed after 1850! New breeds were selected because of a dog's special traits, which made them useful for hunting, herding, protection, or looks.

The environment also affects how living things grow. A tree may inherit the traits needed to grow 12 meters tall. But if the environment does not give the tree the sunlight, water, and soil it needs, it will not reach those heights.

Living things can also learn traits. If you inherit traits for athletic ability, you have the potential to be good at basketball. But you still have to practice to learn to play the game. Learned traits are not passed on through heredity.

Writings and sculptures of the Afghan hound date back to 3500 B.C. The Afghans of the deserts of Egypt were bred to hunt gazelle, deer, and leopards. In the mountains of Afghanistan, the Afghan hound was used to guard sheep and cattle. It was also a hunter of small game.

The colors of these snapdragons are traits inherited from the parent plants.

Asexual Reproduction

All living things die at some point. For that reason, traits are passed on from parent to offspring to help a species live on. The same traits that helped the parent live will also help its offspring.

The living things shown here can reproduce asexually. In **asexual reproduction,** offspring come from one parent, not two. Asexual reproduction takes place by mitosis, the process by which a cell's nucleus copies and divides. The new offspring have exactly the same DNA as the parent.

A bacterium divides into two cells in asexual reproduction. Each one of the two cells is identical to the parent cell. This fast form of reproduction is called fission. Some bacteria can make two new cells in 20 minutes. After 40 minutes, there are four cells. There are eight cells in one hour. In eight hours, one cell will have multiplied to almost 17 million new bacteria! Most of the time conditions change, and the bacteria cannot keep reproducing at this rate.

Another form of asexual reproduction is budding. Yeasts, some plants, and certain animals can reproduce asexually this way.

During budding, a cell in the parent's body makes a small version of the parent. The bud breaks away from the parent to become a new individual. The buds have the same DNA as the parent plant.

The cow you see is a result of selective breeding. Cows have not always made as much milk as they do today. Some people wanted to get more milk from cows, and others wanted to get milk rich in fat. Cows with these traits have been bred through selective breeding and better nutrition.

There are many other uses for selective breeding. It helps make crops that produce more food per plant. Fruits and vegetables are bred to resist disease, pests, and drought. People breed chickens that lay more eggs.

Some bacteria cells split into two cells every 20 minutes.

The hydra is a tiny animal that reproduces by budding.

What traits of this cow do you think were produced by selective breeding?

Choosing Traits

Corn has been around for a very long time. Take a look at the picture. It might surprise you to find out that the corn we eat is very different from wild corn that grew long ago.

In what is now Mexico, about eight thousand to ten thousand years ago, people began to change a grasslike plant they ate. They chose and planted seeds from the plants with traits they liked. Then they grew more plants with the traits they wanted. When those plants grew, they took seeds from plants they liked. They planted those seeds, growing more plants like them. Over time these plants became a better food for people, and eventually became the corn we have today.

Selecting a few living things with desired traits to serve as parents is called **selective breeding.** And it is not used just for plants. It is also used for reproducing animals.

The corn we have today is very different from wild corn long ago because of selective breeding.

There are even more kinds of asexual reproduction. Molds reproduce asexually by forming spores. Spores are reproductive cells that are released by an organism. They are often carried off by the wind. They have a hard coat to protect them. When conditions are right, the spore develops. It becomes a new living being.

Growing new individuals from body parts is another form of asexual reproduction. Some sea stars reproduce this way. When a sea star loses one of its arms, a new individual will grow from the arm.

Some plants use this kind of asexual reproduction too. Buds form on a plant through mitosis. If the bud is cut from the plant it will grow on its own. Potatoes, such as the one on this page, grow this way. The buds form on the outside of the potato and grow into new plants. Some weeds grow this way as well, growing from a piece of root.

Sea stars can grow new arms from just one piece.

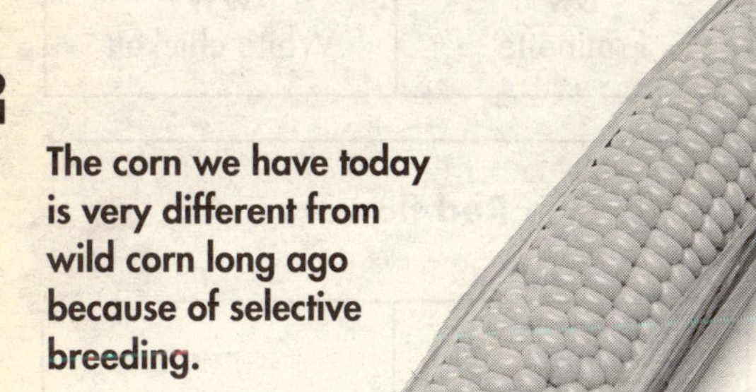

Buds are forming and growing on this potato.

How are traits passed on?

Structure of DNA

We have to look inside the cell to find out how traits are passed on. Most living things have chromosomes in the cell nucleus. Chromosomes tell the cells what to do, giving directions to different parts of the cell. In multicellular organisms, chromosomes tell cells how to work together to form an individual organism.

Chromosomes are made up of proteins and two DNA strands that are tightly wound. DNA stands for deoxyribonucleic acid. The cell's nucleus contains the DNA and proteins that make up chromosomes. Usually, chromosomes are spread out in the nucleus. They only come together during cell division.

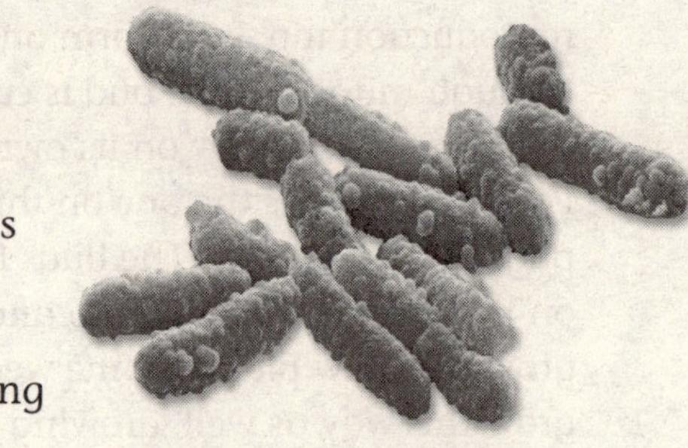

Each *E. coli* bacterium has one chromosome, which contains one thousand genes that are made up of 4 billion base pairs.

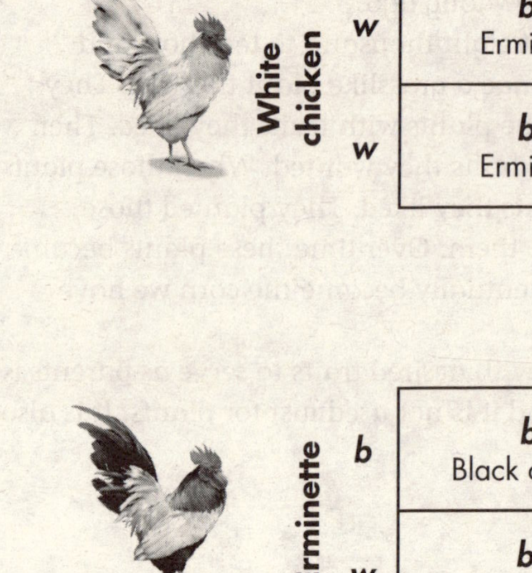

	b	b
White chicken w	*bw* Erminette	*bw* Erminette
w	*bw* Erminette	*bw* Erminette

Black chicken

	b	w
Erminette b	*bb* Black chicken	*bw* Erminette
w	*bw* Erminette	*ww* White chicken

Erminette

	r	r
White flowers w	*rw* pink	*rw* pink
w	*rw* pink	*rw* pink

Red flowers

	r	w
Pink flowers r	*rr* red	*rw* pink
w	*rw* pink	*ww* white

Pink flowers

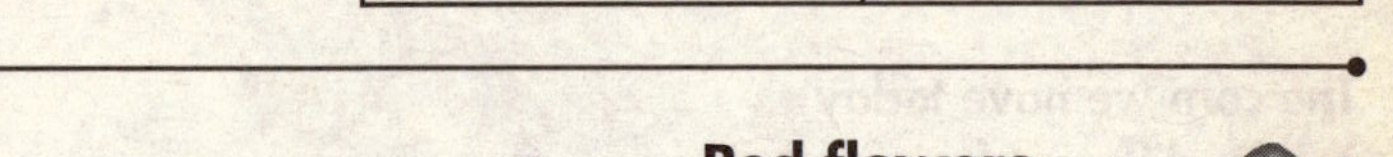

Sharing Dominance

Some gene pairs work differently, such as the feathers of the Erminette chicken you see here. This chicken has gene pairs that decide its feather color. But neither gene is dominant, so the chicken has both feather colors.

The table on the next page shows how the chicken got its feather color. The table is called a Punnett square. For two parents, it shows all the possible offspring gene mixes. On the side axis is one parent. In the first table, it's a white chicken. The top axis shows the other parent, a black chicken. In the cells, you can see the possible gene combinations.

In the first table, two purebred parents, one black, *bb*, and one white, *ww*, would produce young chickens with mixed genes. Each possible combination has one gene from the mother and one from the father, *bw*. So the young will be Erminette chickens, with both black and white feathers.

The second diagram shows what would happen if two Erminette chickens mated. Take a look at the possible mixes of genes. What are they? Do you see anything surprising?

Gene mixes show up in other ways than they do in the chickens. In the four o'clock flowers you see on the next page, the parents have red and white flowers. But the offspring have pink flowers. The genes in this case seem to mix to make a new color. The offspring of the pink flowers can be red, white, or pink. The Punnett square shows how that can happen.

This mixing of genes happens in people too. A child may have a mother with curly hair and a father with straight hair. The child could have a blend: wavy hair. But as you saw with the chickens and flowers, two parents with wavy hair could have a child with straight hair, curly hair, or wavy hair.

As you can see in the picture on this page, DNA looks like a ladder that has been twisted. Two scientists, James Watson and Francis Crick, were the first to describe this shape of DNA using X-ray photographs in 1953. Before the 1950s, scientists could see chromosomes in cells, but they did not know the role of DNA.

On the "ladder" of DNA, there are two sides and many "rungs." Materials called bases make up the rungs. Each rung is made up of two bases, called a base pair, and the bases are labeled with letters: *A, T, C,* and *G*.

DNA is divided into sections called genes. A **gene** is a series of base pairs, or rungs. Genes control what substances the cell makes and when it makes them, determining the traits of a living thing. The genes in the cells of a rose will contain information about the flower's color. The genes tell the flower cells what pigment color to make.

A gene is a series of base pairs, or rungs. The number of rungs varies from gene to gene, but at least one known gene has more than 2 million rungs.

How Many Chromosomes?

Each species has its own unique number of chromosomes. Members of the same species have the same number of chromosomes. The number of chromosomes each cell of a species has is not related to the size of the individuals.

Gorilla: 48 chromosomes, two more than each human cell

Crayfish: 200 chromosomes

Horsetail: 216 chromosomes

Copying DNA

Four bases make up the DNA of all living things. The bases are A, T, C, and G. The order of the pairs changes at different places on the DNA strand. The base pairs are TA, AT, GC, or CG.

The way that these pairs are arranged on the DNA strand determines exactly what directions each gene gives to the cells. A series of base pairs such as TA-CG-GC-TA give different directions than TA-AT-GC-TA. Different living things have different arrangements of base pairs.

Each rung on the DNA ladder is made up of two bases. Only certain bases fit together to form a pair. Base A and base T fit together, and base C and base G fit together. Pairing in this way allows DNA to make a copy of itself when it divides.

DNA Bases

Sometimes, living things have two dominant or two recessive genes. In the picture you can see that the mother guinea pig has two genes for rough fur. Both are dominant, and they are written as *RR*.

The father has two genes for smooth fur. These are recessive and are written as *rr*. When a living thing has two versions of a trait of the same type, as the mother and father below have, they are called purebred for that specific trait.

Each offspring will get one trait for a rough coat from the mother, *R*, and one trait for a smooth coat from the father, *r*, or *Rr*. Because the rough coat is dominant, the young will have rough coats.

But what if the parents are not purebred? What if each parent has an *Rr* gene? The young can have three possible gene mixes. They are *RR*, *Rr*, and *rr*. *RR* and *Rr* will show as a coat because of the dominant rough coat gene. Only *rr* will show up as a smooth coat.

How do genes determine traits?

Dominant and Recessive Traits

Genes control the traits that individuals get from both parents. Like the guinea pigs you see here, living things can get one gene for smooth fur from the mother and another for rough fur from the father. Why does a guinea pig with both of these genes have a rough coat? What happened to the gene for a smooth coat? How an offspring looks depends on how the genes from its parents work together.

For many traits, an individual has a pair of genes. One gene that masks another is called a dominant gene. The other gene is hidden. It is called a recessive gene. For guinea pigs, rough fur is dominant and smooth fur is not. If a guinea pig has one gene for smooth fur and another for rough fur, it will have a rough coat. In fact, the only way it could have a smooth coat is if it has two smooth coat genes.

Take a look at the drawing of DNA below. During mitosis the base pairs come apart. In the nucleus there are free-floating bases. These bases pair up with the divided strands. Soon, there are two full strands of DNA. They are exactly the same as the original strand before it pulled apart.

But sometimes an exact copy is not made. One base might take the place of another base. A base might be added or removed. When this kind of change happens, it is called a mutation. A mutation is a change in the DNA strand.

In a strand with a mutation, the directions a gene sends can be changed. This gene can be passed on to offspring too.

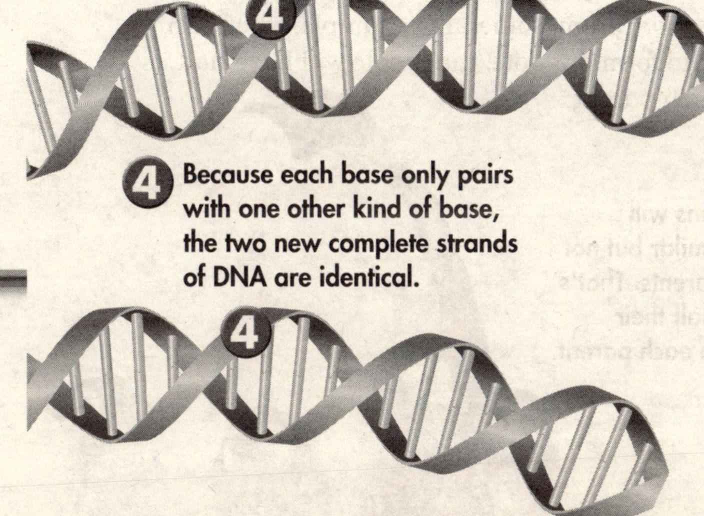

What is sexual reproduction?

Reproduction by Two Parents

A kitten does not look exactly like its mother. This is because cats reproduce through **sexual reproduction,** or reproduction by two parents. DNA from both parents are passed on to the kitten.

Living things that reproduce sexually have sex cells. These are special cells used during reproduction. In the female, these are called **egg cells,** and in the male, they are called **sperm cells.** Each special cell has only half the number of all chromosomes found in regular cells of that species. So if a living thing has 38 chromosomes in all, each sex cell will have 19.

Sex cells develop in **meiosis,** when one cell divides into four cells. The new cells have half the chromosomes of the parent cell. They are sex cells and can be male or female.

A male and female cell join during **fertilization.** When an egg cell and a sperm cell join, they form a new cell. It is called a zygote. It is the first cell of a new offspring. In time it will divide into many more cells.

Remember that each sex cell has half of all the chromosomes found in the cells of that living thing. When the two sex cells join, the zygote has a full set of chromosomes. For example, when two penguin sex cells join to form a zygote, the zygote will have half its chromosomes from each parent.

These baby penguins will grow up to look similar but not identical to their parents. That's because they got half their chromosomes from each parent.

Comparing Sexual and Asexual Reproduction

The simplest form of reproduction is asexual reproduction. It can produce many offspring quickly. Also, only one member from a group of living things is needed for asexual reproduction. Unlike sexual reproduction, asexual reproduction happens with one cell. A cell can reproduce on its own. Asexual reproduction does not require as much energy as sexual reproduction.

All living things coming from asexual reproduction have exactly the same DNA as their parents. So a whole group of living things in one place can come from one original parent cell, they will have the same DNA.

Suppose there were many amebas living in a pond. They all have the same DNA, because they all came from a single parent. If there were a sudden change in the pond's conditions, they might not be able to survive. Since all of them have the same traits, all of them would probably die.

But with sexual reproduction, each offspring has traits that are a little different from the others. What could kill one might only stress another. That way, when something changes, part of the species will still live on. Those members will pass on the traits that helped them live. These traits will help the next group to survive.

Asexual Reproduction	Sexual Reproduction
• Can happen quickly	• Is a slow process
• Requires less energy	• Requires more energy
• Needs just one parent cell	• Must have two parent cells
• Produces offspring with DNA identical to parent	• Produces offspring with unique DNA

Individuals Differ

In asexual reproduction, each offspring is exactly the same as its parent organism. But in sexual reproduction, every individual is slightly different. Think of a litter of puppies. Each puppy looks a bit different from its brothers and sisters, and each one also looks slightly different from its parents. Every dog has a unique set of DNA because of meiosis.

When a sperm or egg cell forms by meiosis, it only gets half a set of DNA. When it combines with another sex cell to form a zygote, it produces a unique DNA combination. Each puppy in a litter will be different because each received a different combination of genes from its parents. For example, one puppy might get its size from the father and its color from its mother, while another might get its mother's size and its father's color.

egg cell   sperm cell

fertilization

zygote

Puppies inherit some DNA from each parent. Notice that no two puppies look exactly alike.

Fertilization in Seed Plants

Flowering plants reproduce sexually. Their flowers have both male and female parts. The female part of a plant is called the pistil. It often has the shape of a bottle. Flowers can have one or more pistils. The pistil produces the egg.

The male part of a flower, called the stamen, produces pollen. Pollen is a powder and contains the male sex cells.

During pollination, pollen moves from the stamen to the pistil. The diagram below shows what happens as the pollen moves into the pistil and an egg is fertilized.

Flowers have special adaptations that help with pollination. For instance, many flowers have bright petals that attract insects. When the insects move around the flower, they move the pollen too. Flowers that are pollinated by the wind or water have different adaptations that help with fertilization.

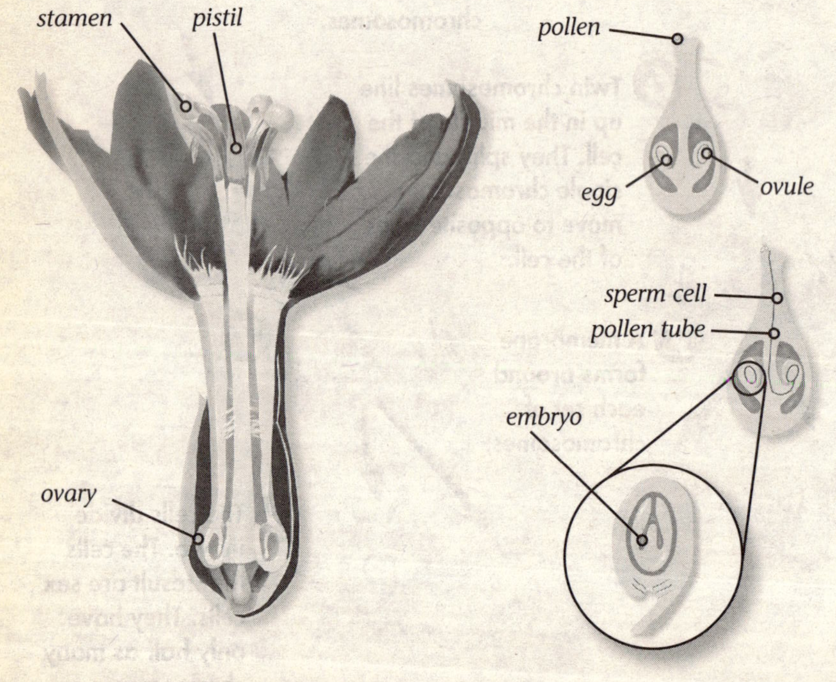

Fertilization in Animals

Like flowers, animals' sperm and egg cells join during sexual reproduction. Depending on the animals, this can take place inside or outside the female.

Fertilization that takes place outside the female is called external fertilization. Many animals that live in or near water use this kind of fertilization. Animals release egg and sperm cells into the water. The sperm cells swim to the eggs and fertilize them.

Staghorn coral, shown in the picture, release sperm and eggs into the water at the same time. Then the sperm cells fertilize the egg cells. These animals release billions of sperm and egg cells. But very few fertilized eggs survive, because of environmental conditions or predators.

For most land animals, fertilization takes place inside the female. Eggs and sperm dry out too quickly on land, and fertilized eggs need moisture.

Some land animals, however, do lay eggs. Birds and turtles lay eggs on land. Fertilized eggs need moisture, so these animals' eggs have hard outer shells that keep them from drying out.

1. Pollen lands on the pistil.

2. The pollen grains grow pollen tubes down toward the ovary. Sperm cells travel down to the ovules.

3. Each ovule within the ovary contains an egg cell. Sperm cells reach the egg cells and fertilization occurs.

4. The fertilized egg becomes an embryo. The ovule forms a seed.

Staghorn coral

Science

Body Systems

by Erin Rogers

Genre	Comprehension Skill	Text Features	Science Content
Nonfiction	Cause and Effect	• Captions • Charts • Diagrams • Glossary	Body Systems

Scott Foresman Science 6.4

ISBN 0-328-13979-3

PEARSON

Scott Foresman

scottforesman.com

What did you learn?

1. What are the different types of tissue found in the body?

2. Name the parts of a neuron, and tell what each part does.

3. What is the difference between voluntary and involuntary muscles?

4. **Writing** in Science Your digestive system breaks down the food you eat so your cells can use it. Write to explain the different ways your body digests food. Include details from the book to support your answer.

5. **Cause and Effect** If a pathogen gets inside your body, what does your immune system do to fight the pathogen?

Illustrations: Title Page: Big Sesh Studios; 13 Big Sesh Studios; 6-7, 10, 14, 19-21 Jeff Mangiat
Photographs: Every effort has been made to secure permission and provide appropriate credit for photographic material. The publisher deeply regrets any omission and pledges to correct errors called to its attention in subsequent editions. Unless otherwise acknowledged, all photographs are the property of Scott Foresman, a division of Pearson Education. Photo locators denoted as follows: Top (T), Center (C), Bottom (B), Left (L), Right (R), Background (Bkgd).
2 ©Jay Dickman/Corbis; 4 (BL) ©Science Photo Library/Photo Researchers, Inc., (BC) ©VVG/Photo Researchers, Inc., (R) ©SIU/Visuals Unlimited; 7 (CL) ©P. Motta/Photo Researchers, Inc., (TL) ©Dee Breger/Photo Researchers, Inc.; 9 ©SIU/Visuals Unlimited; 16 (CL) ©Omikron/Photo Researchers, Inc., (BR) ©Eye of Science/Photo Researchers, Inc.; 17 ©SPL/Photo Researchers, Inc.; 18 ©Dr. Richard Kessel & Dr. Randy Kardon/Tissues & Organs/Visuals Unlimited; 19 ©Science Photo Library/Photo Researchers, Inc.

ISBN: 0-328-13979-3

Body Systems

by Erin Rogers

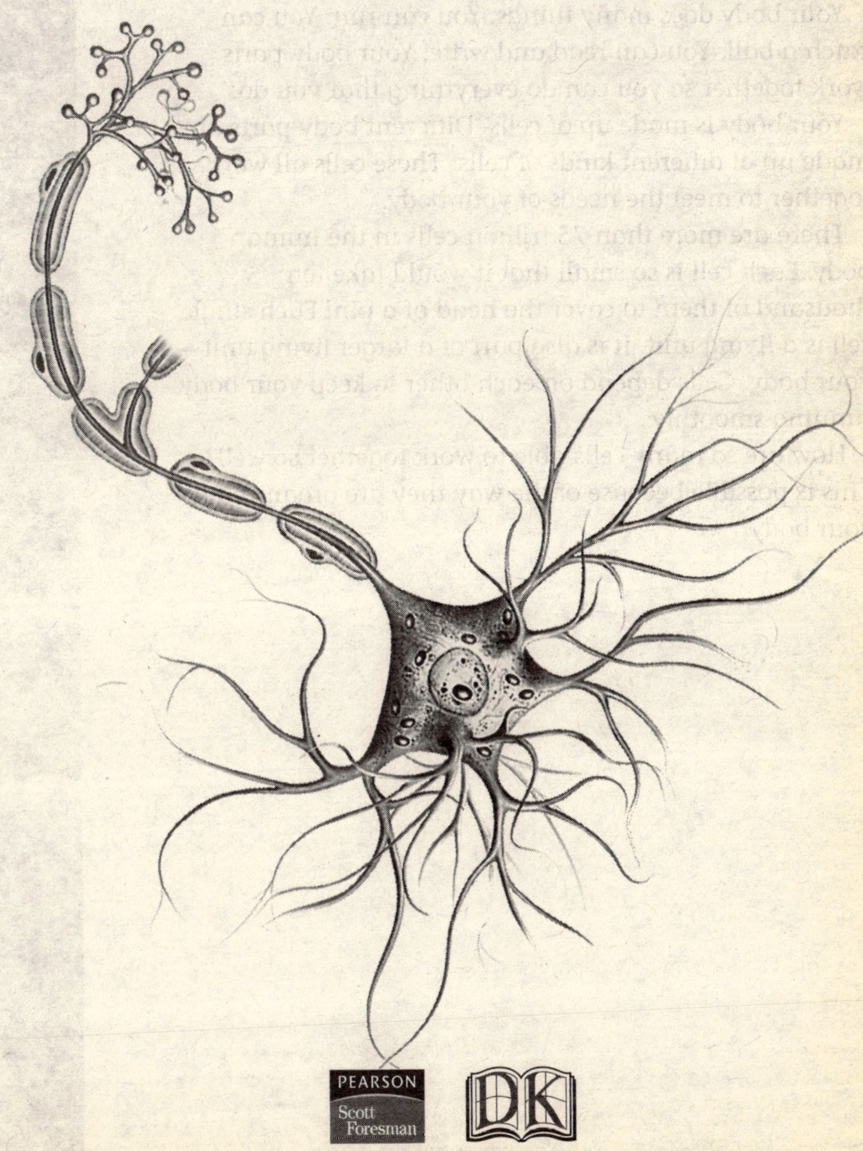

Glossary

alveoli	tiny sacs on the end of bronchioles where oxygen comes into the blood and carbon dioxide leaves
antibody	chemical produced by white blood cells that kills certain pathogens
endocrine gland	organs that release chemical substances directly into the blood
enzyme	a chemical that helps break down food into nutrients
gland	an organ that makes a chemical
hormone	a substance released by endocrine glands into the blood
impulse	a message that travels from one neuron to the next, caused by a chemical change
neuron	a nerve cell that passes messages throughout your body
pathogen	an organism that makes a person sick

37

How is the body organized?

Cells Working Together

Your body does many things. You can run. You can catch a ball. You can read and write. Your body parts work together so you can do everything that you do.

Your body is made up of cells. Different body parts are made up of different kinds of cells. These cells all work together to meet the needs of your body.

There are more than 75 trillion cells in the human body. Each cell is so small that it would take ten thousand of them to cover the head of a pin! Each single cell is a living unit. It is also part of a larger living unit—your body. Cells depend on each other to keep your body running smoothly.

How are so many cells able to work together so well? This is possible because of the way they are organized in your body.

Muscular and Skeletal Systems

The muscles in a person's legs get messages from the brain to contract. As they contract, the muscles pull on the person's leg bones. This is how the leg moves. If the contracting muscles relax, the muscles opposite them contract. The bones then move in the opposite direction.

Respiratory and Circulatory Systems

These systems have to work harder when the body is active. Breathing gets faster in order to provide more oxygen to the muscles and to help get rid of carbon dioxide waste. The heart pumps faster to bring more nutrients and oxygen to the muscles.

Habits for Staying Healthy

- Eat well-balanced meals.
- Get regular physical activity.
- Sleep at least eight hours every night.
- Drink plenty of water.
- Avoid using alcohol, drugs and tobacco.
- Keep your body clean.
- Wash your hands often.
- Wear protective gear when playing sports that require it.
- Wear your seat belt in a car.

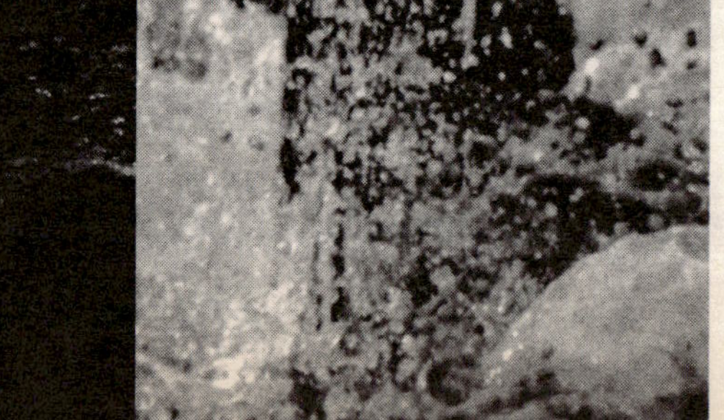

Systems Working Together

The systems of your body are always working together. They are involved in everything you do. It is important to take care of your body every day.

Healthy habits start at a young age. You can start taking good care of your body now. Many adult health problems start when a person is young. It is never too early to care about your health. To find out how to stay healthy, read the list on page 23.

Nervous System

Nerves gather information about the environment. They are in the eyes, ears, nose, and skin. This information is sent to the brain by impulses. Impulses reach the brain through the spinal cord. The brain processes the information and tells the body what to do.

Digestive System

The digestive system prepares the body for activity. Some nutrients are in the blood. They supply energy. Some nutrients get stored in tissue and are used when they are needed.

Endocrine System

Endocrine glands are always checking on the body. Their hormones make sure the muscles have enough energy.

Levels of Organization

All cells are made up of the same basic parts. However, not all the cells in your body have the same job. Many different jobs must be done in order to keep the body in balance, so certain cells are responsible for certain jobs. The way the cells are organized depends on the job that they do.

Cells that do the same job in the body make up tissues. There are many types of tissues that perform different functions in your body. For example, muscle tissue is made up of cells that can contract and shorten. Whenever you move a part of your body, you are using your muscle tissue.

Another type of tissue is called nerve tissue. Nerve tissue is made up of cells that can carry messages from one cell to another. Your brain is mostly made up of nerve tissue. There are many other types of tissue. Some tissues hold body parts together; other tissues support the body. Still other tissues cushion organs or release substances, to keep your body in perfect balance.

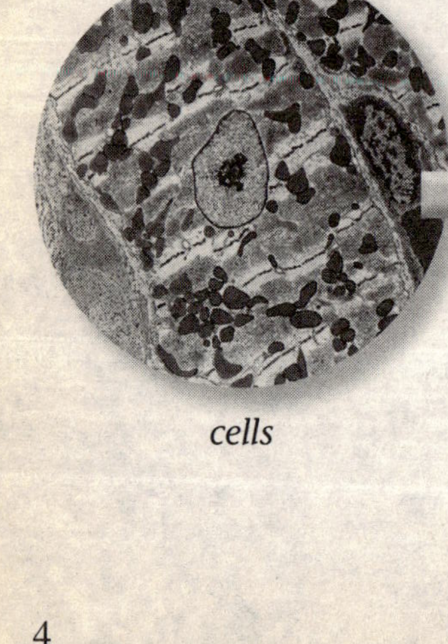

cells

tissues

There are other types of white blood cells that will only fight certain pathogens. They do this by making **antibodies.** Antibodies are chemicals that kill only certain pathogens. Antibodies will recognize and fight that same pathogen if it comes into your body again.

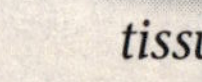

How do systems keep the body healthy?

Immune System

Every day your body fights to keep you from getting sick. It must protect you from the pathogens that are all around you. **Pathogens** are organisms that make you sick. Pathogens can be found everywhere. Your body is good at fighting pathogens so that you will stay healthy. Your body does this in many ways.

The first thing your immune system does to fight pathogens is to prevent them from coming into your body. Your skin keeps many pathogens out of your body. The tears in your eyes have chemicals that kill pathogens. Tears also wash pathogens away. Inside of your nose, mouth, and throat there is mucus that traps pathogens. The saliva in your mouth and the juices in your stomach also kill pathogens. Your body's reflexes, such as sneezing and coughing, help your lungs and throat get rid of pathogens.

Your body is good at keeping pathogens out. However, sometimes pathogens are still able to get in. Once pathogens get into your body, your immune system kicks in. Your immune system causes extra blood to flow to the pathogen. The extra blood tells your white blood cells there is a pathogen there. The white blood cells will then fight and kill the pathogen. This type of white blood cell fights any kind of pathogen.

When a group of tissues works together, it forms an organ. Some examples of organs in your body are the heart, the lungs, the skin, and the stomach. All organs must have muscle tissue for movement. They also have nerve tissue that tells the muscle what to do. Organs also have connective tissue to hold themselves together and carry blood.

Cells make up tissues. Tissues make up organs. Organs are part of organ systems. These systems work together and depend on each other to keep the body working. Look at the chart to see what each system does in your body.

The Body's Major Systems	
System	**Function**
Circulatory	Transports nutrients, oxygen, and cell wastes
Digestive	Breaks down food into a form the body can use
Endocrine	Controls internal conditions, growth, development, and reproduction
Excretory	Removes wastes from the blood
Immune	Defends the body against pathogens
Muscular	Allows body movement and movement of substances within the body
Nervous	Controls body movement, thought, and behavior
Reproductive	Produces sex cells and offspring
Respiratory	Provides the body with oxygen and removes gas wastes from the blood
Skeletal	Provides body protection and support; interacts with muscles to allow movement

What systems help move body parts?

Skeletal System

The bones in your body are made up of living tissues and minerals from your bone cells. Although bones seem hard, blood flows through every part of your bones.

Your skeletal system is made up of bones and a flexible material called cartilage. If you touch the tip of your nose, you might notice that you can push it and bend it with your finger. This is because your nose is made of cartilage. When you were a baby, many of your bones were made of cartilage. As you grow and get older, a lot of that cartilage is replaced by bone.

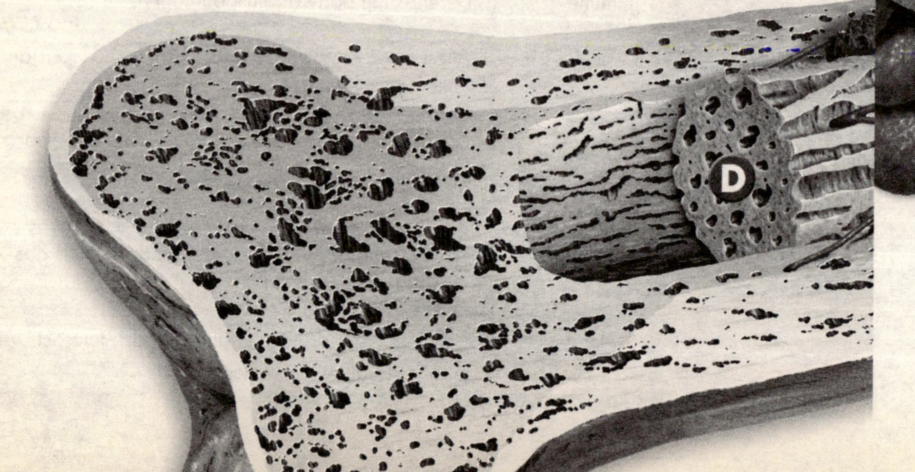

D Red marrow in the long arm and leg bones makes new red blood cells, while yellow marrow stores fat.

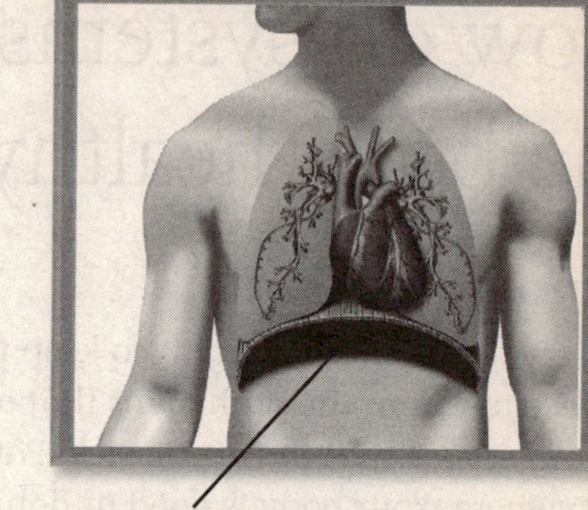

Alveoli occur in bunches in the lung. Tiny bronchioles supply each alveolus with oxygen.

The diaphragm helps the lungs to function. When air enters the lungs, the diaphragm contracts. When air leaves, the diaphragm relaxes.

When you breathe in, air goes into your nose. It moves through your nose, down through your trachea, and into your lungs. Your trachea divides into bronchial tubes, which get smaller and smaller. The smallest tubes in your lungs are called bronchioles. At the end of the bronchioles are tiny sacs. These sacs are called alveoli. In the **alveoli,** oxygen moves into the blood and carbon dioxide leaves. This switch happens very quickly. When you breathe out, you are getting rid of the carbon dioxide in your body.

Respiratory System

Cells in your body need nutrients in order to function. But cells also use oxygen to release energy from nutrients. This process produces carbon dioxide. Carbon dioxide is a waste that must be removed from cells. Your blood carries oxygen to your cells and takes away the carbon dioxide. When your blood travels back to your lungs, it drops off the carbon dioxide. Your blood also picks up more oxygen to bring to your cells.

The job of the respiratory system is to take in oxygen from the air and get rid of the carbon dioxide from your body. Your lungs, nose, trachea, and bronchial tubes are all part of the respiratory system.

Lungs are made of a spongy material with branching tubes, air sacs, and blood vessels.

Bones hold your body up and make you tall. Some bones, such as your skull, protect your organs. Bones can also store minerals that your body needs, such as calcium and phosphorous. These minerals make your bones hard and strong. When bones lack calcium they weaken and a disease called osteoporosis can develop. Some bones can even make new blood cells.

A A thin, tough outer covering of blood vessels and other tissue covers bones and supplies them with materials they need.

B Compact bone is the hardest material in the human body.

C Spongy bone tissue makes the bone lightweight.

A joint is where two bones meet. The shape of cartilage covering the ends of bones at joints determines how they move.

Ball-and-Socket

Hinge

Pivot

Muscular System

You need bones to support your body. You also need muscles so that you are able to move. You have more than 600 muscles in your body. Those muscles and the tissues that attach them to your bones are what make up the muscular system.

There are three different types of muscle tissue. One type of muscle tissue is found only in your heart. This tissue is called cardiac muscle. Cardiac muscle does not get tired even though it contracts time after time. When you feel your heartbeat, you can feel the cardiac muscles working.

The second type of muscle tissue is called smooth muscle. Smooth muscle is in the organs of the digestive system and in blood vessels. Both cardiac and smooth muscles are involuntary muscles. This means that they control the movements in your body automatically.

The third type of muscle is called skeletal muscle. Unlike smooth muscle and cardiac muscle, skeletal muscles are voluntary. This means that you control how your skeletal muscles move. Skeletal muscles work together with your bones to make your body move. Pairs of muscles connect to different sides of your bones near a joint. When you move, one pulls the bone and the other relaxes. Your body will move in the direction that the muscle is pulling.

Circulatory System

Your circulatory system is made up of your heart, blood, and blood vessels. The main task of this system is to move nutrients and other materials throughout your body. These materials flow through blood vessels to your cells.

The part of blood that is liquid is called plasma. Plasma is mostly water, but it contains other substances such as nutrients and waste products. Red blood cells, white blood cells, and platelets also float in the plasma.

Your heart pumps blood to all parts of your body. Your heart is a muscular organ the size of your fist. It beats about 70 times every minute. Blood moves away from the heart through your arteries. Arteries are thick and muscular tubes. Arteries get smaller and smaller as they get farther and farther away from the heart. They eventually become capillaries, the smallest blood vessel in your body. The walls of capillaries are so thin that materials can pass through them. The capillaries give materials to the cells. They also take away materials from the cells. Blood then flows from the capillaries to larger blood vessels called veins. Veins carry blood back to the heart.

44

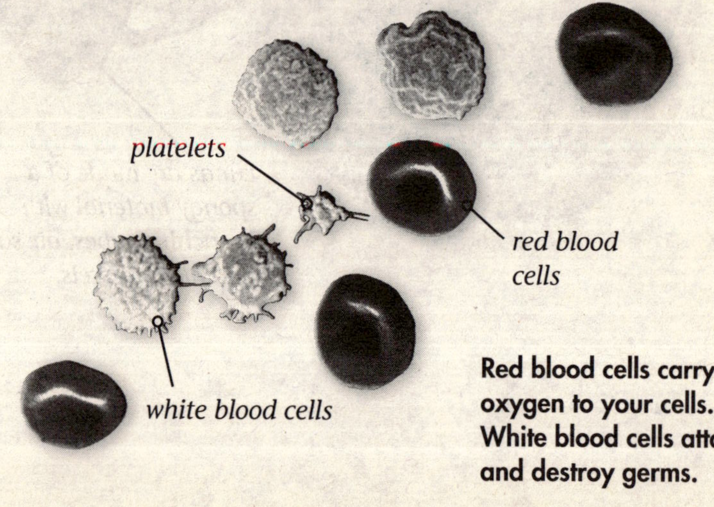

Red blood cells carry oxygen to your cells. White blood cells attack and destroy germs.

A Closer View

Many parts of your digestive system work at the microscopic level. They help break down and absorb food so your body can use it.

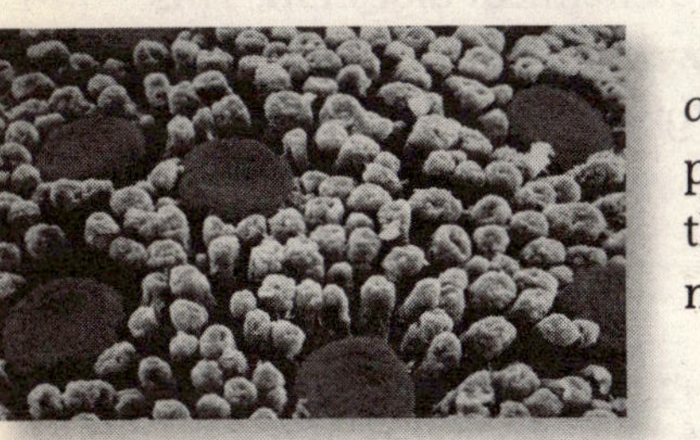

Tongue

The large structures on the tongue are taste buds. The smaller fingerlike projections form a rough surface that helps in the chewing and movement of food.

Stomach

The lining in the stomach contains glands that produce digestive juices. It also secretes mucus that protects the stomach from digestive substances.

Small Intestine

The surface of the small intestine is covered by as many as 40 villi per square millimeter. These structures increase the surface area through which digested food is absorbed into the bloodstream.

Keeping Muscles and Bones Healthy

Sometimes muscles can get hurt. If you push your muscles too hard or stretch them too far, you might strain them. You need to help your muscles stay strong. Some ways of doing this are by eating healthy foods, getting plenty of sleep, and exercising. Also, be sure to warm up before you exercise. Warming up loosens your muscles and other parts of your body so you won't get hurt. Don't forget to stretch after exercising too.

To straighten the leg, the muscle on top of the leg contracts, and the muscle on the back of the leg relaxes.

The muscle on the top of the leg is relaxing. This allows the lower leg to be pulled backward.

The hinge joint of the knee allows the lower leg to move freely.

When the lower leg is pulled back, the muscle on the back of the leg contracts. This pulls on the bones of the lower leg.

How do systems control the body?

Nervous System

Muscles and bones are what move your body, but how does your body know when to move? The nervous system tells your body. Your nervous system is made up of the brain, spinal cord, nerves, and sense organs. Without this system you would not be able to speak, think, taste, hear, or see. The nervous system knows exactly what is going on both inside and outside your body. It is able to make sense of all the information it receives and respond to it.

The nervous system would not work without nerve cells called **neurons.** Neurons pass messages throughout your body. Each neuron has a cell body with short branches sticking out on one side and one long branch on the other side. The short branches are called dendrites. Dendrites get messages from other neurons and give them to the cell body. The long branch, called the axon, moves messages away from that neuron to other nerve cells.

When the dendrite of a neuron gets a message, the chemicals in the neuron change. This change causes an **impulse,** or message, to move across the neuron. The impulse moves from the dendrite to the cell body. It leaves the neuron through the axon. The message then gets picked up by the dendrites of the next neuron and causes an impulse in that neuron. This is how messages move from one neuron to the next.

Process of Digestion

There are two types of digestion. The first is called mechanical digestion. Mechanical digestion involves the tearing, crushing, and mashing of food. An example of mechanical digestion is when you take a bite of food and chew it with your teeth.

The other type of digestion is called chemical digestion. This happens when chemicals, called **enzymes,** help to break food down into nutrients. The nutrients in food give us energy and help us grow.

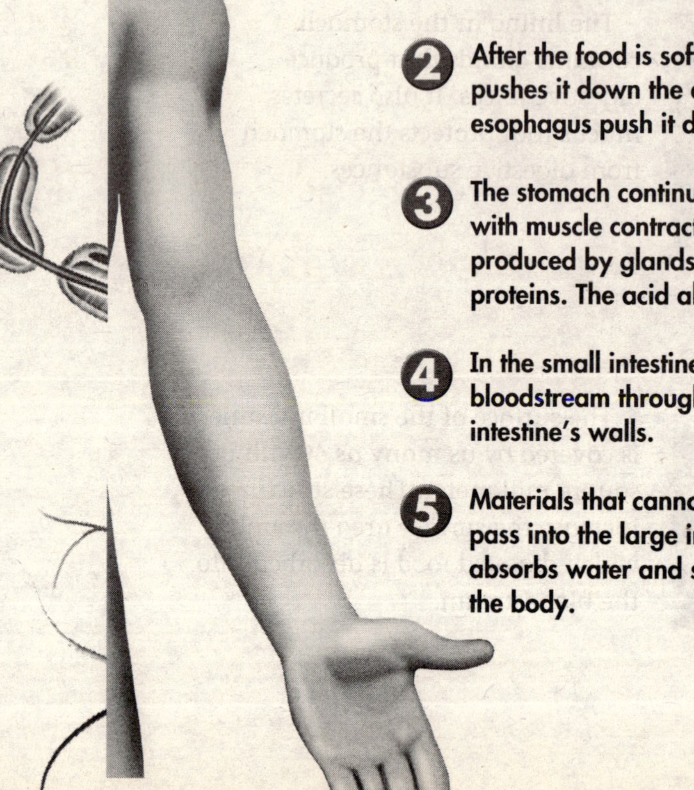

1. Mechanical digestion begins in the mouth. Food is shredded by the teeth, and mixed with saliva. Saliva begins the process of chemical digestion to break down starches into simple sugars.

2. After the food is soft and moist, the tongue pushes it down the esophagus. The muscles in the esophagus push it down into the stomach.

3. The stomach continues the mechanical digestion with muscle contractions. Enzymes and acid produced by glands in the stomach break down proteins. The acid also kills bacteria in the food.

4. In the small intestine digested food passes into the bloodstream through the villi, which line the small intestine's walls.

5. Materials that cannot be absorbed into the blood pass into the large intestine. The large intestine absorbs water and stores waste until it leaves the body.

How do systems transport materials?

Digestive System

The digestive system takes the food that you eat and changes it into a form that cells can use. Organs in the digestive system break down food into a useable form.

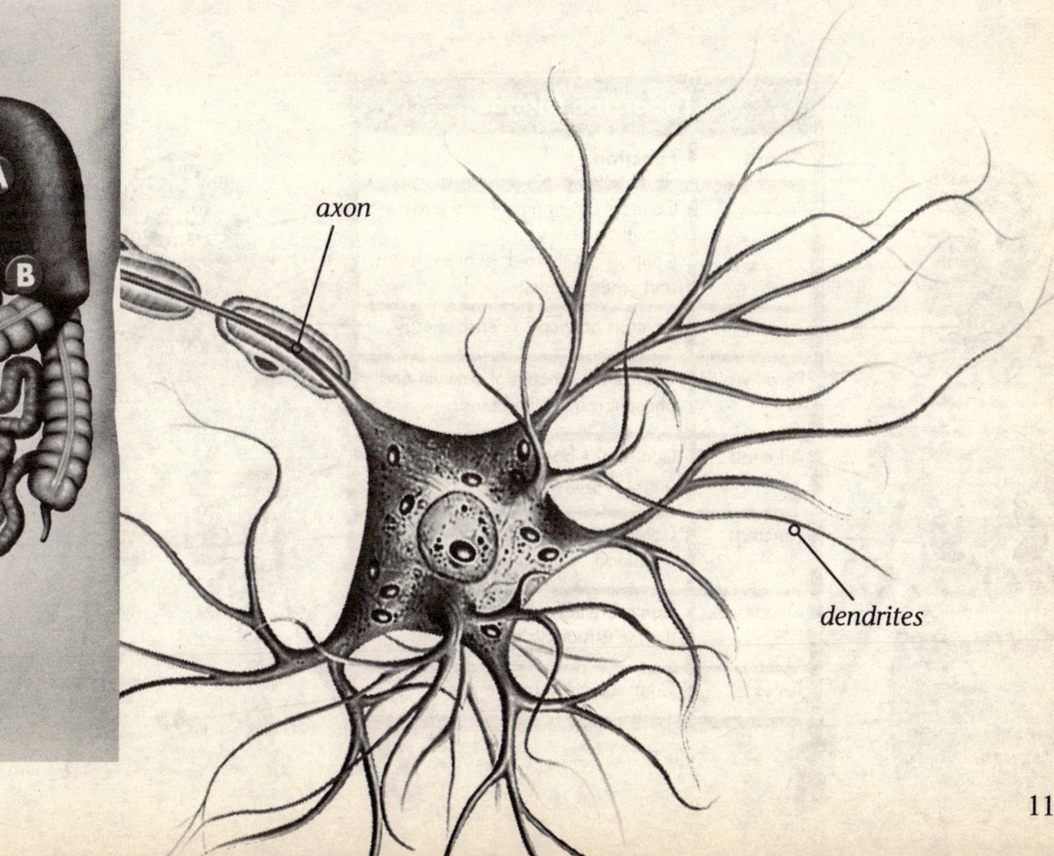

A The liver stores some nutrients and produces bile, which breaks down fat. It also breaks down harmful substances in the blood.

B The gallbladder stores bile produced by the liver and releases it to the small intestine.

C The pancreas produces enzymes that neutralize stomach acid. These enzymes are mixed with the food as it enters the small intestine.

Most of these impulses move along neurons to your brain. Your brain controls almost everything you experience. When your brain gets a message from your nervous system, it makes sense of the message and tells your body how to react.

This message is sent through the spinal cord. The spinal cord is a long bundle of nerves that runs down your back. Some neurons of the spinal cord bring messages to the brain. Others carry messages away.

Reflexes

Not all messages pass through the brain. For example, if you put your hand on something hot, you will move it away quickly. This response is called a reflex. In this situation your brain did not tell you to move your hand away. You did it automatically. Reflexes help you avoid danger.

12

Endocrine System

The endocrine system helps balance everything going on in your body. It controls the slower processes, such as body growth and sugar levels in your blood.

The endocrine system is made up of glands. A **gland** is an organ that makes a chemical. Some glands put their chemicals into tiny tubes, or ducts. But an **endocrine gland** releases its chemicals directly into the blood. These chemicals are called **hormones.** Hormones control many of the body's functions.

The endocrine system is always checking on your bodies. To maintain your body's internal balance, it releases hormones. There are different types of hormones, each with a different job. Some hormones cause bones to grow, and some cause muscles to store sugar.

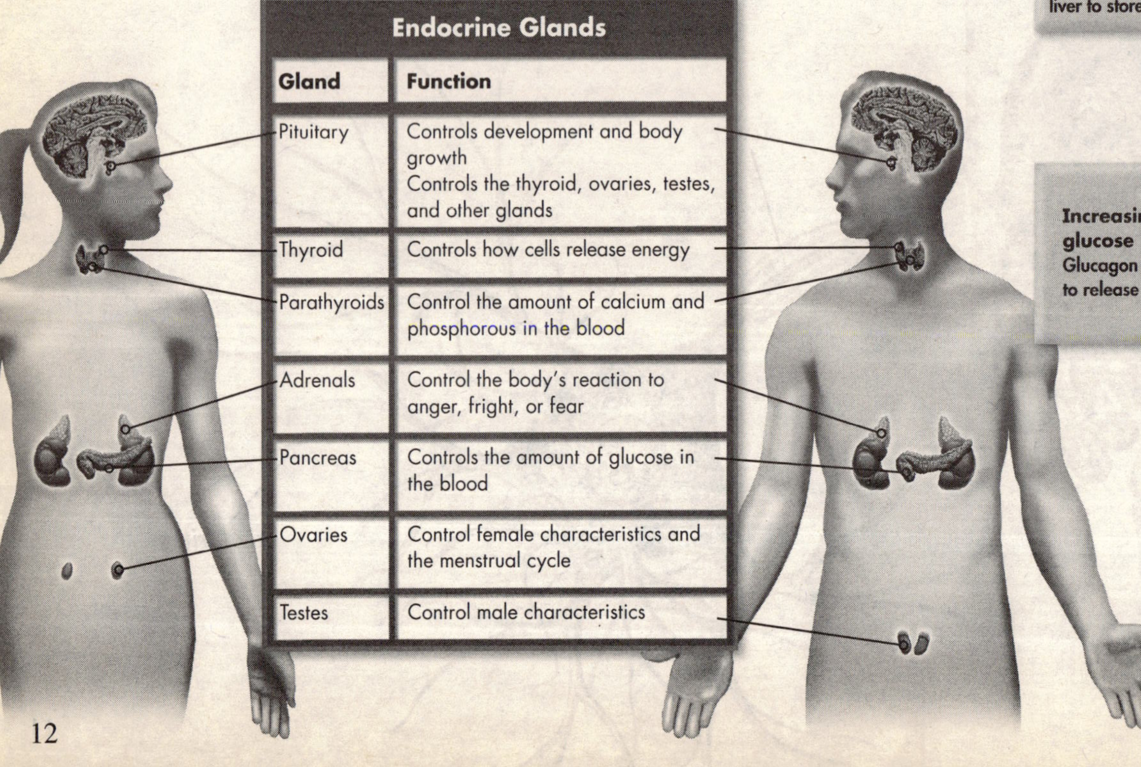

Biofeedback Loop

Endocrine glands have the job of keeping your body in balance. They do this by releasing different amounts of hormones. For example, hormones from the endocrine system control how much sugar there is in your blood. Blood sugar is called glucose. Every single cell in your body needs glucose to work. The diagram below shows how your body balances glucose in your blood. A biofeedback loop is a circular pathway that sends information back and forth from one part of the body to another.

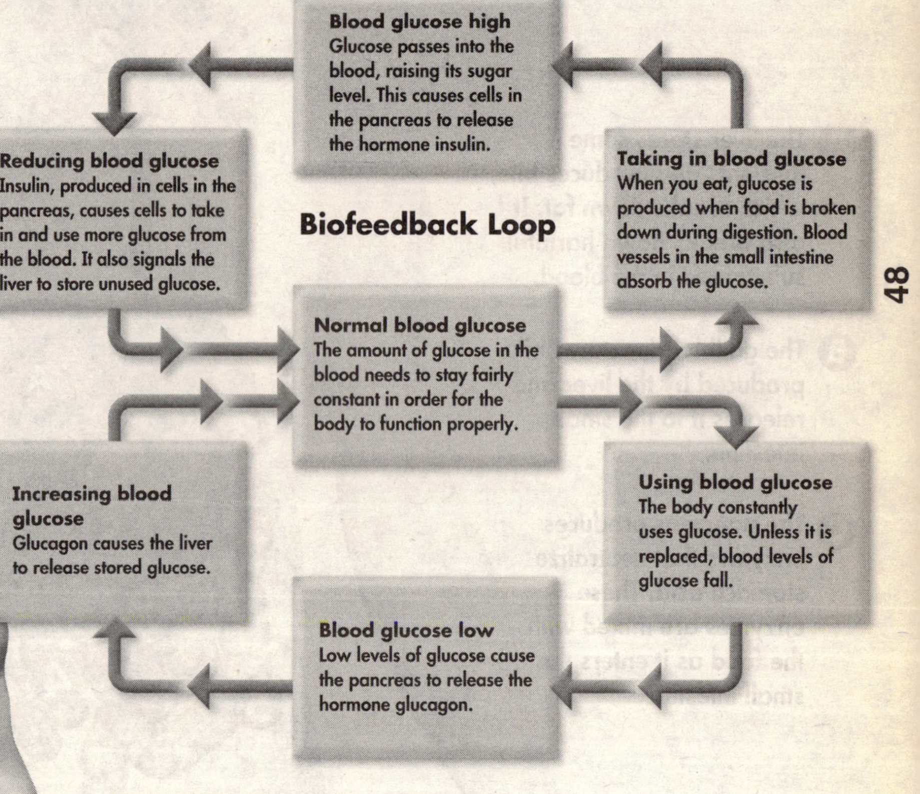

13

Plants

by Kelly Kong

Genre	Comprehension Skill	Text Features	Science Content
Nonfiction	Compare and Contrast	• Captions • Charts • Diagrams • Glossary	Plants

Scott Foresman Science 6.5

PEARSON

Scott Foresman

ISBN 0-328-13982-3

90000

9 780328 139828

scottforesman.com

What did you learn?

1. What happens to the leaf when the stoma opens?

2. What occurs during photosynthesis?

3. What happens when there is uneven growth in a plant's stem?

4. **Writing** in Science During cellular respiration, cells break down food with the release of energy, or glucose is broken down into simpler substances. Write to explain what happens when oxygen is present in the cells.

5. **Compare and Contrast** Compare angiosperms and gymnosperms. How are they the same? How are they different?

Illustration: 5, 8 Sharon & Joel Harris; 6, 14 Tony Randazzo.
Photographs: Every effort has been made to secure permission and provide appropriate credit for photographic material. The publisher deeply regrets any omission and pledges to correct errors called to its attention in subsequent editions. Unless otherwise acknowledged, all photographs are the property of Scott Foresman, a division of Pearson Education. Photo locators denoted as follows: Top (T), Center (C), Bottom (B), Left (L), Right (R), Background (Bkgd).
Title Page: ©DK Images; 2 ©DK Images; 3 ©Runk/Schoenberger/Grant Heilman Photography; 4 ©Dr. Jeremy Burgess/Photo Researchers, Inc.; 6 ©P. Motta & T. Naguro/Photo Researchers, Inc.; 7 (T) ©Bill Brooks/Masterfile Corporation, (CR) ©DK Images; 8 ©DK Images; 9 ©Michael Mahovlich/Masterfile Corporation; 10 ©DK Images; 11 ©Frances Muntada/Corbis; 12 Getty Images; 13 ©Ed Reschke/Peter Arnold, Inc.; 15 ©Adam Jones/Visuals Unlimited.

ISBN: 0-328-13982-3

Plants

by Kelly Kong

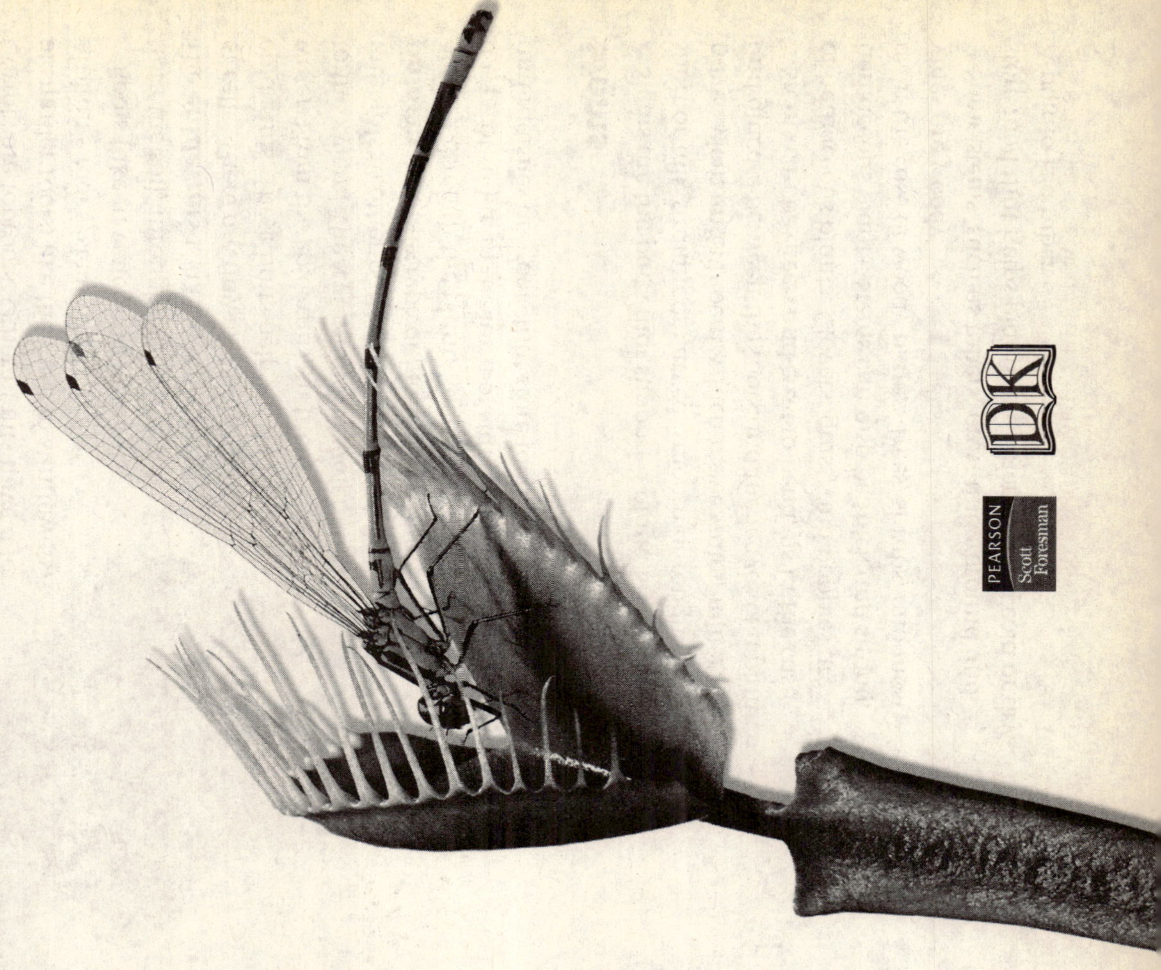

Glossary

cellular respiration the process by which cells break down food with the release of energy

epidermis a thin outer layer of cells

guard cells cells that open and close a leaf's stoma

phloem the part of the plant that carries glucose, which leaves make, throughout the plant

photosynthesis the process in which plants make glucose

stoma the small hole in the epidermis of a leaf (plural, stomata)

transpiration the loss of water from a leaf

tropism the turning or bending movement of a living organism

xylem the part of the plant that moves water and minerals from the roots to other parts of the plant

16

What are the parts of a vascular plant?

Roots

Roots anchor a plant in the ground. Some plants have one main large root, called a taproot. Carrots are taproots. Other plants have a lot of smaller roots, like the roots in sunflowers. A plant's root system can be huge!

Roots take in water and minerals from the soil, through the epidermis. The **epidermis** is a thin outer layer of cells. There are tiny root hairs on the epidermis. These hairs help roots take in water. From the epidermis, nutrients move to the xylem. The **xylem** moves water and minerals to other parts of the plant, while **phloem,** another type of plant tissue, moves glucose through the plant. Roots store glucose, a type of sugar, in the form of starch. Carrots and radishes are roots that store food.

Stems

Stems are the parts that support a plant. Stems can be short or tall, straight or curved, smooth or rough. They have xylem and phloem, which move water, minerals, and glucose between the roots and the leaves of a plant.

Stems can be green and easy to bend, as in the case of herbaceous plants. Clovers, grass, and poppies are herbaceous plants. Stems can also be thick and strong, as in the case of woody plants. Trees, shrubs, and most vines are woody.

Some stems, such as tubers, grow underground and store food that helps plants live when it is too cold or dry. A potato is a tuber.

Some plants have a mechanical response called thigmotropism. A positive thigmotropism makes plants grow toward the surface it touches.

Responding to the Environment

Why do roots grow down? Why do stems grow up? The reason is that plants respond to their environments. Plant behavior is hard to see, but it definitely exists. Have you ever seen plants that bend, droop, twist, or turn? This turning or bending movement is called **tropism.**

Plants do not have nerves to control behaviors like animals. Instead, the chemicals that plants make cause different behaviors. For instance, chemicals can cause cells in different parts of the plant to grow at different rates. Cells on one side of a stem may grow very quickly. Cells on the opposite side may grow very slowly. This uneven growth causes the stem to bend. Stems usually bend toward light, which is called phototropism, while roots bend away from light.

Leaves

Leaves make glucose, which plants use for energy. While making glucose, water and gases move in and out of the plant through a small hole in the epidermis of the leaf, called a **stoma.** Two **guard cells** open and close the stoma. Sunlight causes guard cells to take in water. The extra amount of water puts pressure on the walls of the guard cells, and the stoma opens. Most stomata—plural for stoma— open in the daytime and close at night.

When a stoma opens, gases from the air enter the leaf and water exits the leaf. This loss of water is called **transpiration.** Wind, air temperature, and the amount of water in the air and soil affect how much water is lost in transpiration. When water exits a leaf, more water moves in. This process is like drinking with a straw, it pulls up water through the xylem. If the water lost to transpiration is not gained through the plant's roots, the plant may wilt.

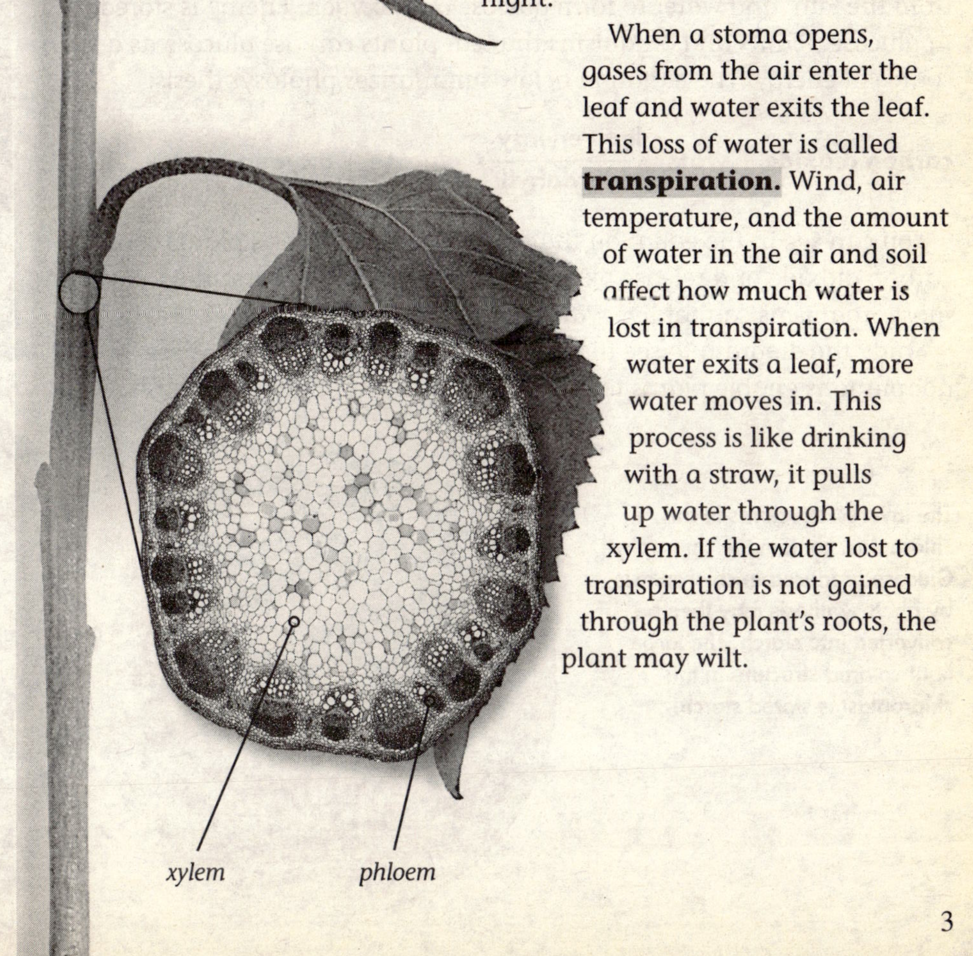

How do plants get and use energy?

Photosynthesis

What is so special about the color green?

Leaves and other plant parts are green due to chlorophyll. Chlorophyll is a substance in chloroplasts. It helps plants make glucose. Glucose is a form of food. Animals cannot make their own food because their cells do not contain chlorophyll.

Photosynthesis is the process in which plants make glucose. In photosynthesis, plants use carbon dioxide from the air, light energy from the Sun, and water to form glucose and oxygen. Energy is stored in glucose. Plants and organisms that eat plants can use glucose as a source of energy. The equation below summarizes photosynthesis:

$$\text{carbon dioxide} + \text{water} \xrightarrow[\text{chlorophyll}]{\text{light energy}} \text{glucose} + \text{oxygen}$$

You can see in the equation that during photosynthesis plants use carbon dioxide and release oxygen. Oxygen is very important as most organisms cannot live without it.

Study the diagram to see the many adaptations of leaves. These adaptations enable plants to carry on the process of photosynthesis.

The layered structures in this chloroplast contain the chlorophyll. Glucose produced in chloroplasts by photosynthesis may then be converted into starch. The large light-colored structure in this chloroplast is stored starch.

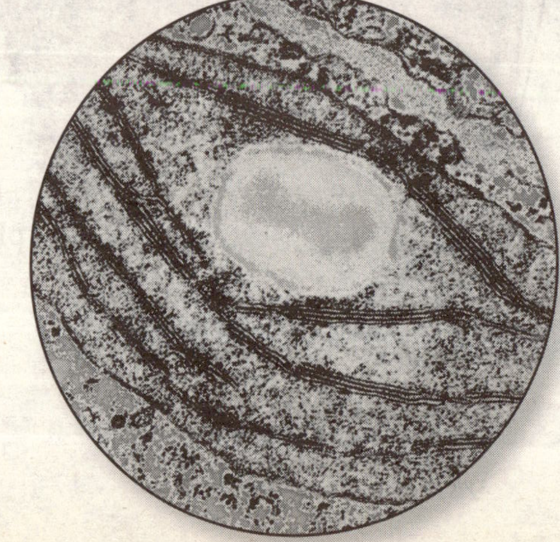

When seeds germinate, roots grow downward and stems grow upward. New cells develop at the tips of roots and stems. Plants get bigger. Branches on a plant's stem may grow from side buds. Some plants also grow wider. To assist with the development process, cells also divide to repair damaged tissue in the plant.

Some plants do not grow from seeds. Plants can also grow from spores. Mosses and ferns produce spores. The table below shows how spores and seeds are different. Like seeds, spores can only become plants if the conditions are just right. Having plenty of water available is usually a good condition for a spore-producing plant.

Spores

Spore	Seed
Contains a single cell that grows into a new plant	Contains a multicellular embryo that develops into a new plant
Does not contain stored food	Contains stored food
Is usually very small	Can vary in size

Germination and Growth

Seeds contain a small plant embryo. The embryo can only grow so large within a seed. Then it must wait until conditions are suitable for germination. Germination is when a plant starts to grow from a seed.

Different plants need different conditions to grow. All seeds need a certain temperature. Seeds that grow in colder regions may not germinate until spring or early summer. Seeds that grow in tropical rain forests need warm temperatures and a great deal of moisture. Seeds that germinate in colder, drier climates do not need as much warmth or moisture.

When a seed coat opens, more oxygen reaches the cells of the embryo. The cells get larger. Then, they divide and make new cells. If seeds get too much moisture, they may not get enough oxygen. If this occurs, growth will not take place and the seeds will rot.

Some seeds may become inactive if conditions are not right. Seeds can remain inactive for long periods to protect the plant. Inactive seeds can survive conditions that would kill a plant. Examples of these types of conditions are droughts, freezing temperatures, and forest fires.

Wheat seeds

Leaf Structure

The top and bottom of the leaf have a layer of cells called the epidermis. This thin layer allows light to pass into the middle of the leaf.

A waxy layer called the cuticle may cover a leaf and slow water loss.

Photosynthesis takes place in the middle of the leaf. These tall, thin cells absorb sunlight that enters the leaf. These cells have chloroplasts that a plant needs to make glucose.

Most leaves have more stomata on the lower epidermis. Less light reaches under the leaf, so the lower part is cooler and less water is lost through transpiration.

The veins of a leaf contain its xylem and phloem. Water and minerals enter the leaf through the xylem. Sugar made by the leaf moves to the rest of the plant through the phloem.

The air spaces surrounding cells in this part of the leaf allow the carbon dioxide that is needed for photosynthesis to move freely throughout the leaf.

Energy from Food

When the Sun is shining, plants can make more glucose than they need. The extra glucose is converted into other sugars and starches. Plants store these sugars and starches. When they want to use the stored food, plants break down the food to release the energy it contains. All organisms break down food to release stored energy. The process by which cells break down food to release stored energy is called **cellular respiration.**

Cellular respiration starts in the cytoplasm of the cells. In the cytoplasm, glucose is broken down into simpler substances. If a cell contains oxygen, the simpler substances move into the mitochondria of the cell. The mitochondria use oxygen to break down the simpler substances even more. In this process, carbon dioxide and water are produced. Energy is also released. The equation below summarizes cellular respiration:

glucose + **oxygen** ⟶ **carbon dioxide** + **water** + **energy**

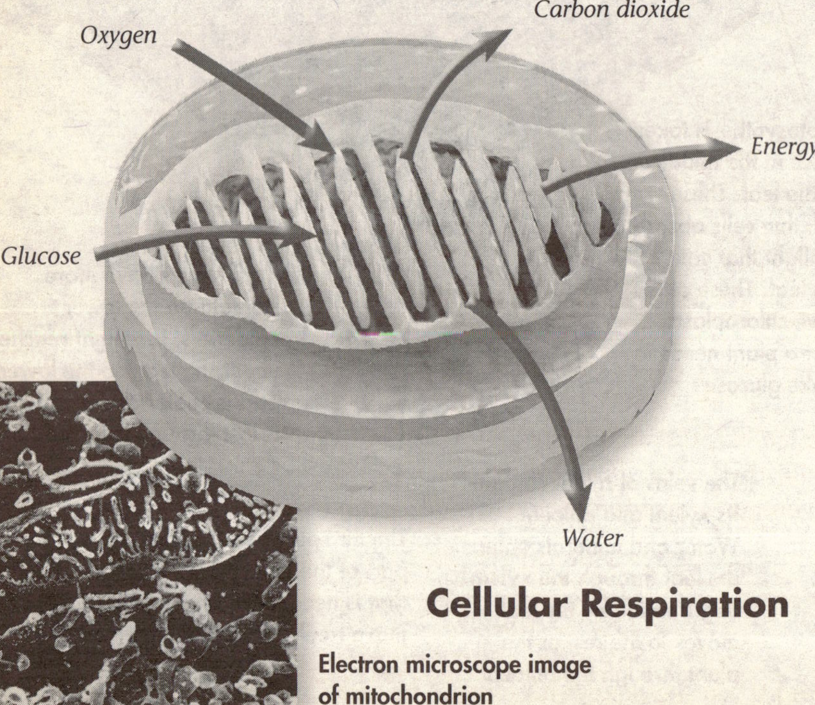

Cellular Respiration

Electron microscope image
of mitochondrion

After fertilization, seeds grow in female cones. Female cones close up and do not open until seeds are mature. This process may take two years! When seeds mature, they are released and fall to the ground. Unlike angiosperms, seeds of gymnosperms are not found in fruits.

Gymnosperms produce a lot of products that are used every day. They are good sources of wood and materials for paper products. They are also used in paints, air fresheners, disinfectants, and scents in soaps and cosmetics. Gymnosperm seeds are a source of food for animals.

Gymnosperms

Have you seen cones like the one in the picture? Plants that develop seeds in cones are called gymnosperms. Gymnosperms do not grow flowers. They can live for a long time. One type, the redwood, lives for thousands of years.

The conifer is a common type of gymnosperm. Conifers are woody plants with needles or scalelike leaves. The Scotch pine in the picture is a conifer.

Conifers have two types of cones—male and female. Female cones have egg cells. Male cones make pollen that contains sperm. Wind carries pollen from male cones to female cones. Then, sperm fertilizes the egg cells.

Carbon Dioxide—Oxygen Cycle

Have you noticed that the equations for photosynthesis and cellular respiration look similar? Let's look at the equations again:

$$\text{carbon dioxide} + \text{water} \xrightarrow[\text{chlorophyll}]{\text{light energy}} \text{glucose} + \text{oxygen}$$

$$\text{glucose} + \text{oxygen} \longrightarrow \text{carbon dioxide} + \text{water} + \text{energy}$$

These equations are almost the reverse of each other. Both processes use the same materials. Together, they form a cycle. Photosynthesis and cellular respiration form the carbon dioxide—oxygen cycle.

To better understand the carbon dioxide—oxygen cycle, think about this: animals breathe oxygen from the air. Plants take in oxygen and carbon dioxide through their leaves. During respiration, animals and plants use oxygen. They use oxygen to change energy in their food to energy they can use. Plants use energy and carbon dioxide to produce more food and oxygen in the process of photosynthesis. The carbon dioxide—oxygen cycle makes sure that living things have enough oxygen and carbon dioxide.

How do plants grow?

Angiosperms

In a plant that produces seeds, the first step of growth occurs when a tiny seedling emerges from a seed. One type of seed plant, called an angiosperm, produces flowers. Angiosperms are common. Scientists have found between 200,000 and 300,000 species of angiosperms. Only insects have more species than angiosperms. Peach trees, tulips, grasses, daylilies, orchids, oak trees, grapes, tomatoes, and apple trees are all examples of angiosperms.

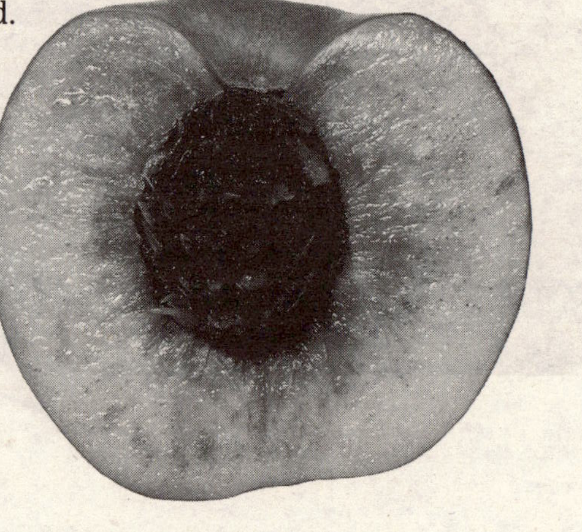

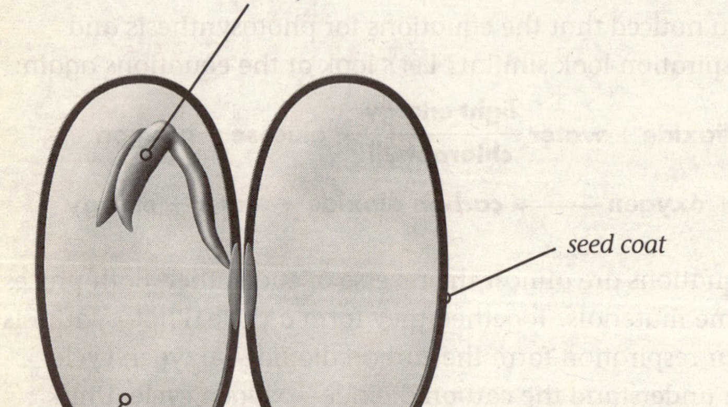

All angiosperms are vascular plants. They have specialized tissues for moving materials around the plant. These tissues—xylem and phloem—were discussed earlier in this book. Most angiosperms have seeds that develop in fruits. Fruits protect the seeds until they are ready to grow.

Humans depend on angiosperms in many ways. We use them as food crops and to make medicines. Lumber, rubber, perfumes, cork, and some fabrics are products made from angiosperms.

Biomes
by Natalie Goldstein

Genre	Comprehension Skill	Text Features	Science Content
Nonfiction	Main Idea and Details	• Captions • Charts • Diagrams • Glossary	Biomes

Scott Foresman Science 6.6

PEARSON
Scott Foresman

scottforesman.com

ISBN 0-328-13985-8

90000

9 780328 139859

What did you learn?

1. What makes up a population of organisms? What makes up a community?

2. What is the difference between a biotic factor and an abiotic factor in an ecosystem? Name one example of each.

3. In what way are the taiga biome and the tundra biome similar?

4. **Writing** in Science The length of a biome's growing season has a huge effect on the number and variety of organisms living there. Explain why a biome with a long growing season has more organisms living in it than a biome with a short growing season.

5. **Main Idea and Details** Plants and animals are adapted to survive in the biome in which they live. Choose one plant or animal you read about and describe the adaptations it has that help it survive in its environment.

60

Illustration: 8 Adam Benton

Photographs: Every effort has been made to secure permission and provide appropriate credit for photographic material. The publisher deeply regrets any omission and pledges to correct errors called to its attention in subsequent editions. Unless otherwise acknowledged, all photographs are the property of Scott Foresman, a division of Pearson Education. Photo locators denoted as follows: Top (T), Center (C), Bottom (B), Left (L), Right (R), Background (Bkgd).
Title Page: (CC) ©Joseph Van Os/Getty Images; 2 ©Ron Thomas/Getty Images; 3 ©DK Images; 5 ©David Paynter/Age Fotostock; 6 ©Jose Fuste Raga/eStock Photo, 7 Jerry Young/©DK Images; 10 (TL) ©Michael Sewell/Peter Arnold, Inc., (BR) ©G.K. & Vikki Hart/Getty Images; 11 (T) ©Cornelia Doerr/Age Fotostock, (B) ©Brian Sytnyk/Masterfile Corporation; 12 (CL) ©Paul A. Souders/Corbis, (B) ©Charlie Ott Photography/Photo Researchers, Inc.; 13 (B) ©Tom Bean/DRK Photo, (CR) ©Frank Greenaway/DK Images; 14 (B) ©Don Pitcher/Stock Boston, (CR) ©Joseph Van Os/Getty Images; 15 (B) ©Doug Sokell/Visuals Unlimited, (CR) ©DK Images

ISBN: 0-328-13985-8

Biomes

by Natalie Goldstein

Glossary

abiotic factor	nonliving part of an ecosystem, such as water or rocks
biome	a large group of ecosystems with similar climates and organisms
biotic factor	living part of an ecosystem, such as a plant or animal
community	a group of populations that interact with each other in a particular area
ecosystem	a community of organisms living together along with nonliving parts of the environment
environment	anything that can affect an organism, including living and nonliving things
population	a group of individuals that belong to the same species and live in the same area

How are organisms on Earth connected?

Connections in the Biosphere

Living things are everywhere, from the highest mountains to the bottom of the ocean. There is a large variety of living things on Earth, from tiny insects to huge whales. The biosphere is the part of Earth where living things are found. The biosphere extends from about 10 kilometers below the ocean's surface to about 10 kilometers above Earth's surface.

Different living things may live in different parts of the biosphere, but they all share Earth's resources. So when something happens to one living thing, it often affects other living things too. Humans are part of the biosphere, so what humans do affects other living things.

All living things interact with other living things and with Earth. Ecology is the study of how living things interact with each other and their environment.

All living and nonliving things are part of this biosphere.

Desert

The main feature of a desert is its lack of precipitation. Most deserts are hot and dry. The driest hot deserts get almost no rainfall. But some deserts can be very cool, especially at night.

Desert plants have adaptations, that help them to live with little water. Cacti have short periods of growth. They have a waxy coating that keeps them from losing water. Many desert animals are active only at night, when it is cooler. Desert birds, snakes, turtles, and other animals have adaptations that enable them to live on little water.

This Sonoran kingsnake lives in Utah, Arizona, New Mexico, and Nevada.

Tundra

The tundra has a very cold climate. Just beneath the surface, the soil is frozen solid all year long. This frozen layer of soil is called permafrost. Water cannot seep through permafrost, so when the topsoil thaws in summer, it turns soggy. During the short summer, mosquitoes and other insects hatch from surface pools. The insects are food for many birds that fly to the tundra in summer to breed. The tundra is so cold and windy that few plants grow there. Short shrubs, moss, and very few short trees grow on the tundra. Animals of the tundra include foxes, hares, many types of birds and lemmings.

The dark feathers of this ptarmigan turn white in winter, which helps it hide from predators in the snow.

Organization of the Biosphere

You probably interact with many living things every day. Do you have a pet? Did you walk your dog or pet your cat today? How many people did you talk to today? It's almost impossible to go through a whole day without interacting with living things.

You also interact with the nonliving things around you. You breathe air, drink water, and are warmed by sunshine. You could not live without any of these things.

Living things, including humans, are called organisms. All the organisms that live together in an area interact with each other. They also interact with the nonliving things in their area. An organism's **environment** is anything that can affect the organism. The environment includes living things and nonliving things.

An individual is a single organism that belongs to one species.
A species is one type of living thing. A **population** is a group
of individuals that belong to the same species. A population of
organisms lives together in the same area. For example, look at the
zebras in the picture. All these zebras make up a population of zebras
that live together in the same place.

Other animals, such as giraffes and elephants, may live in
the same area as the zebras. Giraffes and elephants are different
species. There is a population of giraffes in this area. There is also a
population of elephants in this area. When scientists talk about a
particular population, they define the area in which it lives.

Individuals within a population compete for the resources in
the environment. For example, they compete for food and water.
If resources become limited, some individuals may die. Then the
population gets smaller.

Grassland

Grasslands get too little rain to support many large trees. Yet
grassland soil is very rich in nutrients. Many grasses in this biome
have deep roots. The roots add nutrients to the soil.

Grassland soil is excellent for farming. Every year millions of tons
of wheat, corn, and soybeans are grown on grasslands in the United
States.

Some of the largest animals on Earth live on grasslands. These
include bison, rhinoceros, and giraffes. Coyotes, as well as prairie
dogs and other rodents, are smaller animals of the grasslands.
Insects, such as grasshoppers, are common grassland animals too.

The grassland biome
provides plentiful food
for grasshoppers.

Taiga

The taiga is a biome with long, cold, dark winters. Most trees that grow in the taiga are conifers. These include fir and spruce trees. A few deciduous trees and some shrubs also grow in this harsh, cold biome.

Many taiga animals, such as squirrels and birds, eat the seeds and berries of conifer trees. Large animals, such as elk, deer, caribou, and moose, eat tree bark and plant shoots. Wolves, grizzly bears, and hawks hunt and eat the small animals of the taiga.

The long, thick hair of this caribou helps keep it warm during long taiga winters.

Single populations do not live alone. In any environment, many populations live together and interact with each other. A **community** is a group of populations that interact with each other in a particular area. Zebras, giraffes, and elephants are all part of the same community on an African plain.

If your family has pet dogs, cats, fish, or birds, several populations live in your house. Your house contains a population of humans and a population of each different species of pet. All these different populations are part of the community that is your house.

Communities need the nonliving things in their environment to live. They need air, water, and shelter, among other things. Together, the living and nonliving parts of an environment are called an ecosystem. An **ecosystem** is a community of organisms living together along with the nonliving parts of the environment.

An ecosystem may be as small as a crack in a sidewalk or as large as a huge forest or desert. Earth's biosphere is made up of many ecosystems. Every ecosystem interacts with other ecosystems.

Meeting the Needs of Organisms

All organisms in a community depend on their environment to meet their needs. **Abiotic factors** are the nonliving parts of an ecosystem, such as air, soil, water, sunlight, and temperature. All living things need water to survive. The amount of water in an environment can limit the number of organisms that can live there. Few organisms are able to survive in desert areas.

Plants need sunlight to make their food in the process of photosynthesis. Most organisms cannot make their own food. They depend on plants. Some animals eat plants directly; others eat animals that eat plants. The amount of sunlight an environment gets also affects what kinds of plants and animals that can live there.

An area's temperature is another factor that affects what types of animals and plants can live there. Each species can live only in a particular range of temperature. Polar bears live where it is very cold. Cacti live in desert areas, where it is very hot.

Most organisms need gases in air to live. Land animals breathe oxygen from the air. Organisms that live in water get oxygen that has dissolved in water. Plants need carbon dioxide to make food through photosynthesis.

Deciduous Forest

Deciduous forests grow where summers are warm and winters are cold. Deciduous trees shed their leaves in autumn. They grow new leaves each spring. Oak, maple, and beech trees are common in deciduous forests. Conifers, such as pine trees, also grow here. Shrubs and ferns grow on the forest floor.

Songbirds, deer, bears, and porcupines are common animals in deciduous forests. Because winters are cold, some animal species hibernate to avoid the cold. Many bird species migrate to warmer climates for the winter.

The leaves shed by deciduous trees decay on the forest floor. They add nutrients to the forest soil. The soil beneath deciduous forests is rich in nutrients.

Porcupine

Tropical Rain Forest

Tropical rain forests contain more species than any other biome. Tropical rain forests once covered about 14 percent of Earth's land. Today more than half of these tropical rain forests have been destroyed.

Dead organisms decay quickly in hot, wet tropical rain forests. Plants quickly take up their nutrients. In tropical rain forests, most nutrients are found in plants. The soil is poor in nutrients.

Trees grow very tall in tropical rain forests. Their leafy tops form a dense covering called the canopy. Little sunlight filters through this covering. Though some shrubs grow beneath the trees, few plants grow on the forest floor. Most rain forest animals live in the treetops, where they eat leaves and fruit.

Tree frogs such as these are common in tropical rain forests.

Biotic factors are the living organisms in an ecosystem. Some biotic factors are too tiny to see without a microscope. These include bacteria that live in the soil and algae in the ocean. Mites and protists that live in or on animals are also biotic factors.

Polar bears are adapted to live in a cold environment.

Adaptations

An environment's biotic and abiotic factors shape the communities that live in an ecosystem. All organisms in an ecosystem have adaptations that help them survive there. An adaptation is a characteristic that helps an organism live and reproduce in a particular environment. A polar bear has thick fur that keeps its body warm. Its thick skin absorbs sunlight to warm its body. It has large paws and claws to help it move over the ice and catch food. All these characteristics are adaptations that help the polar bear survive in its cold environment.

What are Earth's biomes?

Climate and Biomes

Different parts of Earth have similar communities. This occurs when places have similar climates and landforms. A **biome** is a large group of ecosystems with similar climates and organisms. Scientists group ecosystems into biomes to help them describe the world.

Climate is the average temperature and precipitation of an area. Climate is very important in determining the characteristics of a biome. For example, the growing season of plants is mainly determined by temperature. Plants can only survive in a biome if they are adapted to its yearly temperatures. Animals depend on plants for food. So when plant populations get larger, animal populations get larger as well.

A tropical rain forest is hot and gets lots of rain. Tropical rain forests have many, many plants. They also have a large variety of animals. Tropical rain forests are one of the richest biomes on Earth.

Characteristics of Biomes

Soil is another important factor in defining biomes. Different types of soil occur in different places. The type of soil an area has determines what plants can grow there. Some soils hold water near the surface. These areas have plants with shallow roots. Plants with deep roots could not survive in these soils.

As you read about different biomes, think about the type of soil found in each. Think about how organisms are adapted to live in a biome. Remember that a biome is not one particular place. A biome is a group of similar ecosystems, which may occur in many places on Earth.

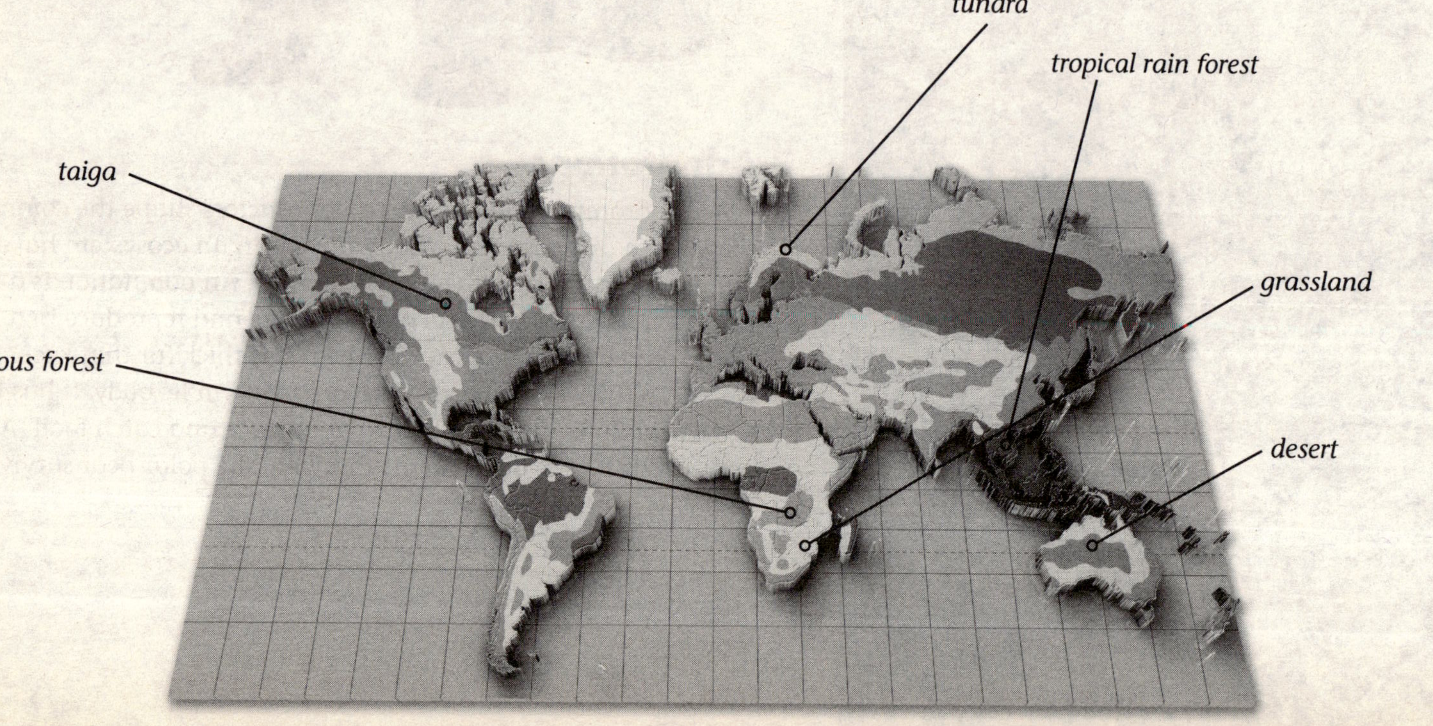

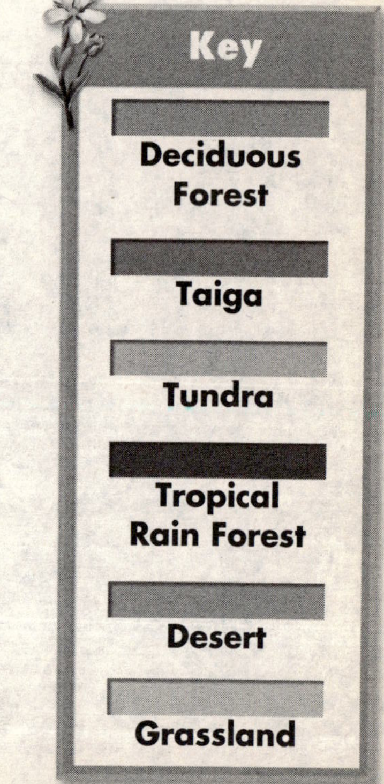

Ecosystems

by Martin E. Lee

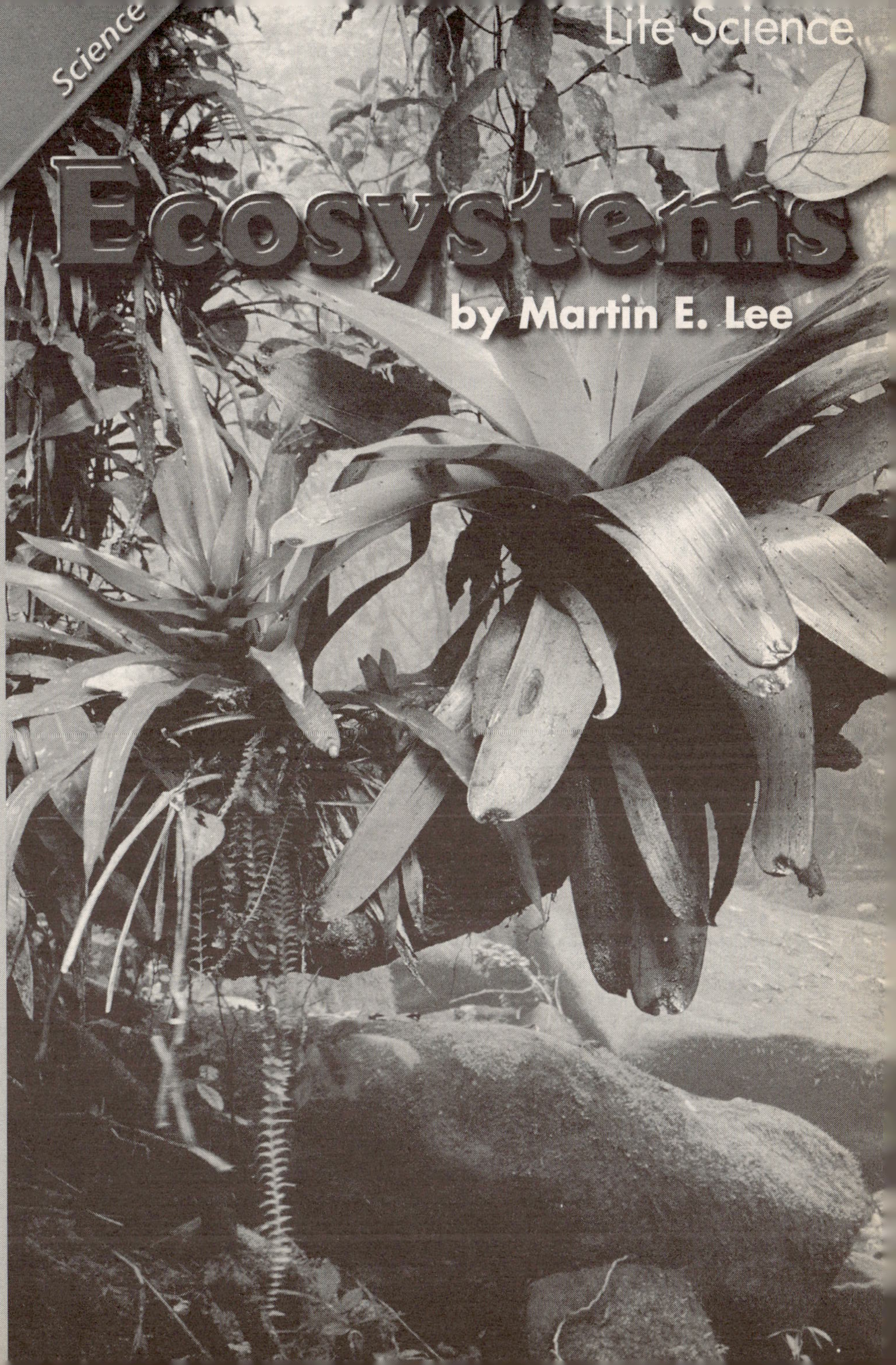

Genre	Comprehension Skill	Text Features	Science Content
Nonfiction	Predict	• Captions • Charts • Diagrams • Glossary	Ecosystems

Scott Foresman Science 6.7

PEARSON

Scott Foresman

scottforesman.com

ISBN 0-328-13988-2

9 780328 139880

90000

Vocabulary

competition

decomposer

energy pyramid

host

parasite

succession

symbiosis

What did you learn?

1. How does most life on Earth get energy from the Sun?

2. What causes competition in an ecosystem?

3. What are some examples of symbiotic relationships?

4. **Writing** in Science Earth recycles many of its resources. Write to describe how Earth recycles nitrogen, carbon, and water. Use details from the book to support your answer.

5. **Predict** What do you think would happen to fennec foxes if their environment got very cold?

Illustration: 15 Clint Hansen
Photographs: Every effort has been made to secure permission and provide appropriate credit for photographic material. The publisher deeply regrets any omission and pledges to correct errors called to its attention in subsequent editions. Unless otherwise acknowledged, all photographs are the property of Scott Foresman, a division of Pearson Education. Photo locators denoted as follows: Top (T), Center (C), Bottom (B), Left (L), Right (R), Background (Bkgd).
Title Page: Norman Banks/U. S. Geological Survey; 2 (BC) ©DK Images, (BR) ©Royalty-Free/Corbis; 3 ©James Balog/Getty Images; 4 ©DK Images; 5 ©Patrick Johns/Corbis; 6 Frank Greenaway/©DK Images, ©DK Images, ©H. Taylor/OSF/Animals Animals/Earth Scenes; 7 ©DK Images, ©Harold Taylor/OSF Limited; 8 (B) ©DK Images, Kim Taylor and Jane Burton/©DK Images, Frank Greenaway/ ©DK Images; 9 Frank Greenaway/©DK Images, Dave King/©DK Images, ©DK Images; 12 ©Norbert Wu/Minden Pictures; 13 ©Michael & Patricia Fogden/Minden Pictures; 14 ©Mike Severns/Getty Images; 15 ©Ralph C. Eagle Jr./Photo Researchers, Inc., ©Eye of Science/Photo Researchers, Inc., ©Biophoto Associates/Photo Researchers, Inc.; 16 ©Richard L. Carlton/Visuals Unlimited; 20 Norman Banks/U. S. Geological Survey, ©1980/Gary Braasch, ©1999/Gary Braasch; 21 ©James Hanley/Photo Researchers, Inc.; 22 © AFP/Getty Images; 23 ©Will McIntyre/Photo Researchers, Inc., Getty Images, ©Tony Freeman/PhotoEdit

ISBN: 0-328-13988-2

Copyright © Pearson Education, Inc.

Ecosystems

by Martin E. Lee

Glossary

competition	the fight among organisms to survive where resources are limited
decomposer	an organism that gets energy by breaking down the remains of dead organisms
energy pyramid	a model that shows how energy moves through an ecosystem
host	the organism that is harmed in a symbiotic relationship
parasite	the organism that is helped in a symbiotic relationship
succession	a series of predictable changes that take place over time
symbiosis	a close, long-term relationship between organisms that benefits at least one organism

Why do adaptations vary among species?

Surviving in the Environment

It can be difficult to stay cool in a hot desert. The fennec fox's large ears help it stay cool? Blood rushes to the fennec fox's ears when it gets hot. Body heat then moves from the fox's blood into the air. So large ears are an adaptation that help keep the fennec fox cool.

By contrast, the arctic fox lives in extreme cold. It must stay warm to survive. Small ears are an adaptation that help the arctic fox. Its small ears reduce heat loss.

The table shows other adaptations of the fennec fox and arctic fox.

Adaptations for Different Environments	
Fennec fox	• Pale fur reflects the Sun's rays. • Fur on feet protects against burning desert sand.
Arctic fox	• Thick fur changes from white in winter to brown in summer to help the fox blend in with its environment. • Thick fur on feet reduces heat loss.

Fennec fox

Arctic fox

Preventing Problems

It's better to prevent problems before they happen in the first place. Here are ways you can help:

- Understand how you affect your ecosystem.
- Learn how to reduce the harm you cause.
- Reuse, recycle, or reduce your use of natural resources.
- Know how ecosystems work.
- Get involved. Join environmental groups to help.

As an adult, you will make decisions that affect yourself and your community. And what your community does will affect other regions in your state and country. These choices may even affect the world at large. Learn to be an informed citizen now. It will make it easier for you to become a responsible adult.

Recycling aluminum saves energy.

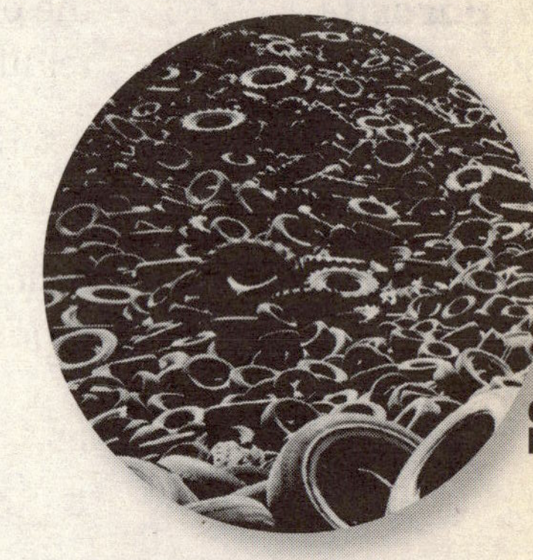

Tires are made from fossil fuels, which cannot be renewed. Ground rubber from old tires can be used as a building material.

Recycling plastic items, such as milk jugs, saves natural resources.

Saving Ecosystems

In 1989 an oil spill damaged the coast of Prince William Sound in Alaska. Millions of gallons of oil leaked from an ocean oil tanker. It polluted the land and water and put a great strain on the ecosystem. Thousands of workers helped to clean up the mess. Many washed oily animals, such as otters, with soap and water. They scrubbed oil from the rocks. But even with all the work and money spent, much of the damage could not be undone. Billions of animals died, including 22 orca whales and 250,000 sea birds. The area still has not fully recovered.

Oil spills must be cleaned up quickly to save an ecosystem.

Bright colors on the mandrill's face help identify him to other mandrills.

Structural Adaptations

Many different environments exist on Earth. Adaptations help species live in their environment. Adaptations develop over many generations. A species changes as individuals are born with new traits that give them a better chance to survive. Individuals that survive pass these traits to their offspring. This process repeats over long periods of time.

Adaptations help living things get energy. They help them to find mates and to reproduce. They protect organisms from dangers in their environments. Adaptations can be related to behaviors, structures, and some body processes.

Behaviors and Body Processes

Behavioral adaptations can be as important as structural adaptations. The male mandrill uses its teeth for more than eating. He shows his large front teeth to warn off other males. Behavioral traits in animals are inherited over generations. Examples of these behaviors include spiders making webs and birds making nests.

Body processes are also adaptations that help animals to survive. Some animals hibernate in winter. Their body temperature falls. Their heart rate and breathing slow down. This helps animals live through the cold.

How do organisms get energy?

Energy Flow in Ecosystems

Most living things on Earth depend on the Sun's energy either directly or indirectly. The leaves of a berry bush use energy from the Sun to make food known as glucose. Plants use the chemical energy in glucose as energy for their life functions. Plants are producers—organisms that can make their own food.

Animals cannot use sunlight to make their own food. Animals are consumers—organisms that get energy by eating other organisms. When a bear eats berries, it gets the energy stored in them. The bear uses energy from the Sun indirectly.

Human Impacts

Humans are part of the ecosystem where they live. Human activity can change the environment. Some organisms cannot survive these changes.

Think of the trash you threw away so far today. In 2001 each American produced about four pounds of trash a day! Much of it ends up in landfills. The advantage of using landfills is that they reduce odor. They are safer than open dumps. But they can cause problems too. Unsafe waste, such as paint and batteries, can leak and harm ecosystems.

Building landfills can cause some organisms to lose their habitats and die. Over time, landfill space gets used up, and new areas must be found for the waste.

People may cause harm without even knowing it. Pollution enters the air when people drive their cars. Power plants cause pollution too. Even ranching and farming can have harmful results. When livestock overgraze, plants die. The soil erodes. Fertilizers can enter the water cycle and pollute lakes and rivers.

Many organisms lose their habitats when new houses and roads are built.

How do ecosystems change?

Natural Changes

Mount St. Helens, located in the state of Washington, erupted in 1980. Ash, smoke, rock, and mud covered the area. The land became suddenly bare. Other natural events can also quickly affect ecosystems. Fires, earthquakes, landslides, and floods cause changes.

Climate changes affect ecosystems more slowly. Climates can get warmer or cooler. Such changes can affect the types of living things that can exist in that place.

Succession is a series of predictable changes that take place over time. Succession happens because living things affect their location. The land near Mount St. Helens didn't stay bare. As organisms die, their decayed bodies help make new soil. After soil forms, seeds may take root and form new plants. In turn, these plants change the environment so that other plants can grow. Over time, animals will come back to the area.

Toadstools cannot make their own food. But they cannot eat other organisms either. When organisms die and fall to the ground, their bodies decay. A **decomposer** is an organism that gets energy by breaking down the remains of dead organisms. Toadstools are decomposers. Decomposers return the materials from the dead organism's body back into the environment. Decomposers help provide materials that other organisms can use. Without decomposers, nothing would ever decay. Dead organisms would just pile up forever!

Mount St. Helens erupted, leveling the forest around it.

Some buried seeds survived.

Slowly, the ecosystem recovers as plants make the soil more fertile and animals move into the area.

Food Chains

In an ecosystem, some organisms produce food, while others consume food. This is how energy travels in an ecosystem. A food chain shows a path of energy through an ecosystem. The arrows on a food chain always point toward the organism that is getting the energy. Follow the food chain from the microscopic organisms to the common mussel, then to the herring gull. What other food chains can you find?

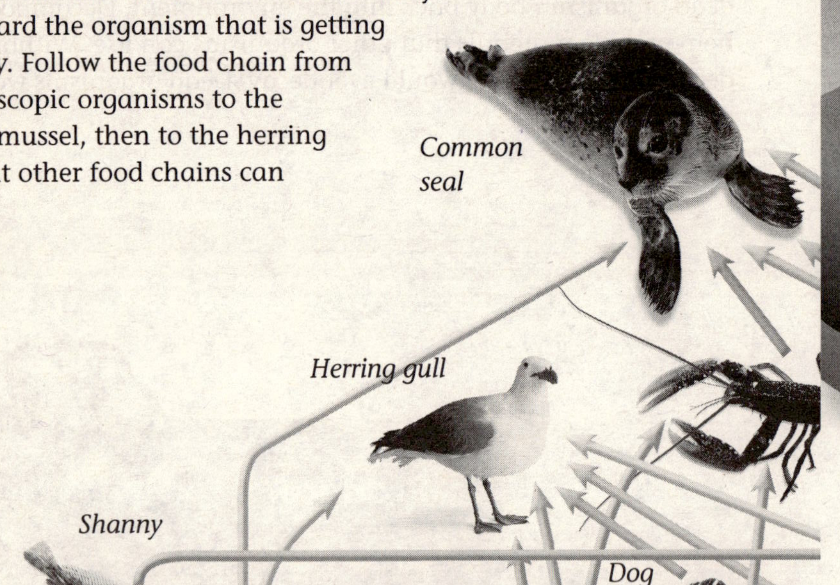

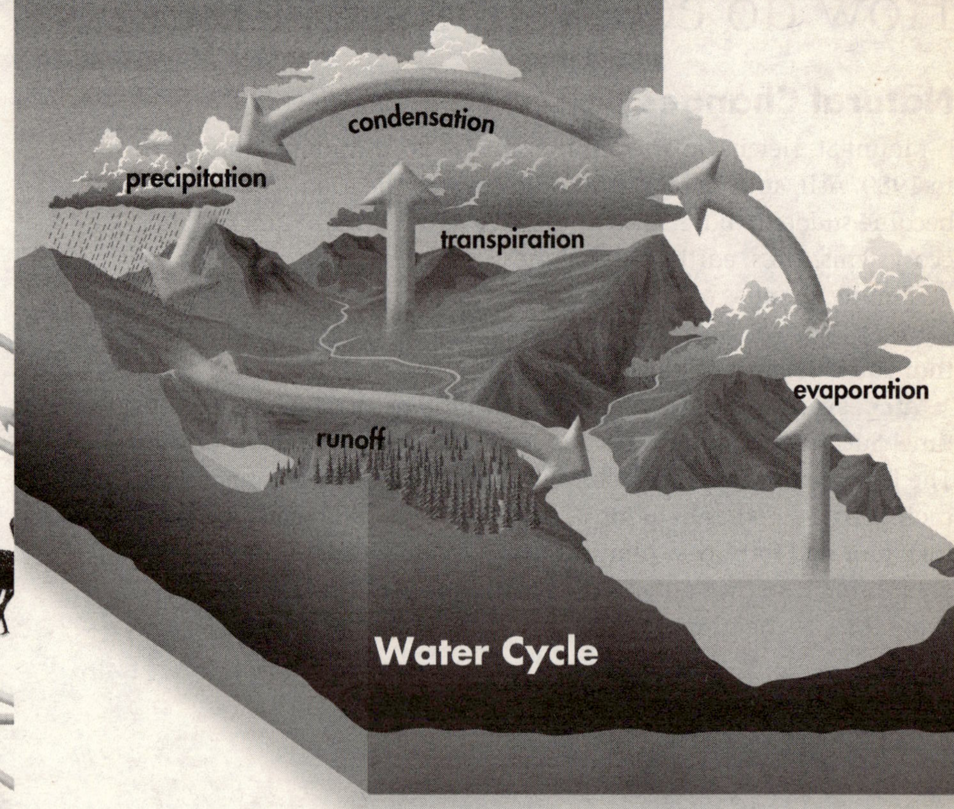

Water Cycle

Life depends on water. Just think about a day without a sip of it! Many chemical reactions that keep organisms alive need water to occur. Water reaches all parts of an ecosystem through the water cycle.

As the Sun heats water on Earth, the water changes from a liquid to a gas. This process is called evaporation. When water evaporates, it forms a gas called water vapor. Water vapor also enters the air when the leaves of plants give off water vapor during transpiration. Your breath contains water. The breath of animals also contains water.

Water in the air rises and then cools. Clouds form when water vapor condenses on dust or salt particles in the air. Water returns to Earth as rain, snow, or hail.

Carbon Cycle

About 18 percent of your body is make up of carbon. Carbon is cycled during photosynthesis and during cellular respiration. It is cycled in other ways too. Decomposers, such as fungi and bacteria, break down waste and dead organisms. Carbon is released during this process. Some organisms do not decompose. Over time, they may form fossil fuels, such as coal, oil, and natural gas. These organisms had carbon in them when they lived. It gets released into the air when the fuels are burned. Carbon is also released as carbon dioxide when volcanoes erupt.

Food Webs

Many different food chains exist in an ecosystem. Food chains have producers and consumers. Consumers often eat other consumers. Organisms may be part of several food chains. A food web is made up of several food chains that are interconnected. Look at this food web. How many food chains include the herring gull?

Energy Pyramid

A food chain shows how energy travels from producers to the top consumer. But a food chain does not show how much energy moves from one organism to another.

Not all of the energy that a green plant takes in from the Sun moves to other organisms. The plant uses some of the energy for its own life processes. Some energy is lost as heat. This repeats throughout a food chain. A snake uses energy to slide along the ground. A wood mouse uses energy to dig itself a hole. Organisms must use energy to grow, move, and reproduce. So, only part of the energy can move to the next level of the food chain.

Nitrogen Cycle

All living things need nitrogen. It is a key part of protein, which all cells must have. Air is about 78 percent nitrogen. But the nitrogen in air is "free." It is not mixed with other elements. Organisms need nitrogen that is "fixed," or combined with other elements.

Bacteria that live in the soil can fix nitrogen. Some bacteria live in nodules, or bumps, on the roots of plants. The bacteria take in food from the plant. The plant gets nitrogen from the bacteria. Animals get nitrogen by eating plants or prey that ate plants.

There are other ways for fixed nitrogen to enter the soil. Lightning fixes a small amount of nitrogen. Rain carries this nitrogen into the ground. Decomposers also put fixed nitrogen into the soil as they break down dead organisms. Then plant roots absorb it.

How does nitrogen get back into the air? Some bacteria live freely in the soil. These bacteria break down fixed nitrogen into free nitrogen that can enter the air. This steady movement of nitrogen through ecosystems is called the nitrogen cycle.

How do materials cycle through ecosystems?

Recycling Matter

The amount of matter on Earth is limited, just as energy is. So why doesn't it run out? The reason is that much of Earth's resources keep moving through ecosystems. Organisms need key materials, such as nitrogen, water, carbon, and oxygen. If the materials did not move in cycles, they would run out. Earth's cycles allow organisms to use the same materials over and over. Three main cycles of nature are the nitrogen cycle, the carbon cycle, and the water cycle.

An **energy pyramid** is a model that shows how energy moves through an ecosystem. The pyramid gets smaller as it nears the top. There is more energy at lower the levels. There is less energy towards the top of the pyramid because most of it has been used by organisms for life processes or has been given off as heat. Only energy stored in the tissues of an organism can pass from one level to the next.

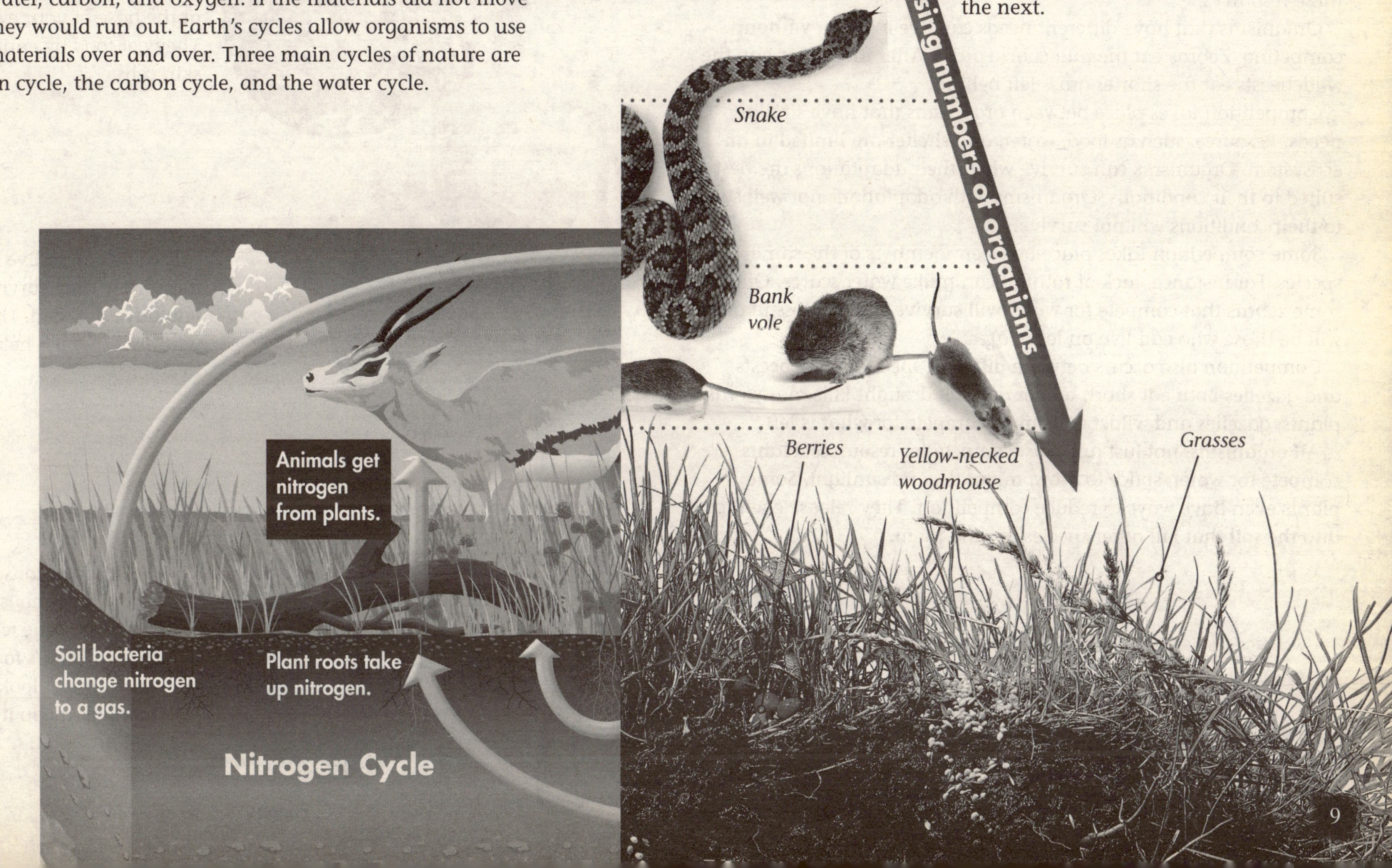

How do organisms compete for resources?

Competition

Competition is the struggle between organisms to survive when resources are limited. Like all organisms, the animals on the African savannah need food, water, and shelter. The animals that survive get these resources.

Organisms that have different needs can live together without competing. Zebras eat the tall, coarse grass. After the zebras eat, the wildebeests eat the shorter grass left behind.

Competition takes place between organisms that have similar needs. Resource, such as food, water, and shelter are limited in an ecosystem. Organisms can survive when their adaptations are best suited to their conditions. Organisms with adaptations not well suited to their conditions will not survive.

Some competition takes place between members of the same species. For instance, lack of rainfall can make water scarce. Only some zebras that compete for water will survive. The successful ones will be those who can live on less water.

Competition also occurs between different species. Wildebeests and gazelles both eat short, tender grass. If drought kills many grass plants, gazelles and wildebeests must compete for what is left.

All organisms, not just animals, compete for resources. Plants compete for water, space to grow, minerals, and sunlight. Some plants even have ways to reduce competition. They release chemicals into the soil that kill other species around them.

Symbiosis in the Human Body

You are part of many symbiotic relationships. Most are harmless, but some can hurt you. Here are some examples:

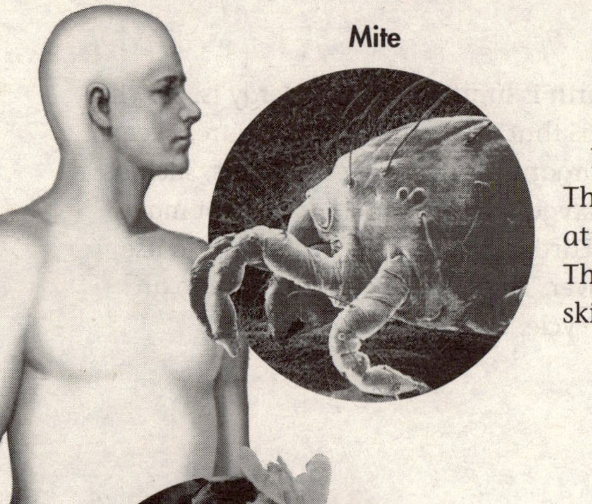

Mite

Mites are very tiny creatures. They can live on your skin or at the base of your eyelashes. They get food by eating dead skin cells.

E. coli bacteria live in your intestines. They survive on food you have digested. They make vitamin K, which helps blood to clot.

E. coli

A fungus causes athlete's foot. This fungus lives on the skin of the foot. If you have athlete's foot, the skin on your feet looks dry and cracked. It can itch and feel hot.

Fungus

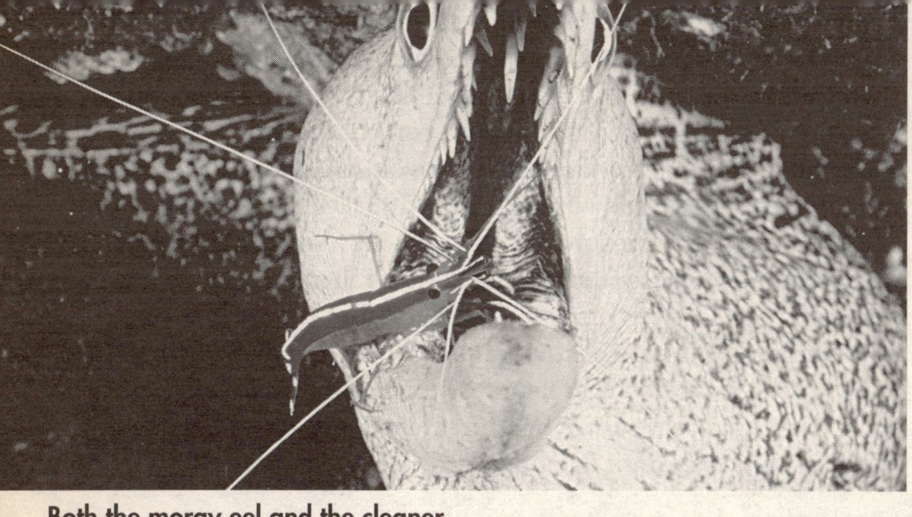
Both the moray eel and the cleaner fish benefit from symbiosis.

Symbiosis

Symbiosis is a close, long-term relationship between organisms that benefits at least one organism. One type of symbiosis is parasitism. In this case, one organism is helped, but the other is harmed. The **parasite** is the organism that is helped. The **host** is the organism that is harmed. Parasites do not usually kill their hosts. This is because they need the host for food.

Parasites may live outside of their hosts. Fleas are parasites that live off the blood of mammals. As the flea gets blood, it can make the host itch. In some cases, the host can become ill. Parasites may also live inside a host. Horses may take in parasites called tapeworms when they graze. The tapeworms live and feed in the horse's intestines. This can cause poor digestion and affect the horse's growth.

When two organisms live together, both may benefit. Mutualism is a symbiotic relationship in which two organisms benefit from living together. The cleaner fish eats bits of dead tissue and parasites from the moray eel's mouth. A relationship that benefits one organism but neither benefits nor harms the other is called commensalism. Barnacles that cling to the side of a whale get food from the water, but do not help or harm the whale.

81

14

Predators and Prey

Animals have different ways to get food. Some animals eat plants. But these plant-eating animals may be the food for other animals. An animal that feeds on other animals is called a predator. The animal a predator eats is called prey.

There must be a balance between the number of predators and prey in an ecosystem. When there are more predators, more prey is eaten. This doesn't leave enough prey for the predators. Some will be unable to find food and will die. Then the numbers of prey will increase because there will be fewer predators.

Predators and prey have adaptations that help them survive. Many predators are adapted to hunt and kill. They may be fast, strong, or have strong senses to find prey. Other predators have behaviors that help them catch prey. Pack animals, such as wolves, work as a group to separate and attack individuals from a herd of prey. An alligator floats with only its eyes and nostrils out of the water. When a frog or other animal comes too close, the alligator suddenly grabs it with its strong jaw muscles and sharp teeth.

Not all predators chase their prey. Hundreds of stinging cells are released into any prey that brushes against a tentacle of a jellyfish. Chemicals in the stinging cells paralyze the prey so that it cannot move out of danger. Then the jellyfish can eat the prey.

Prey have developed adaptations to avoid predators. Some prey animals release a poison when they get attacked. Some have bright colors to warn away predators. Others act like a more dangerous animal. Some prey use camouflage to make themselves look like something else, such as a plant, a stick, or a rock.

Prey animals also use behavioral adaptations to avoid being killed by predators. Have you ever heard the expression, "playing possum?" It means to hold very still. When threatened, possums play dead. Predators that only hunt live prey will leave them alone.

The sea urchin has sharp, hard spikes. Predators that attack it will get jabbed.

The poison dart frog is brightly colored to warn away predators. Glands in the frog's skin release bad-tasting, poisonous chemicals.

Plate Tectonics

by Mary Miller

Genre	Comprehension Skill	Text Features	Science Content
Nonfiction	Draw Conclusions	• Captions • Charts • Diagrams • Glossary	Plate Tectonics

Scott Foresman Science 6.8

PEARSON
Scott Foresman

DK

ISBN 0-328-13991-2

90000

9 780328 139910

scottforesman.com

What did you learn?

1. How did Alfred Wegener explain the formation of continents on Earth in his theory of continental drift?

2. What is the layer called that is made of Earth's crust and upper mantle?

3. What is the place called where two plates meet?

4. **Writing** in Science According to the theory of plate tectonics, Earth has about twenty plates that are constantly moving. Write to explain the different movements that plates can make and what impact these movements have on Earth's surface. Include details from the book to support your answer.

5. **Draw Conclusions** What might scientists conclude if an instrument detected a tremor in Earth's crust?

Illustration: 4, 6, 8, 10, 21, 23 David Preiss
Photographs: Every effort has been made to secure permission and provide appropriate credit for photographic material. The publisher deeply regrets any omission and pledges to correct errors called to its attention in subsequent editions. Unless otherwise acknowledged, all photographs are the property of Scott Foresman, a division of Pearson Education. Photo locators denoted as follows: Top (T), Center (C), Bottom (B), Left (L), Right (R), Background (Bkgd).
Title Page: ©David Parker/Photo Researchers, Inc.; 2 (BL) ©Garry Black/Masterfile Corporation, (R) ©Mitsuaki Iwago/Minden Pictures; 3 ©Roy Ooms/Masterfile Corporation; 6 ©Simon Fraser/Photo Researchers, Inc.; 9 (TR) ©Ken Lucas/Visuals Unlimited, (CL) ©Arnold Newman/Peter Arnold, Inc.; 12 Alcoa, Inc.; 13 U. S. Geological Survey; 16 ©Bernhard Edmaier/Photo Researchers, Inc.; 17 (T) ©David Parker/Photo Researchers, Inc., ©Brad Wrobleski/Masterfile Corporation; 20 (TL) ©Tom McHugh/Photo Researchers, Inc., (CL) ©Yann Arthus-Bertrand/Altitude/Peter Arnold, Inc.; 22 (CL) ©Tony Freeman/Index Stock Imagery, (B) Science Museum-London/DK Images

ISBN: 0-328-13991-2

Plate Tectonics

by Mary Miller

Glossary

continental drift	the theory that continents drifted apart in the past and continue to do so today
core	the center part of the Earth that has a molten outer core and a solid inner core
crust	the top layer of rock that covers Earth
fault	a break in Earth's crust where plate boundaries slide past each other
lithosphere	the section that contains Earth's crust and the upper mantle
mantle	the layer of Earth between the crust and the core which includes an outer mantle of solid rock and an inner mantle of partly melted rock
plate boundary	the edge of one plate, where it meets another plate
plate tectonics	a theory that explains the origin of Earth's features because of plate movement

What are Earth's layers made of?

Earth's Variety

Victoria Falls is one of Earth's many land features. The flat, raised land around the waterfall is called a plateau. A deep crack, called a gorge, splits the plateau. Water flows over the plateau into the gorge.

In the United States a large plateau, called the Colorado Plateau, covers parts of Utah, New Mexico, Arizona, and Colorado. This landform was once flat. Over thousands of years, water washed away some of the rock, making landforms such as the Grand Canyon.

In the African desert of Namib, mountains rise high above the nearby plains. The Napa Valley region in northern California is an example of a valley. Valleys are found between mountains that are close together.

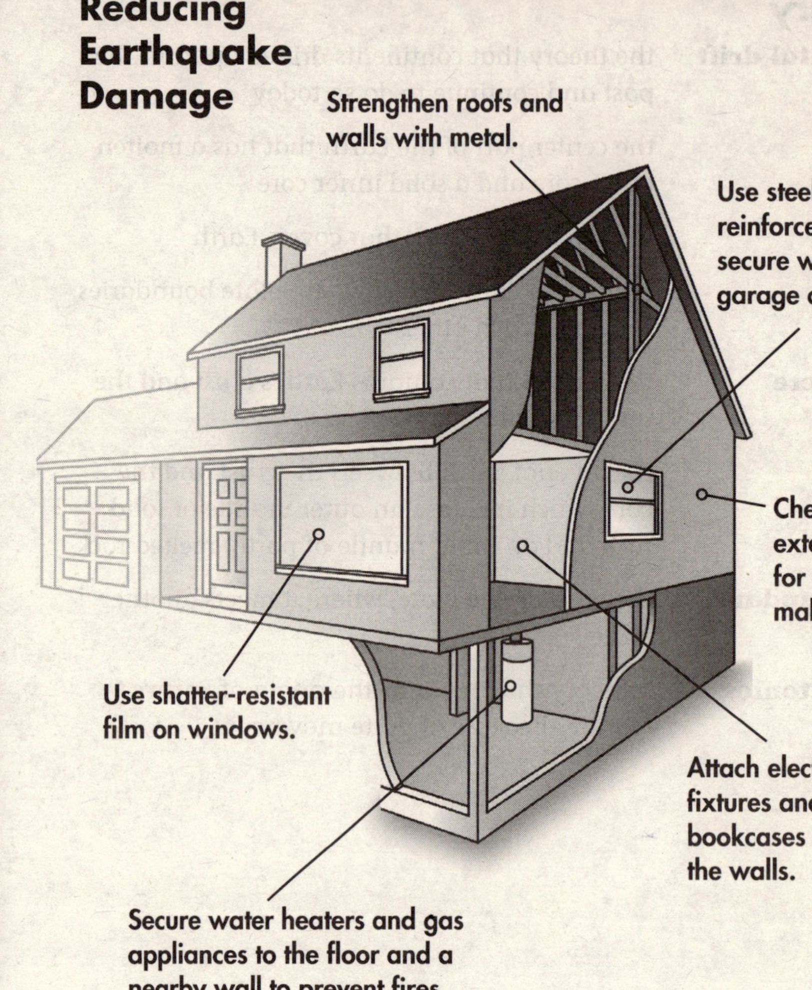

Naukluft Mountains, in
Namib Desert, Africa

Reducing Earthquake Damage

Preparing for Earthquakes

The best way to avoid earthquake damage is to be prepared. Many people take extra steps to protect their homes from earthquakes. The diagram above shows ways that people can do this.

Predicting Volcanoes and Earthquakes

Scientists use many different tools to predict the threat of an earthquake or volcano. A seismometer can detect tremors, or shaking movements, in Earth's crust. Tremors are signals that magma may be rising in a volcano or that Earth's plates are shifting. Scientists use a tiltmeter to detect changes in the slope, or tilting, of the land.

Scientists can often tell where and when a volcano will erupt. Volcanoes often follow a pattern of eruption. So future activity is likely to occur at sites of past eruptions.

Earthquakes are harder to predict than volcanic eruptions. It is difficult to predict when plates will suddenly shift. So scientists listen for tremors with a seismograph. As the ground moves, the free-moving part of the seismograph moves back and forth. The movements are recorded on a sheet of paper.

A ball would drop from a dragon's mouth to a frog's mouth if this ancient seismometer detected a tremor.

seismograph

Not all of Earth's features are visible. Some can be found underwater. Below the surface of the Atlantic Ocean is a long row, called a ridge, of mountains. Some of these mountains are actually volcanoes. There are also long, narrow grooves in the floor of the ocean. These grooves are called trenches.

The landforms that you see may change depending on where you live. You may live in an area that has many mountains. Maybe you live near plains. Valleys, mountains, and plains are very different from each other. But all of them were formed from processes that began deep inside Earth.

Napa Valley, California

Earth's Layers

The surface of Earth is solid. It is made of rock and soil. There are different layers under the surface. Some of these layers are solid; some are not.

Above Earth's surface there is a thin layer of gases called the atmosphere. It contains the air we breathe. Humans could not live on Earth without the atmosphere.

The solid layer of rock that covers Earth is called the **crust.** The crust is the part of Earth that people live on. The thickness of the crust is not the same everywhere on the planet. The crust covered by ocean water is about 6–11 kilometers thick. On dry land, the crust is about 35–40 kilometers thick. Mountain ranges have the thickest crust. Yet, the crust is only a thin shell when compared with Earth's other layers.

Outer Core
Scientists think the outer core is made of iron mixed with smaller amounts of other materials.

Inner Core
The inner core is made of iron.

Magma forms from the melting crust of one plate that sinks underneath another. Gases in the magma can cause pressure to build up. Eventually the pressure is too great for the crust of the overlapping plate. Magma bursts through the crust as a volcano. Magma that reaches Earth's surface is called lava. Many volcanoes are found on the ocean floor. Magma flows out of the volcano. The cooled lava causes new crust to form.

D Caldera
A caldera is a crater that is at least 1.6 km wide. A lake may form in a caldera. The 9.6 km wide Crater Lake in Oregon formed in a caldera of the Cascade Mountain Range.

E Basalt plain
Flows of lava spill out onto nearby ground, forming new crust. Basalt is a dark volcanic rock.

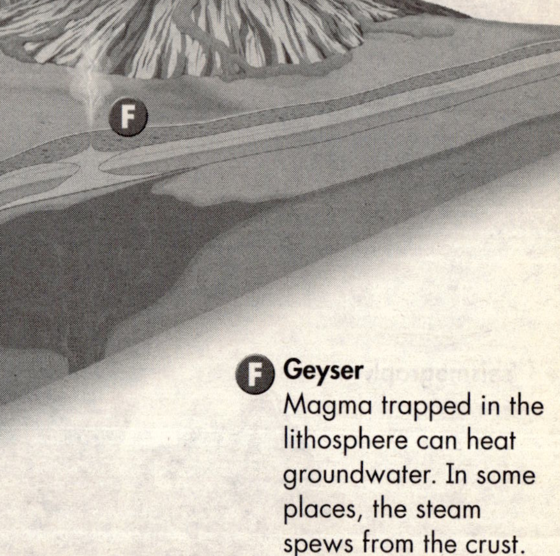

F Geyser
Magma trapped in the lithosphere can heat groundwater. In some places, the steam spews from the crust.

Volcanoes

A volcano is an opening in Earth's surface. Red-hot magma rises out of this hole. Like earthquakes, most volcanoes occur near plate boundaries. The theory of plate tectonics explains why this occurs.

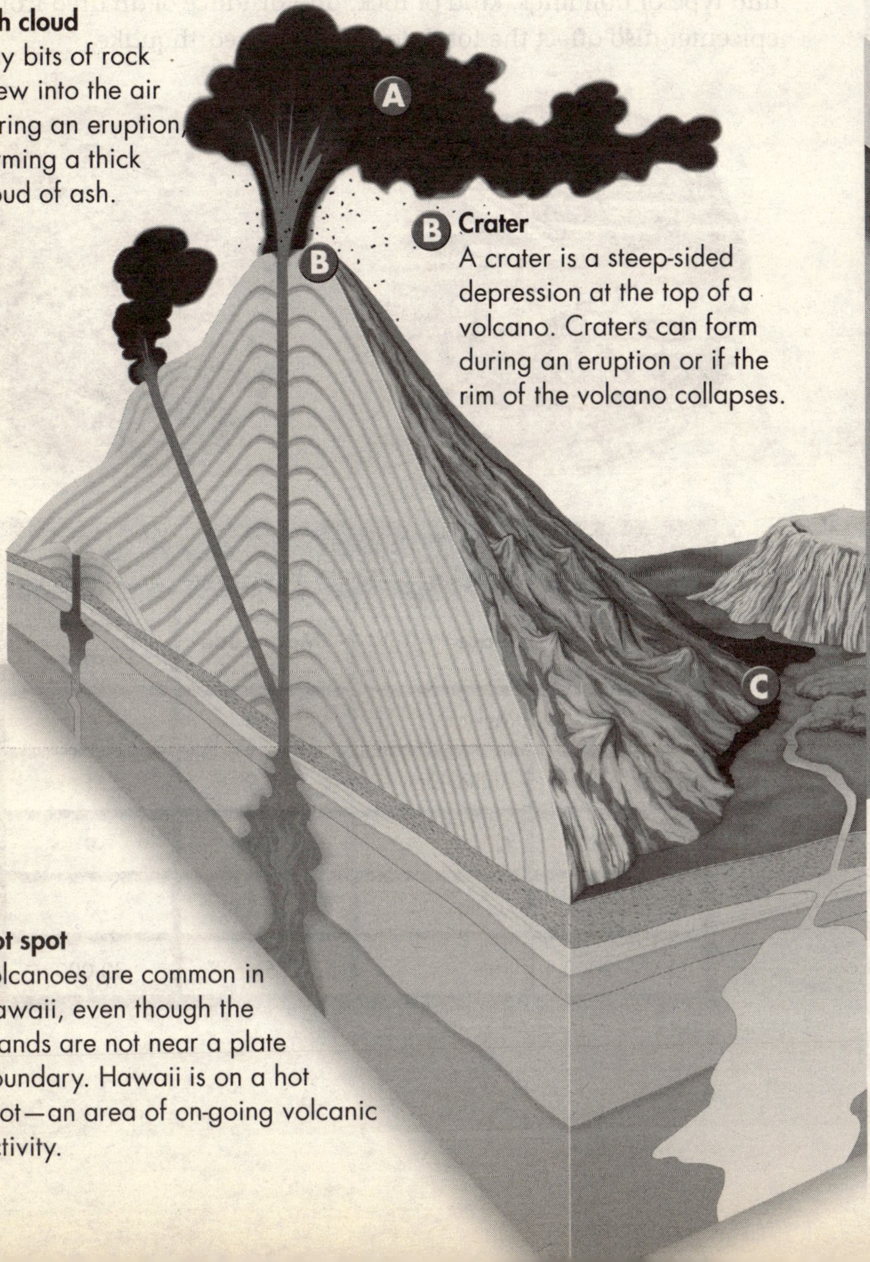

A Ash cloud
Tiny bits of rock spew into the air during an eruption forming a thick cloud of ash.

B Crater
A crater is a steep-sided depression at the top of a volcano. Craters can form during an eruption or if the rim of the volcano collapses.

C Hot spot
Volcanoes are common in Hawaii, even though the islands are not near a plate boundary. Hawaii is on a hot spot—an area of on-going volcanic activity.

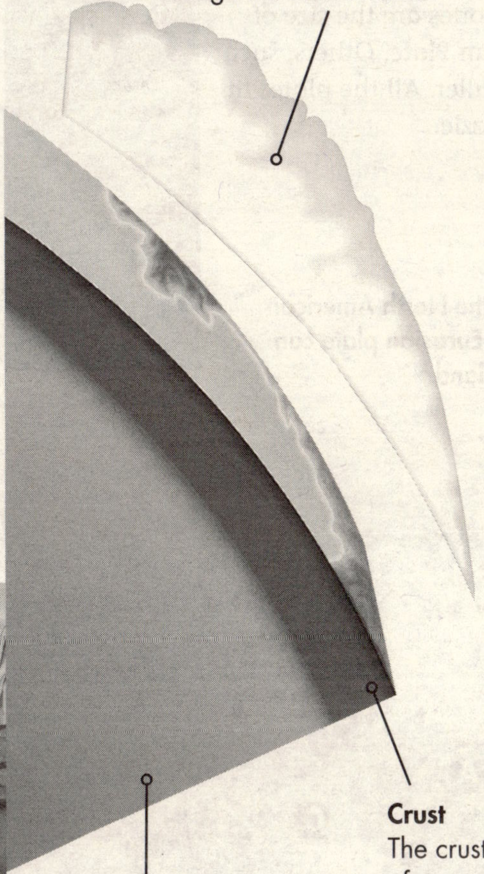

Atmosphere
Earth's atmosphere contains nitrogen, oxygen, carbon dioxide, and water that cycle through the environment.

The layer of Earth just below the crust is called the **mantle.** This thick layer makes up most of Earth's mass. The outer part of the mantle is solid, just as the crust is. The inner part is so hot that the rock can flow slowly over time.

The **core** is at the very center of Earth. The core is very dense. It has been compacted by the weight of all the rock above it. Scientists think that the temperature of the core is about 7,000°C. That is as hot as the surface of the Sun. There is an inner core and an outer core. The outer core is so hot that it is a liquid. The inner core is solid.

Mantle
This middle layer is made mostly of oxygen combined with silicon, magnesium, and iron.

Crust
The crust is made mostly of oxygen combined with other materials—silicon, aluminum, iron, and calcium.

Earth's Plates

Earth's crust and the outer part of the mantle form the **lithosphere.** The lithosphere is not a solid layer. It is broken into pieces called tectonic plates. The plates have different shapes and sizes. The larger ones are the size of continents, such as the South American Plate. Others, such as the Caribbean Plate, are much smaller. All the plates fit together like the pieces of a jigsaw puzzle.

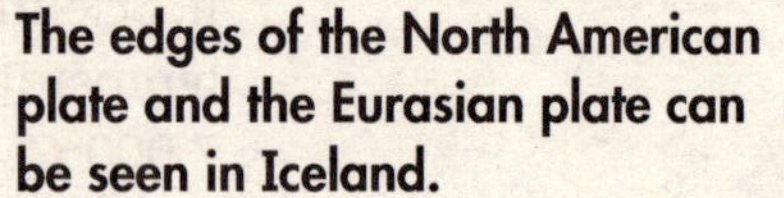

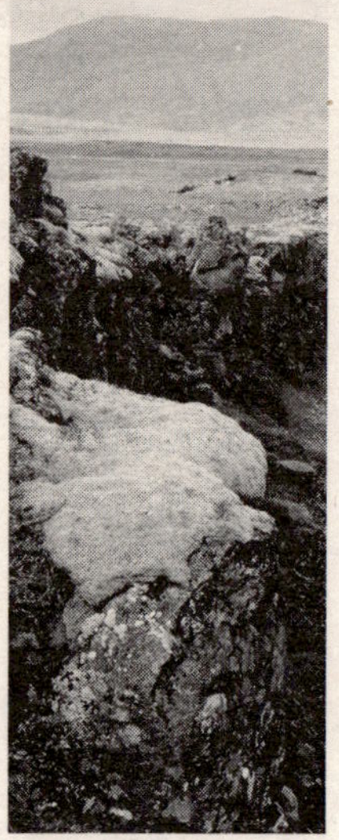

The edges of the North American plate and the Eurasian plate can be seen in Iceland.

Major Tectonic Plates

- A Pacific Plate
- B North American Plate
- C Cocos Plate
- D Nazca Plate
- E South American Plate
- F African Plate
- G Eurasian Plate
- H Indian Plate
- I Australian Plate
- J Antarctic Plate

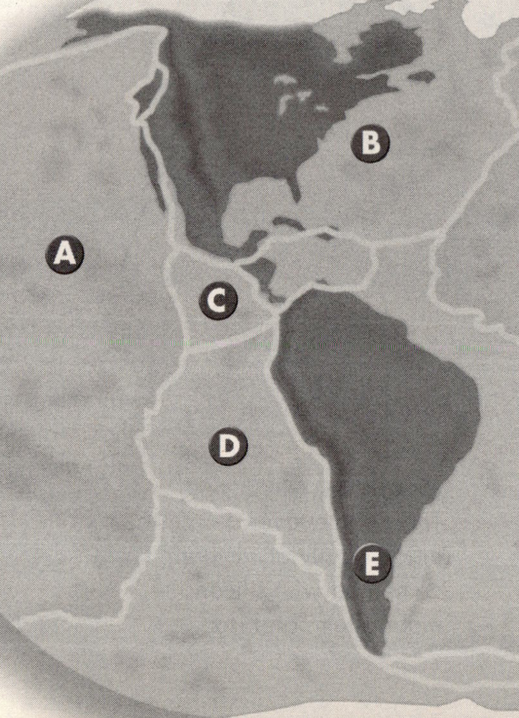

The strength of an earthquake is measured on a magnitude scale. The number tells scientists how much energy is released. For each increase of 1 on the scale, 31 times more energy is released.

The table below shows the magnitude and number of deaths caused by several earthquakes. Magnitude alone does not explain the damage or number of deaths an earthquake will cause. The number and type of buildings, kind of rock, and distance of an area from the epicenter also affect the total damage of an earthquake.

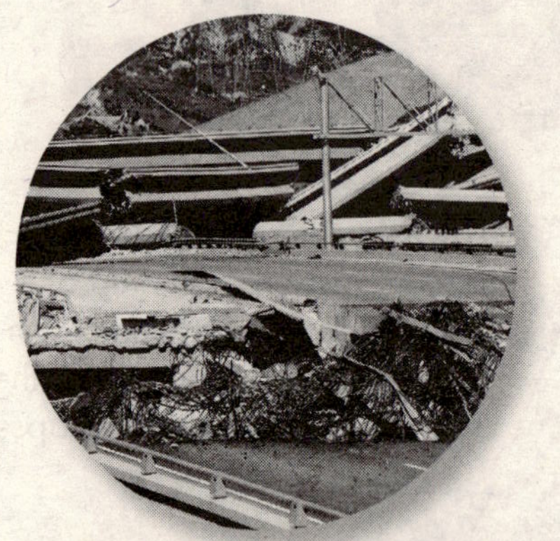

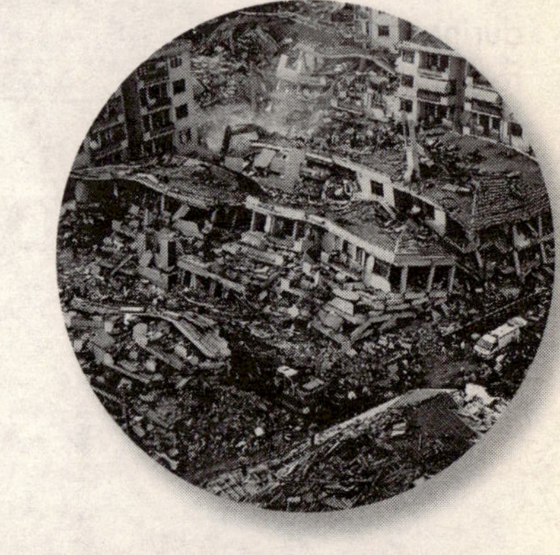

Earthquakes

Date	Place	Magnitude	Total Deaths
1/22/2003	Mexico	7.6	29
3/29/2003	Afghanistan	5.9	1
5/27/2003	Algeria	5.8	9
9/27/2003	Russia	7.3	3
12/26/2003	Iran	6.6	30,000

What causes earthquakes and volcanoes?

Earthquakes

Plate movement is usually too slow to be seen or felt. Sometimes, jagged rock edges in the lithosphere stop a plate from moving. Over time, pressure builds at the jam site. If the pressure grows too strong, the rocks jerk forward. Earth's crust shakes. An earthquake has occurred.

The area underground where the earthquake occurs is called the focus. The spot on Earth's surface directly over the focus is called the earthquake's epicenter.

The energy from an earthquake is carried by waves. The waves spread out from the focus and epicenter. Some waves cause the ground to move back and forth. Other waves cause the ground to move up and down or even in a circular motion.

Waves lose energy as they spread out. That is why the damage from an earthquake is greatest closest to the epicenter.

Most earthquakes take place near the edges of plates. In the United States, most earthquakes occur in California and Alaska. These states are on the boundary between two plates.

There are two kinds of crust, continental and oceanic. The continental crust makes up continents. The oceanic crust makes up the floor of the ocean. The plates do not follow the edges of the continents. Many plates are made of both continental and oceanic crust. Most of the United States is on the North American Plate. Part of the Atlantic Ocean is also on this plate. The western part of California is on the Pacific Plate. The ocean covers the rest of the Pacific Plate. Oceans and other bodies of water cover most of Earth's lithosphere.

The mantle below the lithosphere is made of molten rock. The plates float on the molten rock of the mantle.

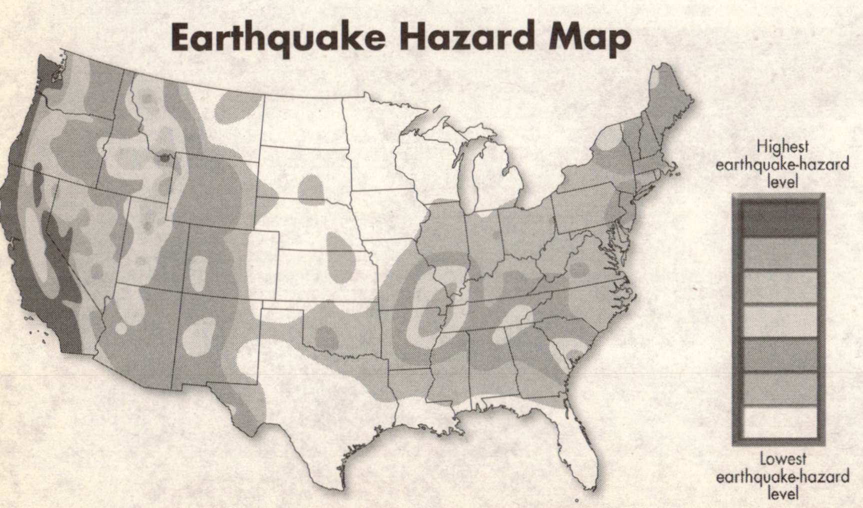

Earthquake Hazard Map

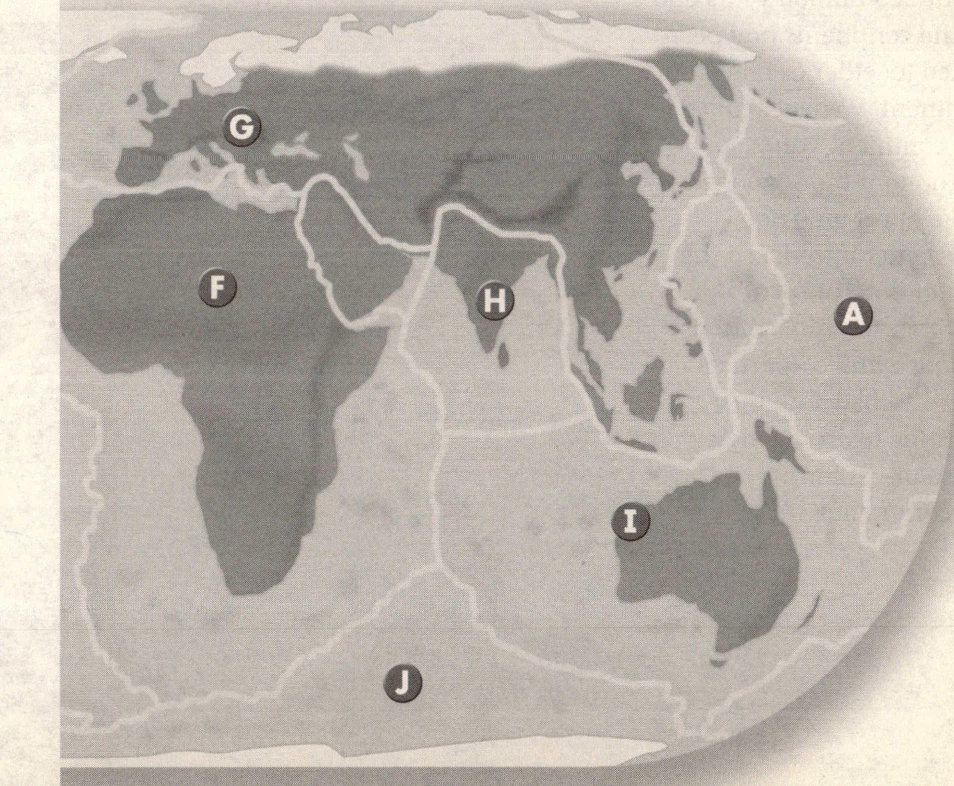

How do Earth's plates help create landforms?

Continental Drift

Long ago, people thought that Earth's continents were always in the same place. Then, scientists noticed that the coastlines on some continents seemed to fit together like pieces of a jigsaw puzzle.

In 1912, Alfred Wegener, a German scientist, came up with an explanation for the fit of the coastlines. He suggested that about 225 million years ago all the continents had been joined together as one giant continent. Wegener called this continent Pangaea. He thought that Pangaea broke apart long ago.

Wegener introduced the idea of **continental drift.** This theory claims that as Pangaea broke apart, its pieces shifted, and they continue to do so today. These pieces form the continents.

250 million years ago

65 million years ago

Today

Plates push against each other at colliding boundaries. The edges of the plates can rise up to form large mountains. One plate can also slide under another plate. This action can cause deep ocean trenches. It can also cause earthquakes or volcanoes.

Fracture Boundary
The San Andreas fault is a boundary between the North American plate and the Pacific plate. The two plates are sliding past each other.

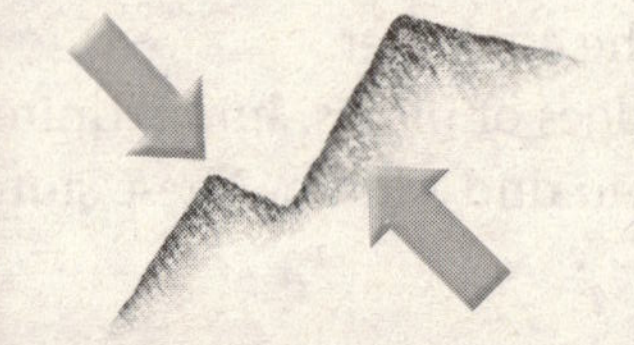

Colliding Boundary
The Himalaya mountains are still rising where the Eurasian plate and the Indian plate are pushing against each other.

Plate Boundaries

A **plate boundary** is the edge of a plate. Plates meet at their boundaries. Plates move slowly in different directions. They can move apart, collide, or slide past each other. Different landforms are made by the changes that slowly take place at each plate boundary.

Plates move away from each other at spreading boundaries. Gaps form between the plates. Magma can bubble up from the mantle through these gaps. Huge valleys can form. This kind of plate movement causes seafloor spreading.

Plates slide past each other at fracture boundaries. Sliding boundaries often cause a break in Earth's crust called a **fault.** Strong earthquakes can occur when these plates move.

Spreading Boundary
The Mid-Atlantic Ridge cuts across Iceland at the boundary between the Eurasian plate and the North American plate. These plates are moving away from each other.

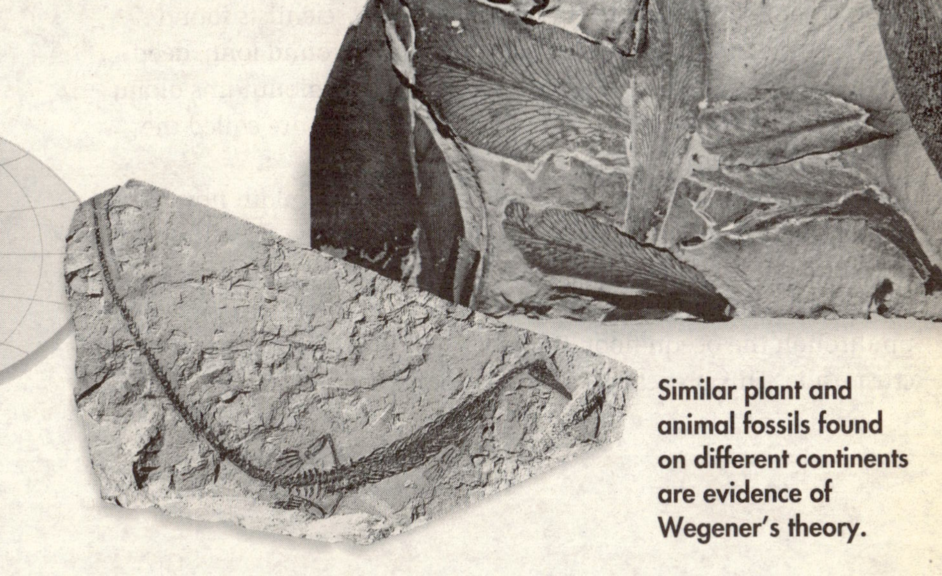

Similar plant and animal fossils found on different continents are evidence of Wegener's theory.

Wegener had evidence other than the shape of the continents to support his theory. Some plant and animal fossils were found on the eastern coast of South America. They were almost identical to fossils found on the western coast of Africa. Wegener did not think that these identical fossils were a coincidence. He thought that the animals had once lived together when the continents were joined as Pangaea.

Evidence to support Wegener's theory was also found in rocks. Layers of rock along the eastern coast of South America matched layers of rock along the western coast of Africa. Wegener believed this showed that the coastlines might have once been joined.

Wegener was not able to explain the forces that caused continents to move. Because of this, most scientists rejected Wegener's ideas.

The Spreading Ocean Bottom

For some time there was no new evidence to support the theory of continental drift. But things changed when scientists found better ways to map the ocean's floor. Scientists found long, deep ocean trenches. They also discovered a chain of mountains along the floor of the Atlantic Ocean. These mountains are called the Mid-Atlantic Ridge.

In 1960 a scientist named Harry Hess tried to explain how the trenches and ridges came to exist. He said that new crust forms at ocean ridges. Molten rock called magma pushes up through Earth's crust. As the magma cools, it forms new crust. More magma comes up through the ocean floor. It pushes both the new crust and the old crust aside. This process is called seafloor spreading.

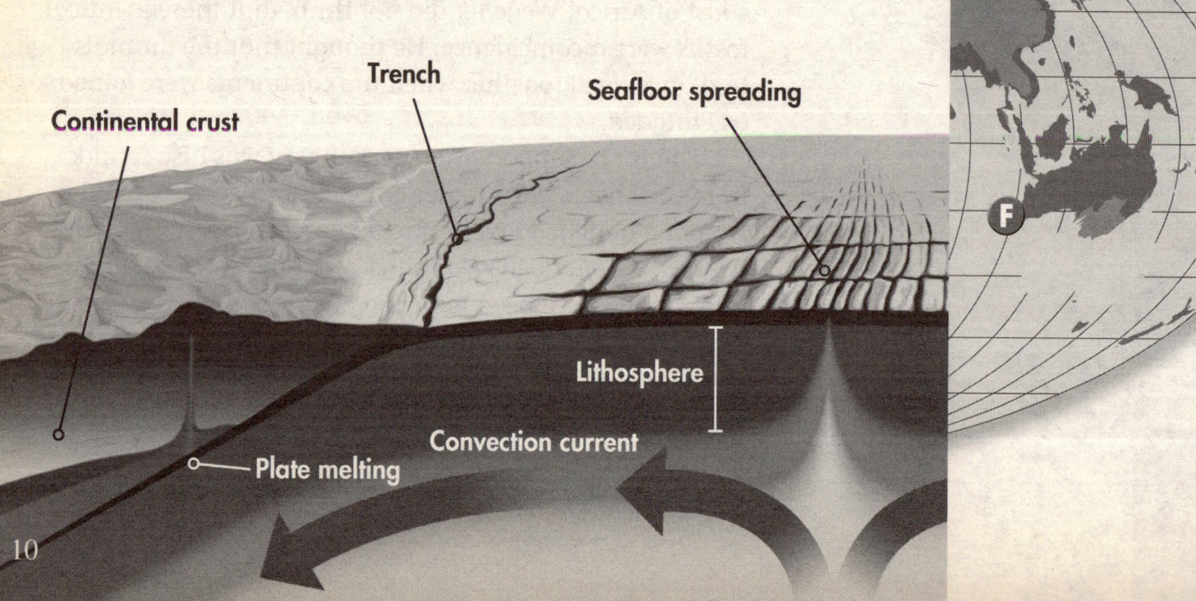

Earth in the Future

The map shows how Earth might look 50 million years from now.

A The Atlantic Ocean will widen.

B The part of California that lies on the Pacific plate will move north.

C North America and South America will split apart.

D Africa and Asia will no longer be joined.

E Parts of western Africa may become an island.

F Australia will move northward and collide with Indonesia.

Earth's plates are constantly moving, but in different directions. Some plates move toward each other, and other plates move away from each other. Other plates just slide past each other.

Scientists receive radio signals from Global Positioning System (GPS) satellites in space to figure out how the plates move. The laser beams can measure the distance between plates. Using laser beams, scientists have measured the North American plate and the Eurasian plate. They are moving away from each other about two centimeters a year. Earth's features can change over time as plates continue to move.

The theory of plate tectonics explains many of Earth's features. For example, mountain chains can form where plates move together. But if plates move apart, hot magma can rise to the surface. This is one way a volcano can form.

Scientists believe that plate movement has always taken place at about the same rate. They predict that the plates will continue to move. The continents may one day come together to form another Pangaea-like continent.

How do scientists explain Earth's features?

Theory of Plate Tectonics

Wegener's idea of continental drift suggested that continents moved. It did not explain many other parts of Earth's crust, such as mountains and volcanoes. Today, scientists use the theory of plate tectonics. **Plate tectonics** explains why Earth's features look the way they do.

This theory states that Earth's lithosphere is broken into about 20 moving plates. The continents and ocean floor make up the surfaces of these plates.

As Earth's plates move, the ocean floor spreads apart. Magma rises up to fill the gap in the ocean floor. Plates move because of currents caused by melted rock in the mantle.

When a liquid is heated, its particles move faster and spread apart. Because hot liquids weigh less, they can float above cooler liquids. The hot liquid rises and cools. It becomes heavier and sinks. More hot liquid can then rise above it. This process is called convection. Earth's mantle is not a liquid, but the hot rock flows slowly, resulting in currents that constantly rise, circle around, and fall. When the mantle moves, the plates floating on it also move. Convection is the force that moves Earth's plates.

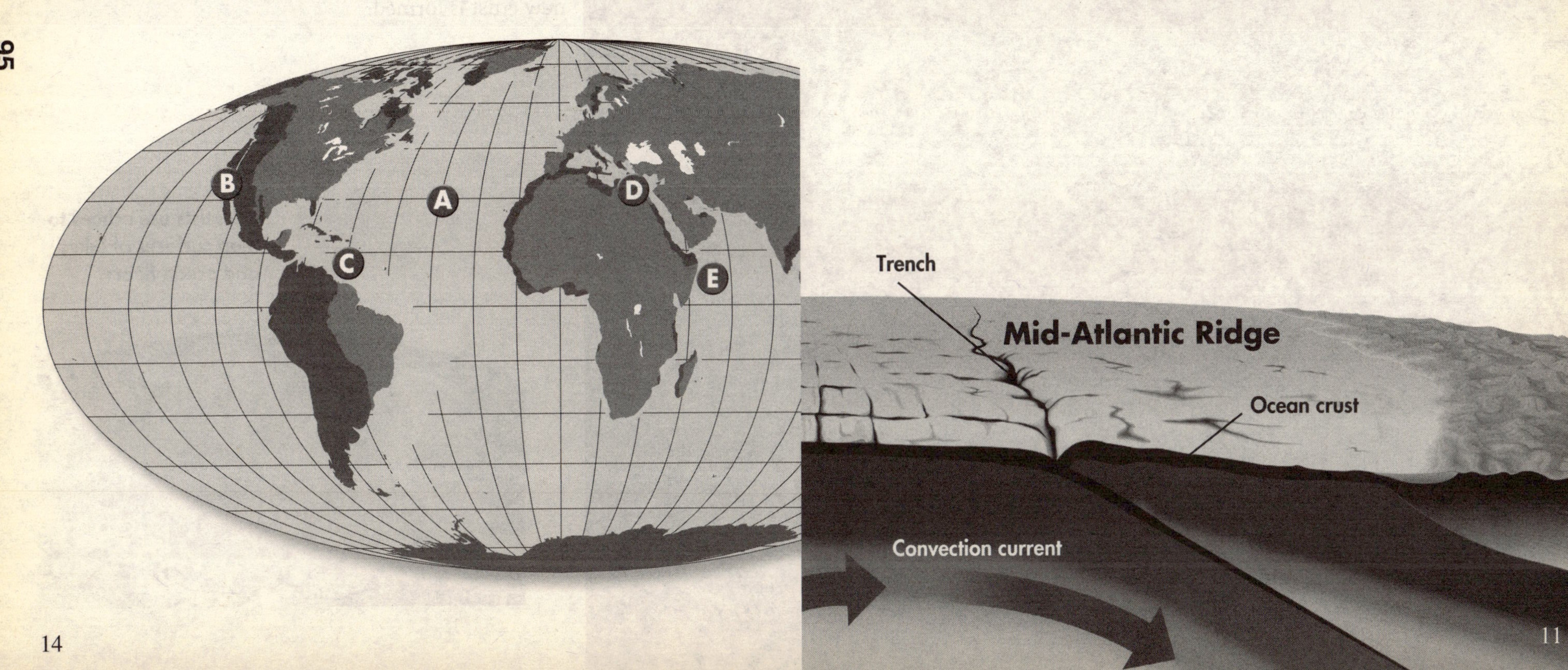

Proof of Continental Drift

Seafloor spreading helped support Wegener's ideas. Yet scientists wanted more proof for continental drift. In the early 1960s some scientists were studying the magnetism of rocks near the Mid-Ocean Ridge. They noticed a pattern. In some places, the magnetism faced north. In other places, it faced south. Scientists found alternating rows of north/south patterns. These rows spread out from the ridge.

Earth's magnetism "flips" about every half million years. If the planet's magnetism faced north, it would flip to face south. A half million years later, Earth's magnetism would flip to face north again. And so the cycle goes. As lava cools, rocks are formed. The particular magnetic pattern at that time is "frozen" into the rocks. The rows of alternating magnetic patterns are evidence that rocks slowly spread as new crust is formed.

Scientists use echoes to map surfaces of lakes and ocean floors.

Genre	Comprehension Skill	Text Features	Science Content
Nonfiction	Compare and Contrast	• Captions • Charts • Diagrams • Glossary	Rocks and Minerals

Scott Foresman Science 6.9

PEARSON

Scott Foresman

scottforesman.com

DK

ISBN 0-328-13994-7

90000

9 780328 139941

Rocks and Minerals

by Marcia K. Miller

crystal

humus

igneous rock

metamorphic rock

mineral

organic matter

rock

sedimentary rock

What did you learn?

1. How can a piece of tile help identify a mineral?

2. How do scientists use the positions of rocks to learn about Earth's history?

3. Why must contaminated soil be cleaned as soon as possible?

4. **Writing** in Science You can sort all of Earth's rocks by how they were made. Name the three types of rocks. Write to tell how each is formed. Include details from the book to explain the main traits of each type of rock.

5. **Compare and Contrast** How are humus and loam alike and different?

Illustration: Title Page: Tony Randazzo ; 6, 10-11 Tony Randazzo
Photographs: Every effort has been made to secure permission and provide appropriate credit for photographic material. The publisher deeply regrets any omission and pledges to correct errors called to its attention in subsequent editions. Unless otherwise acknowledged, all photographs are the property of Scott Foresman, a division of Pearson Education. Photo locators denoted as follows: Top (T), Center (C), Bottom (B), Left (L), Right (R), Background (Bkgd).
2 ©E.R. Degginger/Color-Pic, Inc.; 3 (CR, BR) ©DK Images; 4 (TL, BCL, C, BR, CR) ©DK Images, (BL) ©Charles D. Winters/Photo Researchers, Inc.; 5 (BL, BR, CL, CR) ©DK Images, (BC) Natural History Museum/©DK Images, (TR) Richard M. Busch; 8 ©Brian Sytnyk/Masterfile Corporation; 9 (TL) ©DK Images, (BR) ©Charles O'Rear/Corbis; 12 ©Barry L. Runk/Grant Heilman Photography; 14 ©Breck P. Kent/Animals Animals/Earth Scenes

ISBN 0-328-13994-7

Glossary

crystal	an arrangement of particles with a pattern that repeats
humus	the dark-colored organic part of soil formed from rotted plant and animal remains
igneous rock	type of rock formed when molten rock cools and hardens
metamorphic rock	type of rock formed when pressure, heat, or chemical reactions change one type of rock into another
mineral	a natural, nonliving solid that has a specific chemical structure
organic matter	any substance made of living things or the remains of living things
rock	a solid natural material made of one or more minerals
sedimentary rock	type of rock made when bits of rocks and minerals settle in layers and harden

Rocks and Minerals

by Marcia K. Miller

PEARSON
Scott Foresman
DK

What are rocks and minerals?

Minerals

A **mineral** is a natural, nonliving solid that has a specific chemical structure. A substance must fit all parts of this definition to be called a mineral. For example, coal is not a mineral because it comes from plants that lived long ago.

You may be familiar with more minerals than you think you are. The crust of Earth has more than four thousand kinds of them! Yet only about two dozen are common. Gold is a valuable mineral. Copper is a familiar mineral. Did you ever look closely at sand? If so, you probably saw a mineral called quartz. You may have heard of ruby, emerald, and diamond. These rare, beautiful minerals are called gems.

The mineral magnetite is magnetic.

Factors That Affect Soil

Climate is a key factor that affects the soil in an area. Weathering happens faster where there are heavy rains and high temperatures.

It rains a lot in tropical climates. Heavy rains wash minerals from the topsoil into the subsoil. So tropical topsoil is thin. Not much grows in it. On the other hand, desert areas get little rain. Weathering is slow in the desert. The rain that does fall dries quickly. Minerals in rainwater collect on the soil.

The type of soil that forms also depends on the parent rock below it. The minerals in the rock can affect how it weathers. They also affect its makeup. For example, reddish soils come from rocks that are rich in iron.

Soil color depends on the organic matter it contains. Soils with more organic matter are darker. Soils from the forests of the eastern United States have lots of dark brown humus. Tropical soils have little humus, so they are much lighter in color.

Landforms also affect the soil on them. Mountains usually have thin layers of topsoil. This is because much of the soil has worn away from their slopes. Flat land usually has a thick layer of topsoil.

Earthworms help the soil. They mix the soil as they move through it. They also break down organic matter.

Kinds of Soils

Did you ever dig a hole in the ground? If so, you know that soil can look and feel different. Most soils are a mix of clay, silt, and sand.

- Clay soils are fine-grained. Clay soils hold water very well. But clay soils can get waterlogged in heavy rains.
- Silt soils have medium-sized grains. They drain fairly well.
- Sandy soils are large-grained. They hold water poorly. They have little organic matter.
- Loam is a type of soil that mixes clay, silt, and sand in nearly equal parts. This is the best kind of soil for plants.

Minerals are made up of crystals. A **crystal** is an arrangement of particles with a pattern that repeats. The shape of a crystal is determined by this repeating pattern.

Crystals can be large if they form under just the right conditions. But most crystals are tiny. You would need a microscope to see them.

Identifying Minerals

Minerals have properties that set them apart. Scientists use some key properties to identify minerals.

Scientists rank minerals by hardness. A mineral's hardness tells how difficult it is to scratch its surface. The hardness scale goes from 1 (the softest) to 10 (the hardest). Diamond has a hardness of 10. In fact, diamond is Earth's hardest known natural substance. Talc is a very soft mineral. It has a hardness of 1.

Cleavage is also used to identify minerals. Many minerals tend to split, or cleave, along flat planes. They split in patterns that scientists can recognize. Other minerals do not split. They break into uneven bits instead.

You can also tell a mineral by the shape of its crystals. For example, quartz crystals look like hexagons.

Mineral Hardness

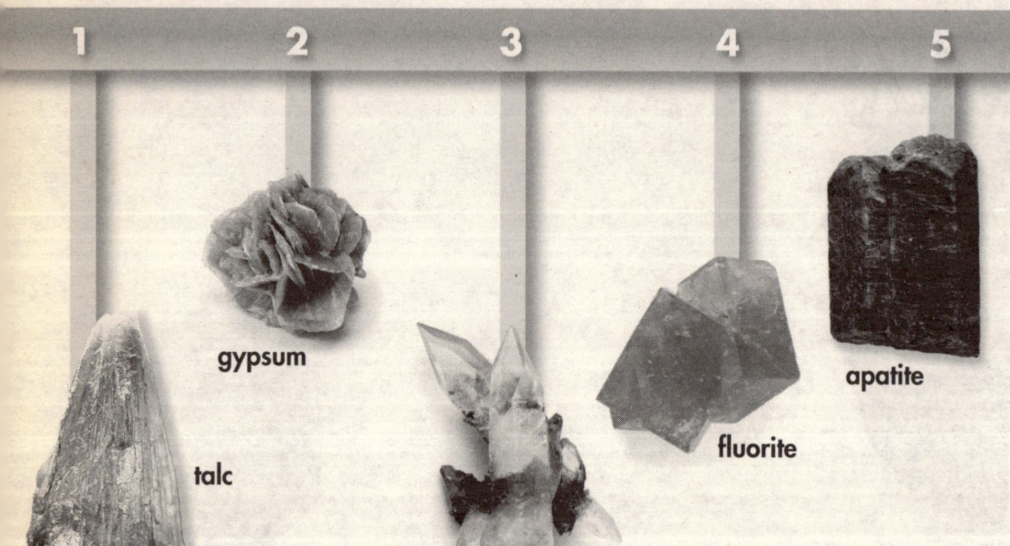

Over time, bacteria, fungi, and plants grow in the particles. When these organisms die, they rot. **Organic matter** is any substance that is made of living things or the remains of living things. **Humus** forms from rotted plant and animal remains. Humus has important nutrients that plants need.

Soil forms in three layers. The first layer is the topsoil. Topsoil is a mixture of small bits of rock, humus, and other organic matter. Most of the living things in soil are found in the topsoil. Loose organic matter, such as dead leaves and twigs, covers the topsoil. Rainwater sinks into the topsoil and washes minerals into the second layer.

The second layer is the subsoil. Subsoil has less organic matter than topsoil. This causes subsoil to have a lighter color. Minerals carried away from the topsoil build up in the subsoil.

The third and lowest layer is called parent rock. This layer has very little organic matter.

3 Mature soil is home to many living things. It is rich in organic matter and holds many plant roots.

Why is soil important to living things?

Forming Soil

Soil is made up of weathered rock, air, water, and the remains of living things. Almost all land organisms need soil to live. Plants get water and minerals from soil. Animals need plants for food. Insects, small animals, fungi, and bacteria live in the soil.

You have read about the rock cycle. Rocks are also part of the process that forms soil. New soil begins when rock starts to break down. This process, called weathering, can be caused by physical changes such as frost, drought, or high heat. Rainwater and the chemicals it carries can also break down rock. Rock bits get smaller and smaller as they weather. Air and water fill the spaces between the bits of rock. These tiny bits of rock, along with the air and water, are the nonliving parts that make up soil.

1 First small bits of rock collect on the surface. Tiny plants start to grow. They break down the rock some more. This is the beginning of soil.

2 More soil forms. Larger plants appear. Layers form. Humus is the dark brown soil.

The four mineral samples look different, but the reddish brown streaks show that all are hematite.

You can use color to identify minerals. But sometimes different samples of the same mineral can have different colors. For example, pure corundum has no color. But when its crystals have some chromium in them, corundum forms a ruby, which is a red gem. A mineral's streak shows its true color. The streak is the mark made when you rub it against a tile.

Luster is how a mineral looks in reflected light. A mineral may look like metal, greasy, or even waxy.

Some minerals have special properties. Fluorescent minerals show colors under ultraviolet (UV) light. A few minerals, such as magnetite, are magnetic.

Rocks

Most minerals are not found in their pure form. They are usually mixed into rocks. A **rock** is a solid natural material made up of one or more minerals.

Sedimentary rock is made up of bits of rocks and minerals. It forms in layers. The oldest rock is at the bottom. Newer layers sit on top of the older ones. Sedimentary rock is a kind of "history book." Past events can be found in each of its layers. Some evidence is the remains of dead animals or plants. Such remains, known as fossils, appear only in sedimentary rock. Limestone is a sedimentary rock is made up of the shells of tiny sea animals. It also comes from materials that settle out of seawater.

Sedimentary Rock

Trilobites are ancient relatives of insects. Trilobites had three body segments. You can see the hard outer skeleton.

Fossils

Fossils are made when animal or plant remains are covered in mud. Most fossils are formed from hard parts, such as bones, shells, or wood. These parts are slow to rot away. When fossils form underwater, minerals may replace the animal's shell or bones. You may also see fossils of burrows and footprints.

Many fossils were made from organisms that no longer exist. Scientists have learned how long ago these organisms lived. Finding these fossils in a rock can help scientists figure out the age of the rock. For example, trilobites were ocean animals that lived about 500 million years ago. When scientists find a trilobite fossil, they know that the rock around it is from that period of time.

Space Rocks

Some rocks fall from space and land on Earth. They can make a giant hole called a crater. Barringer Meteor Crater is a huge bowl-like pit in the Arizona desert. It is almost 1.6 kilometers wide and about 180 meters deep. The crater formed when a giant rock hit Earth between twenty thousand and fifty thousand years ago.

Clues to the Past

Every rock tells a story. Rocks offer clues to the past. Suppose you find a rock that has tiny shells in it. This means that the area where the rock formed was once an ancient sea. Scientists can learn much about Earth's history by studying rocks.

Sedimentary rocks hold a lot of information. Scientists know that the deepest layers are the oldest. They use this fact to compare the age of each layer and the materials in it. This method allows scientists to put past events in time order. But it does not show how long ago each event took place.

The Grand Canyon is one place that shows Earth's history very clearly. The canyon formed 5 million years ago when the Colorado River cut through many layers of sedimentary rock. Because so many layers of rock are exposed, today visitors to the Grand Canyon can see more years of rock history than anywhere else on Earth. Each layer holds clues about events that took place long ago.

Igneous rock forms when molten rock from inside Earth cools and hardens. Some igneous rocks form below Earth's surface. They appear only after the rocks above them wear away. Other igneous rocks form when lava cools on Earth's surface.

Metamorphic rock forms when pressure, heat, or chemical reactions change one type of rock into another. Metamorphic rock can be made from sedimentary rock or from igneous rock. Marble is a metamorphic rock often used for buildings and sculpture. Marble is formed from limestone, a sedimentary rock.

Igneous Rock

Metamorphic Rock

Rocks are always changing in a
pattern called the rock cycle. Over time,
they break down. The minerals in them
get recycled to form new rocks. These
processes can take millions of years.

The rock cycle does not always follow
the same pattern. Any type of rock
can change into any other type in any
order. For example, igneous rocks may
erode, and their particles may form
sedimentary rocks. Igneous rocks may
also be buried and crushed to form
metamorphic rocks. Or they can sink
deep into Earth and melt to form new
igneous rocks. Study the diagram of the
rock cycle to see all the ways that rocks
can form and change.

Rock Cycle

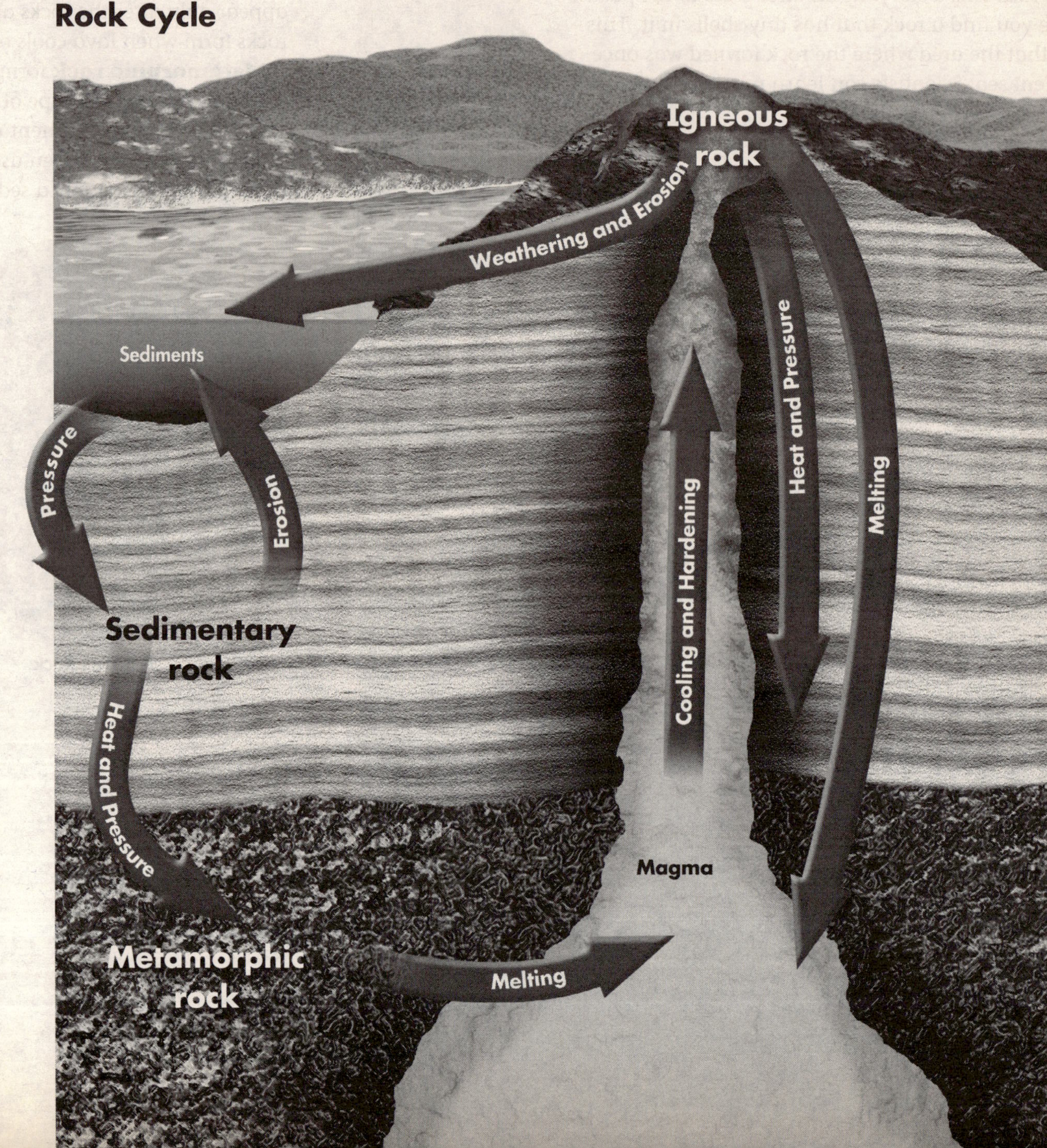

Reshaping Earth's Surface

by Martin E. Lee

Genre	Comprehension Skill	Text Features	Science Content
Nonfiction	Draw Conclusions	• Captions • Labels • Diagrams • Glossary	Earth's Surface

Scott Foresman Science 6.10

PEARSON
Scott Foresman

DK

scottforesman.com

Vocabulary

chemical weathering

deposition

erosion

mechanical weathering

sediment

weathering

What did you learn?

1. Describe three ways that landforms are shaped on Earth's surface.

2. Why do sediments settle out of flowing water as it slows down?

3. What are the sources of energy for ocean waves?

4. **Writing** in Science During the 1930s much of the Midwest and Southern Plains of the United States was known as the Dust Bowl. Write to explain what caused the Dust Bowl, and what its effects were. Use details from the book to support your answer.

5. **Draw Conclusions** Suppose a beach has white sand. What can this tell you about the surrounding rocks?

Illustration: Title Page: Clint Hansen; 7, 14 Clint Hansen
Photographs: Every effort has been made to secure permission and provide appropriate credit for photographic material. The publisher deeply regrets any omission and pledges to correct errors called to its attention in subsequent editions. Unless otherwise acknowledged, all photographs are the property of Scott Foresman, a division of Pearson Education. Photo locators denoted as follows: Top (T), Center (C), Bottom (B), Left (L), Right (R), Background (Bkgd).
2 Getty Images; 3 ©Gabe Palmer/Corbis; 5 Corbis; 6 Muench Photography, Inc; 8 (B) Martin G. Miller, (TR) Corbis; 9 ©Jacques Langevin/Sygma/Corbis; 10 ©Brian Sytnyk/Masterfile Corporation; 12 ©R. Ian Lloyd/Masterfile Corporation; 13 ©Theo Allofs/Corbis; 15 (TR) ©Ted Mead/PhotoLibrary, (BR) ©Geoff Higgins/PhotoLibrary

ISBN: 0-328-13997-1

Reshaping Earth's Surface

by Martin E. Lee

Glossary

chemical weathering	the process by which water, oxygen, or other substances cause changes to the minerals in rock
deposition	the process of dropping sediments from one place to a new place
erosion	the process by which soil and sediments are moved from one place to another
mechanical weathering	the process by which forces such as wind, water, and ice break down rock without changing its makeup
sediment	solid particles that are moved from place to place
weathering	the process of breaking down rock into smaller pieces

16

How does Earth's surface change?

Earth's Features

Look at the picture of Badlands National Park. Do you see the river? You can't because it is far below the tops of the canyons. The canyons began to form when water flowed over flat land. Over many years the water dug deeper into Earth's surface to carve out the canyons you can see today.

Frozen water can also change Earth's features. The five Great Lakes that lie between the United States and Canada were formed by glaciers. A glacier is a huge mass of slow-moving ice. As they move, they can scrape away the land, digging out lake bottoms.

Landforms on Earth have been shaped and changed in many ways. Flowing water is a main force. Rivers carry and drop materials as they go. **Sediment** is solid particles that are moved from place to place. Sediment can change the surface of Earth. It settles to form new features.

Badlands National Park

Wind can also change the landforms along a coast. The wind can shape cliffs and large rocks into amazing shapes. Along quieter, sandy coastlines, wind can blow loose sand into piles called dunes. Beach dunes are usually small. But they can grow to be very large in some areas.

Not all beaches are the same. The color and texture of a beach depend on the sources of its sand and rock. The black sand of Hawaii's beaches comes from black volcanic rock. Even major structures along a beach, such as rocky cliffs or flat patches of sand, can differ from beach to beach.

Lagoons are separated from the open ocean by sand, rocks, or islands. Waves and currents build the barriers that form a lagoon.

The dunes at this quiet cove are stable enough to support plants.

Beaches: Dynamic Systems

Waves carry enormous amounts of energy as they move. They can change an ocean beach. Vast amounts of energy in large waves can cause cracks in rocks. Over time the cracks can grow until pieces of rock finally break off.

Waves also carry sediments, such as stone and sand. When these sediments hit coastal features, they can wear down the rock.

Waves also build up or change beaches by moving the sand around. The way the sand moves depends on the angle at which the waves hit the shore. When waves move toward the shore at an angle, they push water along the shoreline. This movement of water is called a longshore current. It can move materials outward from the shore. This is how a landform known as a sandbar forms. The top of a sandbar may appear either above or below the water.

This sandbar formed when waves carried sand.

Weathering and Erosion

Many changes on Earth's surface take place because of weathering. **Weathering** is the process of breaking down rock into smaller pieces. There are two kinds of weathering.

Mechanical weathering takes place when forces such as water and ice break down rock. This type of weathering does not change the makeup of the rock as it breaks down. Mechanical weathering can begin in tiny cracks in rocks. Water can seep in and freeze. The ice pushes against the crack, making it larger. Water gets back into the cracks again after the ice melts. Rocks freeze and thaw over and over. This process makes the cracks larger each time and eventually splits the rock.

Sometimes soil forms in the cracks of rocks. Plants may take hold there. As the plants grow, their roots push the cracks open even more. Some plants can also produce chemicals that eat into rocks.

In **chemical weathering,** the minerals that make up the rock change. This type of weathering takes place when water, oxygen, and other materials react with the minerals in the rock.

After rock has been broken down by weathering, another process can begin. **Erosion** is the process by which soil and sediments are moved from one place to another. Wind, water, ice, and gravity can carry the eroded materials great distances.

Weathering and erosion are always at work to change the surface of Earth. Erosion can flatten mountains. It can dig deep canyons in layers of rock. But these changes generally take place over long periods of time.

Soil Erosion

When areas of soil have no plants on them, the soil is easily eroded. It can be washed away by water or blown away by wind. Plants help hold soil in place. Farmers who know this may plant cover crops. These are crops planted between harvests to slow down soil erosion. Cover crops also add nutrients to the soil.

When soil erodes, serious problems can result. One example of this happened in the plains of the United States in the 1930s. Years of drought and poor farming methods left many areas of soil nearly bare. That part of our country became known as the Dust Bowl. Harsh dust storms blew for eight years. The blowing dust was so heavy that children wore masks to school. People slept with wet cloths over their faces to keep from choking. The dust was so thick in places that people couldn't see even during the day. Dust piled up like snow drifts.

The drought affected more than the land. People suffered many health problems. Some died. Dust damaged cars and farm equipment so badly that they could not be fixed. Farmers lost their land. Millions of people lost their jobs.

People have learned from those bad years. Farmers learned to use better farming methods. People found new ways to take care of the land. An era of soil conservation began.

Cover crops prevent soil erosion.

The waves you see at a beach are often caused by wind. Wind can form waves in the open ocean too. As winds touch ocean water, their energy transfers to the water. This process forms waves. The size of a wave depends on the speed of the wind and on how long it blows. It also depends on how much of the sea the wind blows over.

Waves are also formed by tectonic activity in Earth's crust. Volcanic eruptions, earthquakes, and landslides may take place along coasts or under the water. These events of nature can cause tsunamis to form. A tsunami is a wave that travels very fast and reaches great heights before it crashes into the shore. Tsunamis are very dangerous. They can cause a lot of damage and loss of life. On December 26, 2004 a powerful earthquake happened in the Indian Ocean. It caused a deadly tsunami to hit the shores of several countries, killing more than 100,000 people.

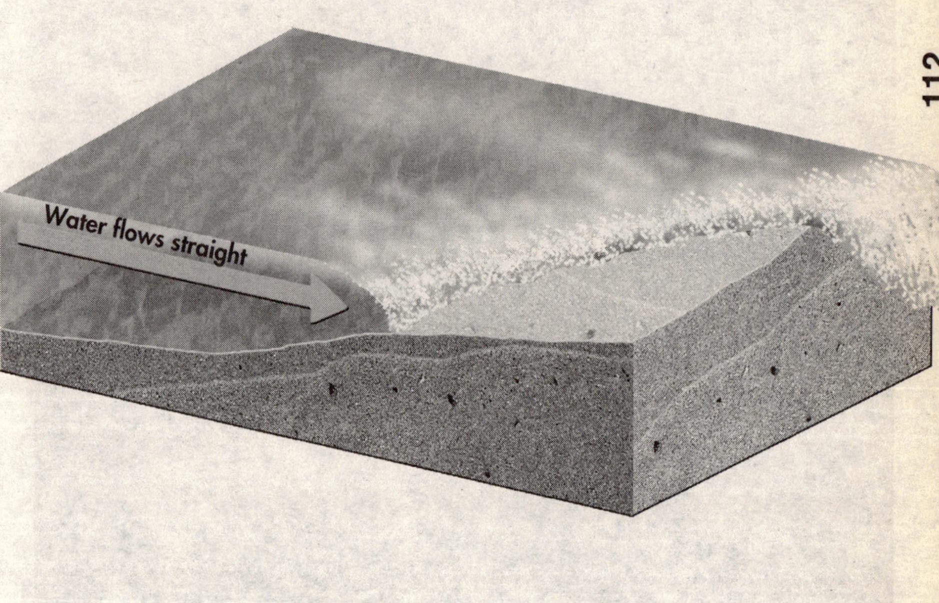

Wave Characteristics

All waves can be described by their characteristics. Scientists also use certain characteristics to describe water waves. Look at this diagram as you read about each characteristic.

The highest part of a wave is the crest. The lowest part is the trough. The position of the water before a wave passes through it is represented by a dotted line. The distance between this line and the crest, or this line and the trough, is called the wave's amplitude. When the ocean is calm, the amplitude of the waves is small. But when a strong wind blows, the waves have more energy and the amplitude of the waves will greatly increase.

Wavelength is the distance from one crest point to the next, or from one trough to the next. For small ripples of water, the wavelength of waves can be measured in millimeters. Large waves can measure several meters in wavelength.

Dust Bowl

1930
Little rain falls in the Southern Plains, but crops flourish.

1931
Severe drought hits the Midwest and Southern Plains. Dust begins to blow.

1932
Fourteen dust storms hit the area.

1933
Thirty-eight dust storms occur.

1934
Fewer dust storms, but they spread as far as New York. About 35 million acres of farmland are destroyed.

1935
Many cattle are destroyed because crops cannot be grown to feed them. About 850 million tons of topsoil blow from the southern plains. The Soil Conservation Service is established to develop conservation programs.

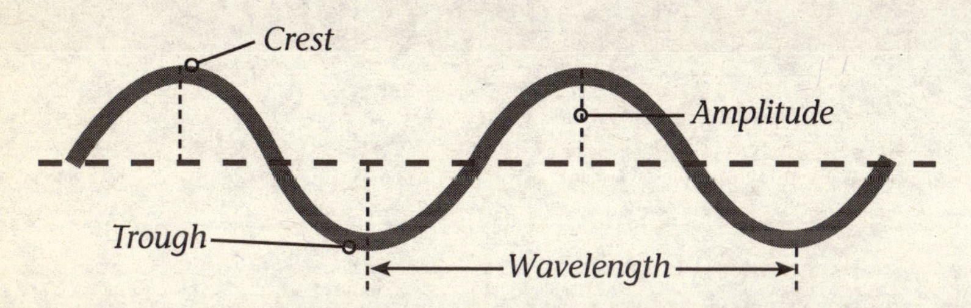

1936
The number of dust storms increases.

1938
Conservation methods, including replowing farmland into furrows and planting trees, result in 65 percent less soil blowing.

1939
Rains arrive, bringing an end to the drought.

How does water affect Earth's features?

Deposition

All moving water has energy. Water flowing downhill is the main force that shapes Earth's surface. The energy of moving water breaks down rock and soil into bits of sediment. This is an example of mechanical weathering. Water can also chemically weather rock. It does this when dissolved minerals act on materials in the rock. This process changes the makeup of rock.

The sediments that form during weathering are carried to other locations. This process of dropping these sediments in a new place is called **deposition.** Deposition often changes the shape and direction of a river's flow. Look at the diagram to see examples of some of these changes.

The diagram below shows how the water in waves moves. As a wave nears, the water moves slightly forward, and then downward, and then back. The water makes a loop. Each time a wave passes, the water ends up just about where it began.

As waves move toward the shore, the ocean bottom gets in the way. It interferes with the pattern of the waves' movements. The ocean floor makes the bottom parts of waves slow down. But the tops of the waves keep moving quickly. This causes the tops to tumble forward. Finally the waves crash at the shore in the form of breakers.

New Mexico's Carlsbad Caverns contain stalagmites and stalactites formed from minerals in water.

Falling water can cause mechanical and chemical weathering.

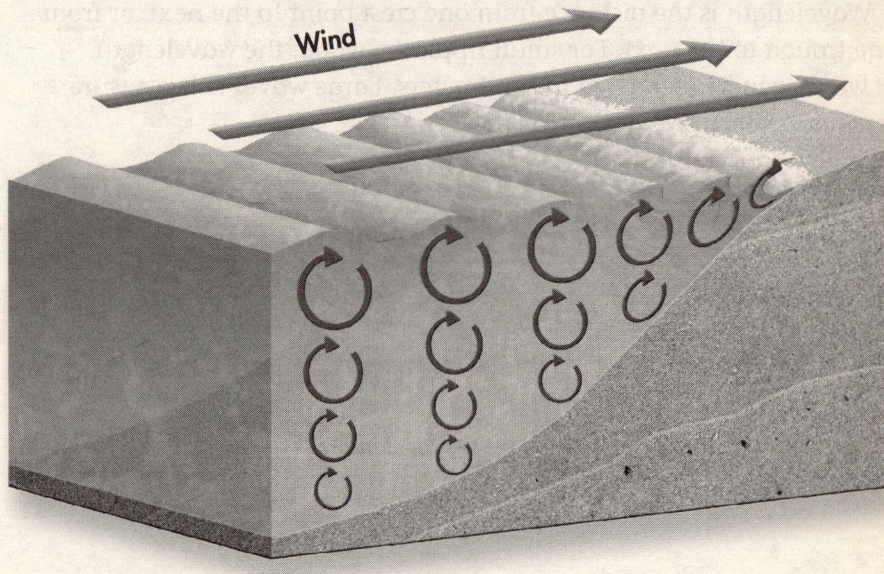

The circular movement of water gets smaller as you go deeper into the water. Wave energy is strongest at the water's surface.

How do waves affect coastal landforms?

Wave Energy

All waves carry energy. Ocean waves carry and pass along a great deal of energy. The waves formed during big storms are especially strong.

Many people who watch ocean waves think that the water moves forward with the waves. But this isn't so. Only the energy moves. The water stays in the same spot. It seems to move toward the shore, but actually it is only moving up and down. The water rises and falls in a circular motion.

Minerals in Lakes and Oceans

As rivers flow to the ocean, they carry sediments and dissolved minerals. Ocean plants and animals need some of these minerals to live. Some of the sediments and minerals settle on the ocean floor. Others settle out of the river water along the way. They form deposits in lakes and along the coast.

Salt is a common mineral on Earth. Moving water carries a lot of salt as it flows. Scientists say that rivers carry about four billion tons of dissolved salts to the oceans each year. Ocean water then leaves behind dissolved salts and other minerals as it evaporates. This cycle has been repeating for thousands of years. It has caused the amount of salt in the ocean to increase.

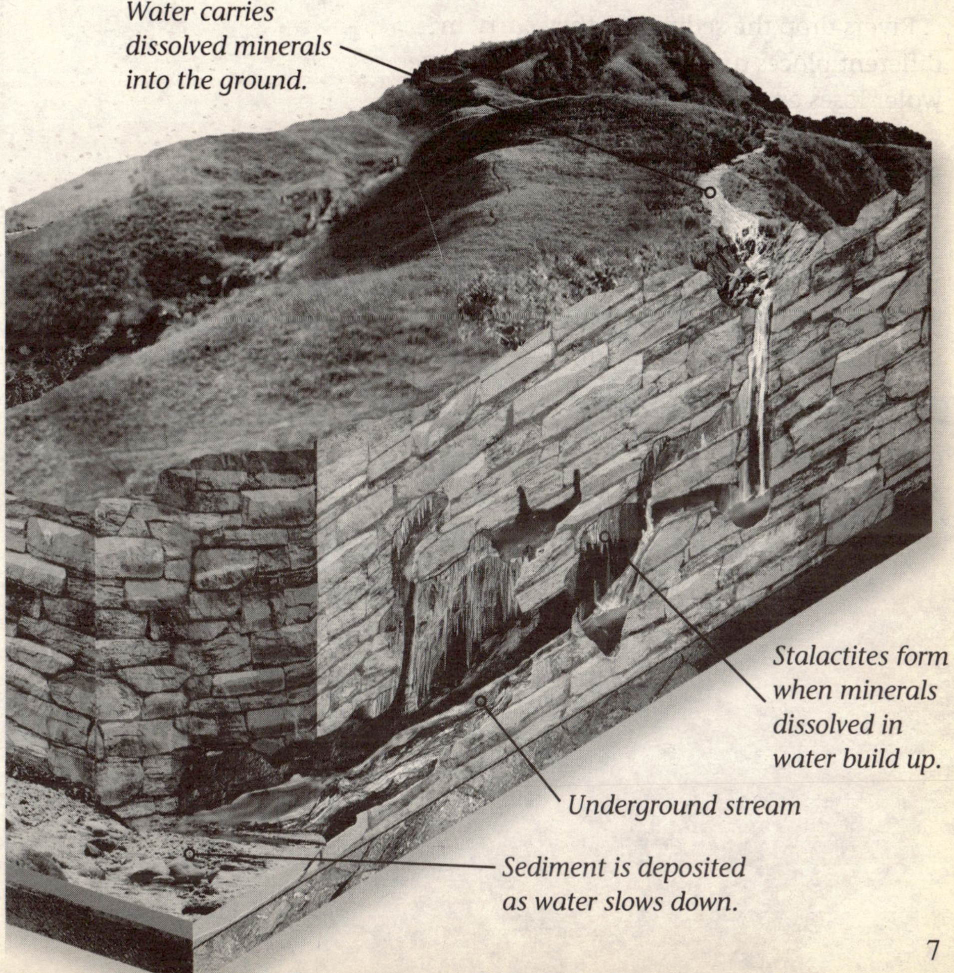

River Systems

You may picture a river as a flat, quiet body of moving water. In fact a river can change quite a lot over time. Rivers and streams are always changing.

A stream begins on land that is higher than sea level. Its water flows because gravity pulls the water downward. As a stream flows along, other streams may join it. Eventually, a river forms. The flowing river wears down soil and rock. It carries the sediments away.

Rivers drop the sediments they carry in different places as they flow. This is because water loses energy as it slows down. Slower water can carry less sediment. The heavier sediments settle out first. Rivers can carry the lighter ones over great distances.

Water often slows down when it reaches the mouth of a river. The fine sediments settle there in areas known as deltas. A delta is shaped like a wide fan.

Mississippi River Delta

This fan-shaped deposit of sediments in Death Valley, California, is made of sediment carried from far upriver.

The Nile River has flooded local homes here in Sudan.

Floodplains

Rivers and streams sometimes overflow their banks. When this happens, the water slows down and deposits many sediments. Floods can move huge amounts of sediment to places that would never get these materials otherwise. These places are known as floodplains. A floodplain is a part of the land that is likely to get the extra water and sediment from a flooded river.

Most people think of floods as total disasters. But farmers in some places depend on flooding. This is because the sediments add important nutrients to the soil. Growing crops need these nutrients. Still, floods can be very destructive. People who live in a floodplain can lose their homes, their towns, or even their lives.

Earth's Resources

by Natalie Rompella

Genre	Comprehension Skill	Text Features	Science Content
Nonfiction	Main Idea and Details	• Captions • Charts • Diagrams • Glossary	Natural Resources

Scott Foresman Science 6.11

PEARSON
Scott Foresman

ISBN 0-328-14000-7

9 780328 140008

90000

scottforesman.com

Vocabulary

acid precipitation

coal

fossil fuel

geothermal energy

natural gas

nonrenewable resource

petroleum

renewable resource

What did you learn?

1. Describe three ways that forests supply resources for organisms that live on Earth.

2. How can water get polluted?

3. How can you help reduce the negative impact that humans can have on the environment?

4. **Writing** in Science Nonrenewable resources cannot be replaced as fast as they are used. Give an example, and write to explain the benefit and cost of using these resources. Include examples from the book to support your answer.

5. **Main Idea and Details** Which source of energy do you think has the most benefits? Support your answer with details from the book.

Illustrations: Title Page, 12, 19, 23 Peter Bollinger
Photographs: Every effort has been made to secure permission and provide appropriate credit for photographic material. The publisher deeply regrets any omission and pledges to correct errors called to its attention in subsequent editions. Unless otherwise acknowledged, all photographs are the property of Scott Foresman, a division of Pearson Education. Photo locators denoted as follows: Top (T), Center (C), Bottom (B), Left (L), Right (R), and Background (Bkgd).
3 ©EPA; 4 ©Pascal Goetgheluck/Photo Researchers, Inc.; 5 ©W. Cody/Corbis; 6 ©Tom Collicott/ Masterfile Corporation; 7 Corbis; 8 ©Beth Wald/Aurora Photos, ©Eric Sanderson/Wildlife Conservation Society and Center for International Earth Science Information; 10 Data courtesy Marc Imhoff of NASA GSFC and Christopher Elvidge of NOAA NGDC. Image by Craig Mayhew and Robert Simmon, NASA GSFC/NASA; 12 ©Bettmann/Corbis; 13 Getty Images; 14 ©Steve Craft/Masterfile Corporation; 15 ©J. Mead/Photo Researchers, Inc.; 16 ©L. Lefkowitz/Getty Images; 17 (C) ©Tom & Pat Leeson/Photo Researchers, Inc., (BR) ©Royalty-Free/Corbis; 18 ©Robert Garvey/Corbis

ISBN: 0-328-14000-7

Glossary

acid precipitation	rain or snow that has a large amount of acid in it
coal	a solid fossil fuel formed from swamp plants
fossil fuel	an energy source made from the remains of living organisms
geothermal energy	heat energy from deep inside Earth
natural gas	a fossil fuel that is a mixture of gases
nonrenewable resource	a resource that cannot be replaced as fast as it is used
petroleum	a liquid fossil fuel, also called oil or crude oil
renewable resource	a resource that is replaced through natural processes almost as fast as it is used

Earth's Resources

by Natalie Rompella

What are Earth's natural resources?

Renewable and Nonrenewable Resources

There are many resources on Earth. Three of the most important are air, water, and land. A resource that can be replaced through natural processes almost as quickly as it is used is called a **renewable resource.** Wood and paper come from trees. New trees can be planted in place of the used ones. Cotton also comes from a plant. Trees and cotton are renewable resources because they can be replanted.

A **nonrenewable resource** cannot be replaced as quickly as it is used. Minerals and fossil fuels can be used quickly, but they take millions of years to form.

Before using resources it is important to consider the cost and benefits. When trees are cut down for lumber to build houses, the benefit is that people will have new homes to live in. The cost is that the trees might have been a habitat for plants and animals.

During Mining

G Mining Laws
Miners must restore the land either to its original state or to a suitable, agreed-upon land use.

H Closing Mine Shafts
Mine shafts are filled back in with the rocks removed, and sealed.

I Sculpting the Land
Topsoil is replaced to prevent erosion.

J Planting the Land
Species of plants are selected and planted to cover the reclaimed area.

L New Land Uses
Reclaimed mining sites serve new purposes. Stone quarries become lakes. Other areas are converted into wetlands, farms, ranches, and recreational sites.

Reclaimed Land

Coal Mining and Reclamation

Coal is removed from the ground differently than petroleum and natural gas. Since it is solid, coal that is buried deep below Earth's surface is dug out making underground tunnels. If the coal is within thirty meters of Earth's surface, it is usually removed in a process called strip mining. Unfortunately, these methods for removing coal can be harmful to the environment and living organisms. It can cause soil erosion, loss of habitat, and water pollution.

Federal and state laws require that land that has been mined through strip mining or underground tunnels be reclaimed, or put to productive use.

A Water Management
Mine operators develop methods to ensure that water flows naturally and without pollution through mining areas.

B Water Treatment
Facilities at the mining site treat water before it is reintroduced to streams.

C Waste Storage
Some waste can be buried underground.

D Chemical Recovery
Chemicals used to remove minerals are collected and disposed of properly.

E Protecting Air Quality
Federal and state laws and regulations include strict guidelines for maintaining air quality.

F Ecosystem Protection
Care ensures that wildlife populations are not permanently affected.

Air Resources

Nitrogen, oxygen, and carbon dioxide are gases in the atmosphere that are essential to life on Earth. Although these gases are renewable, the air can become polluted.

Air pollution is a result of harmful substances being released into the air. This can happen when fuels such as coal, oil, and natural gas are burned. Plants, animals, and humans can be affected by air pollution.

The Environmental Protection Agency (EPA) helps to keep people aware of the quality of their air. An Air Quality Index (AQI) color is used to show the quality of the air. The different colors are indicators of whether the air is clean or polluted.

Land Resources

We depend on land in many ways. Many foods that we eat are grown in the soil. Soil takes hundreds of years to form. Soil erosion can easily happen when wind and water cause soil to blow or wash away. Farmers try to reduce soil erosion by rotating the crops they grow.

We use many minerals from inside Earth. They take thousands of years to form. Automobiles and bicycles are just two of the many things made from the mineral iron. Cement, which is used in buildings and sidewalks, is made from limestone, a rock containing the mineral calcite. Iron and calcite are only two of many minerals we encounter daily. Because they take thousands of years to form, minerals are nonrenewable resources.

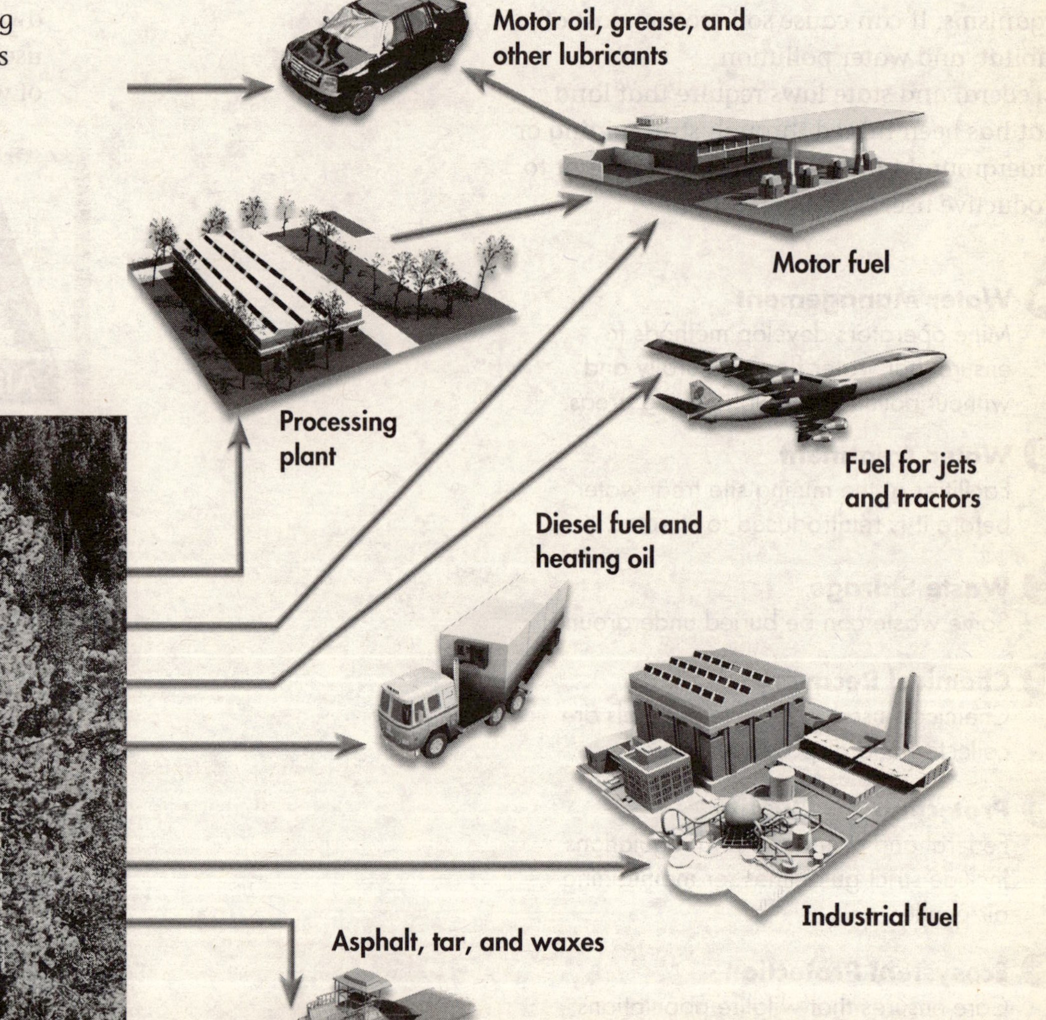

Quartz

Processing and Delivering Petroleum

Petroleum is a combination of many different products. These are separated at a refinery plant. The crude oil is heated; then, different parts of the oil can be removed at different temperatures.

To make the various substances pure, the water, salts, and oxygen they contain must be removed. Products are then kept at refineries until they are sent to gas stations, airports, and factories. Below is a diagram of how petroleum is processed.

Oil and Natural Gas

Oil and natural gas formed in processes similar to those that produced coal, but they formed from the remains of tiny organisms that lived in ocean water. Because natural gas is lighter than oil, it is often found on top of oil deposits. Drilling into Earth collects both.

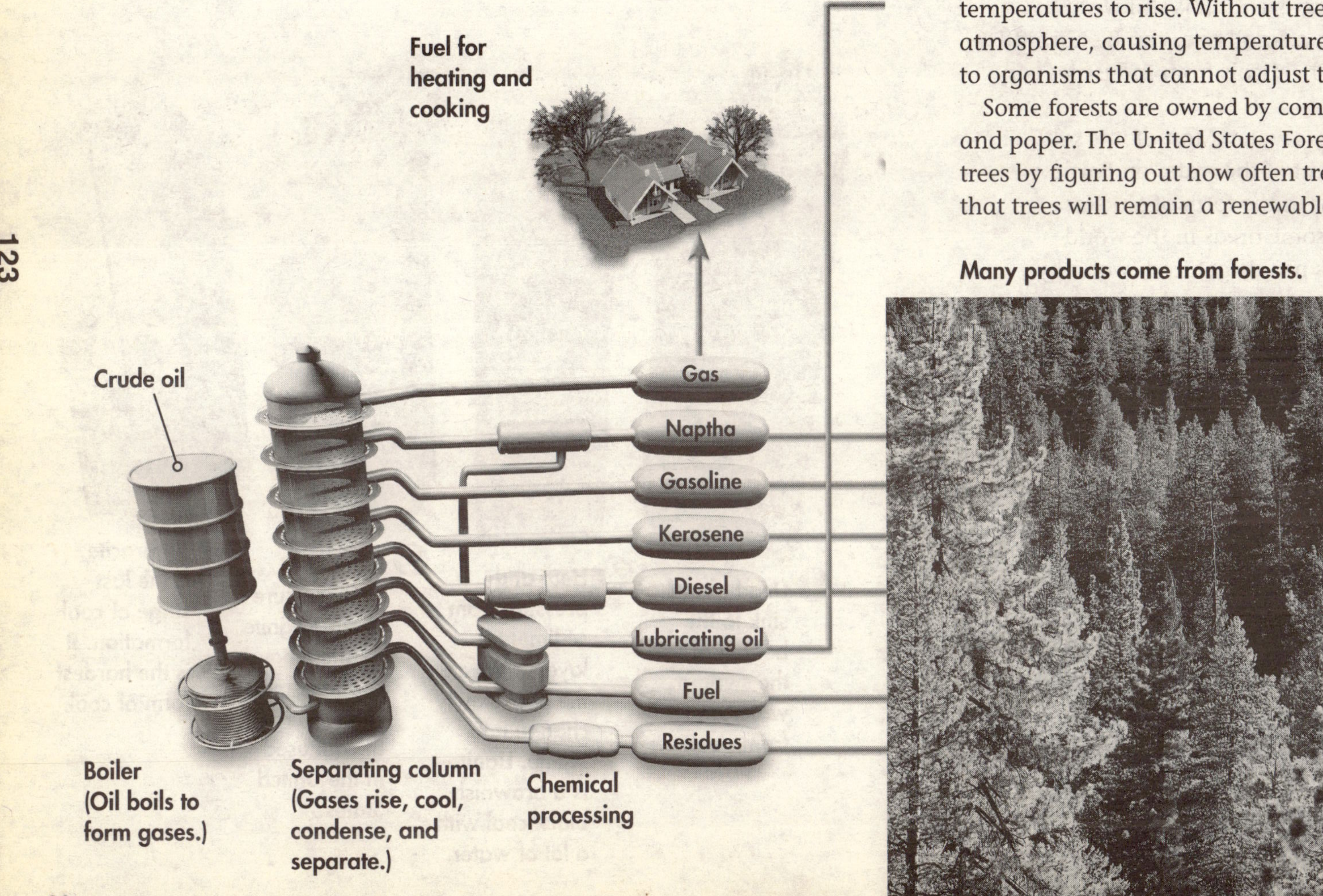

Forests

Forests provide us with many products we use every day, such as paper, wood, and rubber. Rain forests, in particular, provide us with many medicines, nuts, and fruits.

Many animals use the forest as their home. They rely on it for shelter and food. When forests are cut down, these animals lose their habitats. Some animals may have trouble adjusting to a new environment. Because of this, some species may become extinct.

Forests also help to control the amount of carbon dioxide in the atmosphere. Trees use carbon dioxide and release oxygen into the air in the process of photosynthesis. Carbon dioxide traps heat, causing temperatures to rise. Without trees, more carbon dioxide stays in the atmosphere, causing temperatures to increase. This may be harmful to organisms that cannot adjust to the increased temperature.

Some forests are owned by companies that use trees for lumber and paper. The United States Forest Service helps companies conserve trees by figuring out how often trees can be cut down. This ensures that trees will remain a renewable resource.

Many products come from forests.

Water Resources

We use water for bathing, drinking, cooking, cleaning, and growing crops. The cells of all living organisms need water to work properly.

Water is reused over and over in a process called the water cycle. As water washes over the land, it can become polluted. It then empties into rivers and lakes. This pollution can end up in our waterways, where various organisms live and rely on the water.

Industries can also pollute the water. Water is often used to cool down machinery. Once the water is no longer needed, it is emptied back into the lakes and rivers, even if it is still warm. A change in water temperature, even a small one, can be harmful to an ecosystem and its organisms. Chemicals from industries can also pollute water.

About 75 percent of Earth's surface is water. Most of it is salt water in the oceans. Only three percent of the water on Earth is fresh water; and this includes water in the form of glaciers. Because there is so little fresh water, some areas in the world have a water shortage. In these areas people get fresh water by removing salt from ocean water or having it brought in from other locations.

Fish are one of the many organisms that live in water.

How Coal Forms

Millions of years ago, organisms died and became buried in the ground. Swamp plants that were buried under mud and water formed a substance called peat. Through the years, other sediments, including sand and mud, built up on top of it. Pressure and heat changed the peat and sediments to lignite, a soft form of coal.

Coal has many stages. The more carbon coal has, the harder it is and the cleaner it burns. Anthracite is the hardest and cleanest-burning form of coal.

1 Dead plants sink to the bottom of the swamp water and form peat.

2 Heat and pressure from sediment layers above the peat slowly change it to lignite. Lignite is a brownish-black coal with a lot of water.

3 More heat and pressure change lignite to bituminous coal, the most common form of coal used in the United States.

4 Anthracite is the last stage of coal formation. It is the hardest form of coal.

124

Using Fossil Fuels

When fossil fuels are burned, they produce gases. These gases can trap heat in the atmosphere, which can make Earth warmer. This warming of Earth is called the greenhouse effect. Scientists are concerned that as Earth gets warmer, organisms that cannot adjust to the changes of the temperature in their environment may not survive.

In addition, when fossil fuels are burned, other gases are released into the air and can combine with water vapor, resulting in **acid precipitation.** This rain or snow that contains acid can harm living organisms and can damage buildings and statues. The burning of fossil fuels can also cause a haze called smog, which is harmful to living organisms.

Reducing Fossil Fuel Problems

You can make a difference in reducing the amount of fossil fuels used. Carpooling, riding a bike, taking a bus or train, or walking cuts down on the amount of gasoline burned in automobiles. Turning off appliances when they are not being used reduces the amount of electricity needed. As an adult you will be able to make more informed decisions about energy sources. Learn more about other sources of energy, such as the Sun, wind, and water.

Moving water can be used to generate electricity.

Ocean Resources

Oceans also provide us with minerals. One of these minerals is salt. Salt can be removed from ocean water by evaporating water.

Other minerals, such as tin, magnesium, iron, and copper, can also be found on the ocean floor. Oil and natural gas can also be found below the ocean floor. To collect these resources, wells are drilled into the bottom of the ocean.

The ocean is a great source of energy. We can generate electricity from moving ocean water. Tidal energy is an excellent renewable resource because it is both inexpensive and does not pollute the environment. It is not a common form of energy because few places on Earth have the coastline and tides needed to build tidal power stations.

Connections Among Resources

Humans can have a negative effect on Earth's resources. People have caused pollution and destruction of habitats, and have used up materials faster than they can be replaced.

A map produced by scientists called The Human Footprint shows humans' effects on Earth's ecosystems. The scale ranges from 0 to 100, 0 representing the least impact. Scientists found that 83 percent of Earth's total land has been affected by humans. This study was done to inform people how the choices they make affect the environment.

Human Footprint Map

Human Influence
0 - 1   Most Wild
1 - 10
10 - 20
20 - 30
30 - 40
40 - 100   Least Wild

Coal is a solid fossil fuel. It was once commonly used to heat homes and to power trains. Today it is still used in power plants for electricity.

Petroleum, often called crude oil or oil, is a liquid fossil fuel. Ancient Egyptians used it as medicine for wounds and for fuel in lamps. Today we use it for gasoline, jet fuel, home heating, and kerosene.

Natural gas is a mixture of gases. The Chinese used it long ago to heat seawater to separate out the salt. Today it is used for heating homes and for generating electricity. You might use it in your home if you have a gas stove, a gas clothes dryer, or an outdoor gas grill.

Oil is transported through pipelines from where it is found to where it is processed.

Natural gas is stored in tanks and then piped to houses and businesses.

How are fossil fuels formed and used?

Types of Fossil Fuels

Fossil fuels are a nonrenewable resource because they take millions of years to form. Fossil fuels formed from organisms that lived long ago. Some were plants that got their energy from the Sun. Some were animals that got their energy by eating plants. Others were animals that got their energy by eating animals that ate plants. When the organisms died, this energy was stored in their bodies. When we burn fossil fuels, we release energy from the Sun that was stored millions of years ago.

Coal is used in power plants to produce electricity.

Reducing the Impact

Earth's land, water, air, and living creatures are all interconnected. Changes that affect one of these things can affect the others. A forest might be cut down for timber. Without the trees, the soil may begin to erode and wash away. Other plants and trees may not be able to grow without that soil. Organisms that rely on trees and soil may not survive.

Many resources we use daily are nonrenewable. Minerals, coal, oil, and natural gas need to be conserved so they do not run out. This means we need to use them only when necessary. One way to remind yourself of this is the three Rs: Reduce, Recycle, and Reuse.

Where do we get energy?

Energy Needs

Energy comes from many different sources: fossil fuels, wind, water, solar energy, nuclear energy, and geothermal energy.

How do we use energy? One of the ways is shown below. To make this picture, hundreds of satellite pictures of Earth at night were put together. It shows human-made lights. These lights use a lot of energy.

Energy has many other uses. Did you ride the bus to school today? Is your house heated or cooled? Do you watch television? These actions all require energy.

Businesses also use energy. Computers, fax machines, phones, and copiers need energy to work. Restaurants use it to cook and keep food cold; theaters use it to show movies; and ships, trucks, and trains use it to transport people and goods around the world.

Have you ever seen a windmill? The wind causes its blades to spin. Energy from the wind can be transformed into electricity. Like hydropower, wind can turn turbine blades and generate power. Even though wind power is a non-polluting renewable resource, a steady wind is necessary in order to produce electricity consistently. Much of this type of energy is generated in the state of California.

A large number of wind turbines can be placed together to form a wind farm.

Energy from Sunlight and Wind

Solar energy, or energy from the Sun, requires no turbines. It is a renewable resource and does not pollute. With our current technology, however, solar energy can't be used everywhere. In 2002 solar energy represented less than one percent of the energy used in the United States.

Solar collectors gather heat from the Sun. The panels heat water that runs through pipes throughout homes and buildings, providing both heat and hot water.

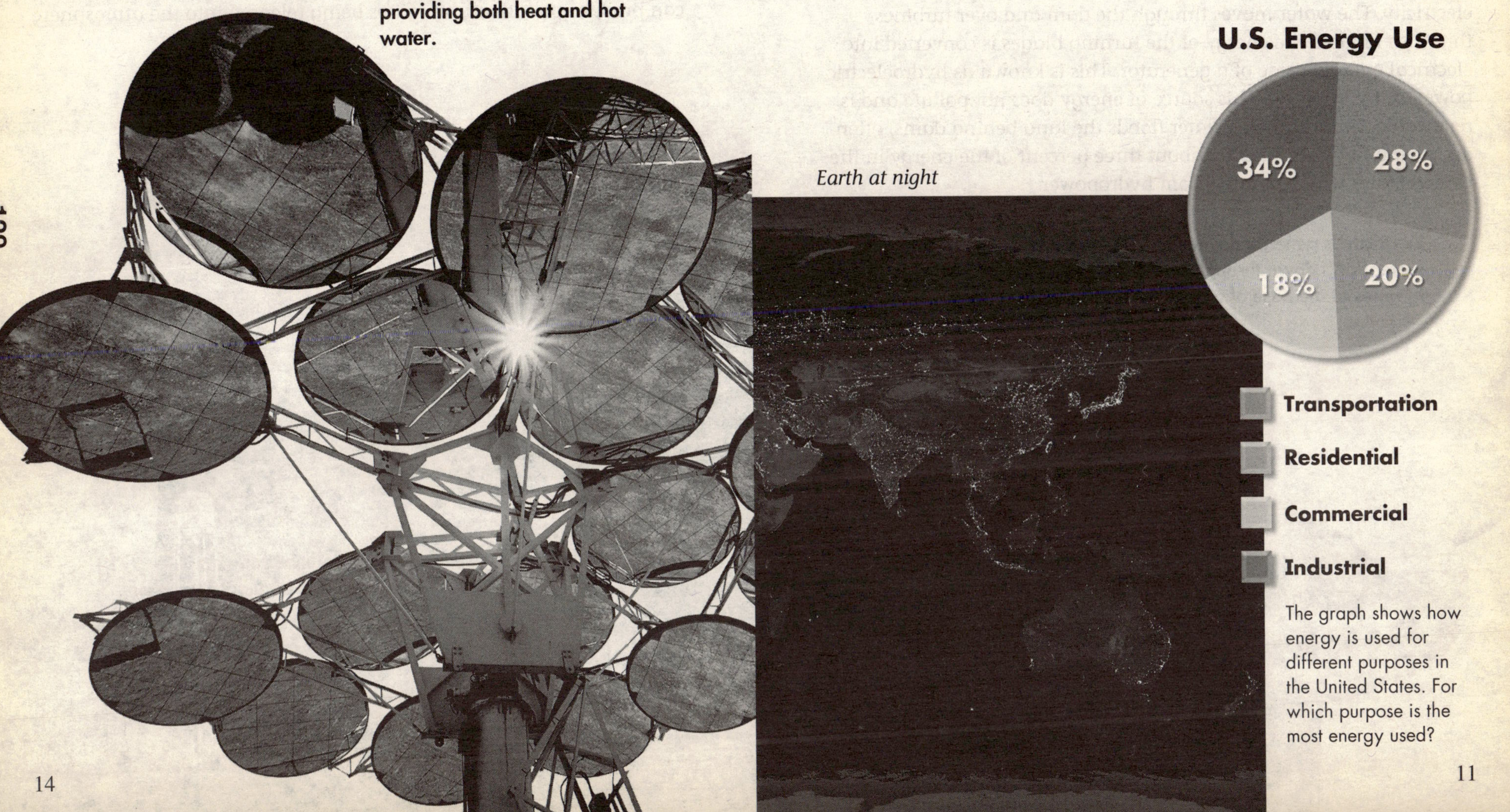

Energy Needs Over Time

Over the years, energy needs have changed. Early societies used wood for lighting, heating, and cooking. Early farms used animals to pull their plows and other tools.

By the 1700s, machines and factories had been built in the United States that could make clothing, furniture, building materials, and farming equipment quickly.

Today the needs for energy have increased even more. Electricity is a major source of energy. Our society depends on it for light, for heat, and to power many appliances. Unlike other forms of energy that are found naturally on Earth, electricity must be produced.

U.S. Energy Use

The graph shows how energy is used for different purposes in the United States. For which purpose is the most energy used?

Sources of Energy

There are many sources of energy on Earth. Fossil fuels are one of the most common. A **fossil fuel** is an energy source made from the remains of living organisms. Coal, oil, and natural gas are fossil fuels.

Energy from Moving Water

Moving water is a source of energy. Electricity can be produced from the movement of ocean tides or from the movement of water in rivers.

Dams built across waterways can use moving water to generate electricity. The water moves through the dam and over turbines that turn blades. The energy of the turning blades is converted into electrical energy inside of a generator. This is known as hydroelectric power, or hydropower. This source of energy does not pollute and is renewable. Unfortunately, water floods the land behind dams, often destroying habitats. In 2002 about three percent of the energy in the United States was generated from hydropower.

Electricity is generated when water flows down through turbines at the base of a dam.

Energy from Atoms and Earth's Heat

Nuclear energy is a source of energy from the heat produced when atoms are split apart. Nuclear energy is a nonrenewable resource. Although nuclear energy does not pollute, the waste produced must be disposed of properly. It can be harmful to organisms, including humans. In 2002 only 8 percent of the energy in the United States came from nuclear energy.

The heat from inside Earth can also be used as an energy source. This is called **geothermal energy.** Scientists drill into Earth's crust, releasing hot steam. This steam can turn turbines and run generators to make electricity. Geothermal energy is a renewable resource, but it can produce pollution from gases being released into the atmosphere.

Clouds of water droplets are forming from the cooling towers of this nuclear power plant.

Science

by Carol Levine

Climate and Weather

Genre	Comprehension Skill	Text Features	Science Content
Nonfiction	Cause and Effect	• Captions • Charts • Diagrams • Glossary	Climate and Weather

Scott Foresman Science 6.12

ISBN 0-328-14003-1

PEARSON
Scott Foresman

scottforesman.com

131

What did you learn?

1. What are the layers of Earth's atmosphere?

2. What is the difference between sleet and glaze?

3. What are some of the tools meteorologists use to predict the weather?

4. **Writing** in Science Climate and weather are different. Write to describe the differences between the two. Use details from the book in your answer.

5. **Cause and Effect** Why do hurricane winds spiral, and why do they gather strength as they pass over warm water?

Illustrations: 7, 10, 12, 14, 20 Peter Bollinger
Photographs: Every effort has been made to secure permission and provide appropriate credit for photographic material. The publisher deeply regrets any omission and pledges to correct errors called to its attention in subsequent editions. Unless otherwise acknowledged, all photographs are the property of Scott Foresman, a division of Pearson Education. Photo locators denoted as follows: Top (T), Center (C), Bottom (B), Left (L), Right (R), Background (Bkgd).
Title Page: ©NASA/Photo Researchers, Inc.; 2 ©J. A. Kraulis/Masterfile Corporation, ©Sherman Hines/Masterfile Corporation; 8 ©NASA/Photo Researchers, Inc.; 9 ©Carl & Ann Purcell/Corbis; 16 ©Graham French/Masterfile Corporation; 17 ©A. & J. Verkaik/Corbis; 18 ©Annie Griffiths Belt/Corbis; 19 ©Christopher J. Morris/Corbis; 21 Brand X Pictures; 22 ©Gary Braasch/Corbis, (TLB) NOAA, (CLT, CLB, BLT) ©Royalty-Free/Corbis, (CL) ©Galen Rowell/Corbis, (BL) Corbis

ISBN: 0-328-14003-1

Climate and Weather

by Carol Levine

Glossary

air mass a very large body of air with similar temperature and humidity throughout

air pressure the measure of the force with which air particles push on matter

atmosphere the blanket of gases that surrounds a planet

climate the average condition of the weather at a place over a long period of time

front a boundary that forms between air masses

humidity the amount of water vapor in the air

meteorologist a scientist who studies the weather

relative humidity the ratio of the amount of water vapor actually present in the air to the greatest amount possible at its current temperature

weather the condition of the atmosphere at a particular time and place

What is Earth's atmosphere?

Gases in Air

An **atmosphere** is a blanket of air that surrounds a planet. Earth's atmosphere is mostly made up of nitrogen and oxygen. The rest of the atmosphere is made up of tiny amounts of about ten other gases. Gravity keeps Earth's atmosphere in place.

Many of the gases in Earth's atmosphere come from the molten rock within Earth. Nitrogen, water vapor, and carbon dioxide were released as molten rock cooled down. For more than four billion years, many gases have escaped Earth during volcanic eruptions.

Climate and weather are vital to life on Earth. It is important to know as much about them as we can. We need ways of predicting weather so we can be prepared for severe weather. Science is advancing all the time, providing new technology to help meteorologists study and forecast the weather in our world.

Water from oceans and other bodies of water evaporates and helps make the climate more humid. As moist air moves over land, it can cause precipitation.

When forests burn, carbon dioxide is released into the atmosphere. And when forests burn or are cut, fewer trees remain to absorb carbon dioxide. Increasing levels of carbon dioxide in the atmosphere may be causing global warming.

Low clouds reflect sunlight, which makes Earth cooler. However, high clouds help keep Earth warm by trapping heat in the atmosphere.

Factors that Affect Climate

Volcanic eruptions release large amounts of ash and smoke into the atmosphere. These materials can block sunlight, causing Earth to cool.

The Gulf Stream current brings warmth from the equator toward the poles. Air warmed by this current helps keep the climates of England and Ireland mild in winter.

Earth's polar regions receive less solar radiation, and ice reflects much of it. This keeps these areas cold.

As air rises over mountains, it cools and water vapor condenses. The western slopes of mountains receive a lot of rainfall. The eastern slopes are generally dry.

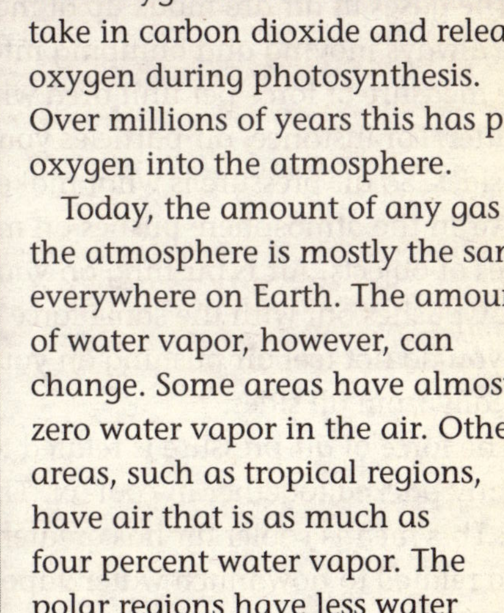

At one time, the atmosphere had little oxygen in it. Plants on Earth take in carbon dioxide and release oxygen during photosynthesis. Over millions of years this has put oxygen into the atmosphere.

Today, the amount of any gas in the atmosphere is mostly the same everywhere on Earth. The amount of water vapor, however, can change. Some areas have almost zero water vapor in the air. Other areas, such as tropical regions, have air that is as much as four percent water vapor. The polar regions have less water vapor in the air than the tropical regions do.

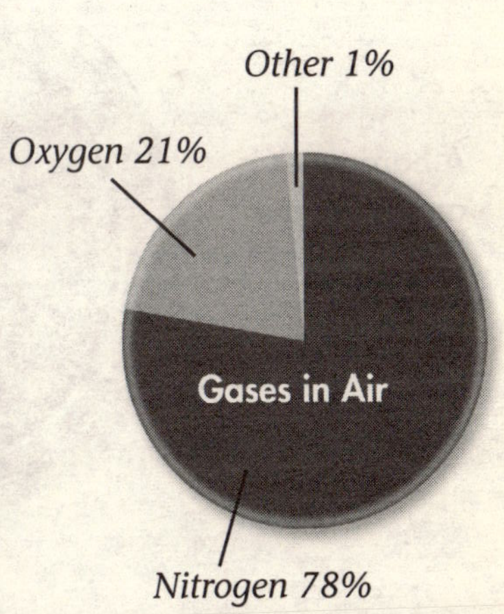

Air Pressure and Temperature

The gases in air are made up of moving particles. These particles are always moving and bumping into other matter. **Air pressure** is the measure of force per unit area with which air particles push on matter. For instance, air particles you blow into a balloon push on its sides. So air pressure is what makes a balloon get bigger.

Air in the atmosphere pushes on matter too. Air pushes on all sides of objects. Air is pushing on your body right now. Air in your body pushes out with the same force that air outside pushes in. So you do not feel air pushing on your body because it is pushing equally from all sides.

The force of air pressure is related to air temperature. Particles are tightly packed together in cool air. They are farther apart in warm air. This means cooler air has greater air pressure. Air pressure is also related to how much water vapor is in the air. Dry air has more pressure than moist air.

The higher you are above Earth's surface, the lower the air pressure is. The pressure is greatest near the surface because more particles are pushing down from above.

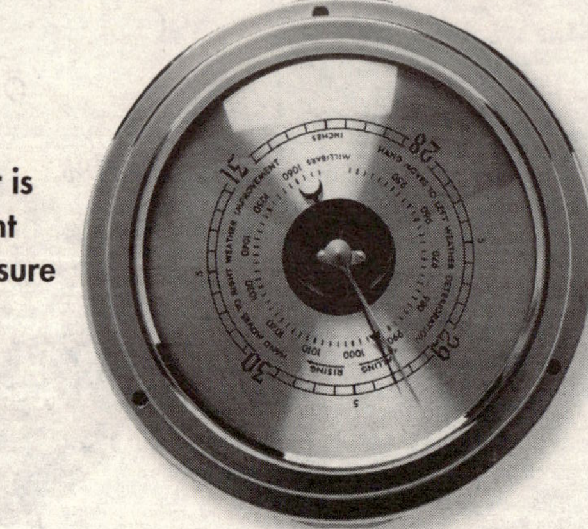

A barometer is an instrument used to measure air pressure.

Climate

Weather and climate are different. Weather can change constantly. **Climate** is the pattern of weather that occurs in an area over a long period of time. This period is usually thirty years or longer. Climate is usually described as average temperature and average precipitation.

Different areas of Earth have different climates. Sunlight, ocean currents, and gases in the air, among other things, affect climate. Large bodies of water affect climate because water warms and cools more slowly than land does. So climates close to the ocean are milder than those farther inland.

Pollution can affect climate. Carbon dioxide, which results from the burning of fossil fuels, can contribute to increased temperatures worldwide. This is called global warming. People can control some factors that affect climate, such as the production of carbon dioxide.

GOES-8

Gathering Data

Meteorologists use tools to predict the weather. Weather is the result of many complicated processes, but many of the tools used to predict weather are very simple. Thermometers measure temperature. Barometers measure air pressure. Anemometers measure wind speed. Rain gauges measure the amount of precipitation.

Meteorologists also measure factors above Earth. Weather balloons are released from weather stations all over the world. They gather information about the weather in the upper troposphere.

Technology has helped weather forecasts become more accurate. Doppler radar uses radio waves to measure wind speed and precipitation, and to tell what direction storms are moving.

Weather satellites track weather data. One group of weather satellites is called GOES. Each GOES satellite stays fixed in orbit over the same part of Earth. Data from all of the satellites can be combined to see almost all of Earth.

Air Pressure and Altitude

In the photo below, the metal can has had the air pumped out of it. This caused the air pressure inside the can to be lower than the pressure outside the can. The higher air pressure outside pushed in, crushing the can.

You may have felt changes in air pressure while driving up or down a mountain, flying in a plane, or riding a fast elevator in a very tall building. As your altitude changed, changing air pressure may have caused your ears to "pop." As you go up, the pressure around you gets lower. As you go down, it gets higher. The "popping" in your ears happens when the pressure inside your ears changes to match the pressure outside.

Airplanes fly at high altitudes, where the air pressure is about half of what it is at Earth's surface. Airplane cabins are pressurized to keep passengers comfortable at these very low pressures.

Layers of the Atmosphere

The atmosphere is made up of layers. The layers have different characteristics.

The thermosphere is the highest layer. The air particles there are far apart. Sometimes electrical energy from the Sun disturbs gas particles in this layer. This causes auroras, or glows, to happen.

The mesosphere is the coldest layer. The higher you go in this layer, the colder it is. The stratosphere contains most of the ozone in the atmosphere. Ozone is a gas that takes in the Sun's harmful ultraviolet rays. As you increase in altitude in this layer, temperature also increases.

The troposphere is the lowest layer. People live in this layer. More than 75 percent of the air in the atmosphere is in the troposphere. Weather happens here. It is warmest near the surface. As you go higher in the layer, it gets colder and air pressure decreases.

Predicting Weather

Weather can change quickly. People use forecasts to prepare for weather. There are weather forecasts on radio and television, in newspapers, and on the Internet. These sources also give instructions and information about severe weather.

Weather forecasting begins with looking at weather all over the world. Meteorologists examine temperature, wind speed, humidity, and air pressure. They use computers to study the data. This helps them make weather predictions. In the United States, the National Weather Service gathers this information. Forecasters across the country use this information to predict both national and local weather.

Scientists observe the weather at this station atop Mount Washington in New Hampshire.

Hurricanes

A hurricane is a large, spiraling storm that forms over warm ocean waters. It starts as a tropical storm over the southern Atlantic Ocean, Caribbean Sea, Gulf of Mexico, or eastern Pacific Ocean. The winds blow at least 119 kilometers an hour. These winds cause lots of damage when the storms move over land.

Hurricanes begin as thunderstorms in areas of low pressure. Winds blow in and spiral because of the turning of Earth. Evaporation of ocean water adds moisture to the air. The water condenses as the warm air rises. This process releases a lot of energy. Large amounts of warm, moist air keep a hurricane moving. The storm loses energy and dies as it moves over colder water and drier land.

Severe-Weather Safety

Hurricanes

- Prepare a disaster plan and a disaster supply kit ahead of time.
- Evacuate if told to do so. If you don't need to evacuate, stay indoors.
- Avoid using the phone except for emergencies.

Hurricane

A Thermosphere
Sometimes, particles of gas in the thermosphere are disturbed by electrical energy from the Sun. When this happens, glows, or auroras, occur that can be seen in the night sky at high latitudes.

B Mesosphere
The mesosphere is the coldest layer. Temperatures get cooler as you move higher in this layer.

C Stratosphere
Temperature increases with altitude in the stratosphere. This layer contains most of the atmosphere's ozone.

D Troposphere
The troposphere is the layer in which you live. More than 75 percent of all the air in the atmosphere is in this layer. All weather takes place here.

Global Winds

Wind is moving air, caused by differences in air pressure. Winds generally move from areas of high pressure to areas of low pressure. When air rushes out of a balloon, it is moving from an area of higher pressure to an area of lower pressure.

Changes in air temperature change air pressure. Heated air is lighter. As its particles move faster, they move farther apart. Warmer air rises, while colder, heavier air sinks. Heat being transferred by moving air is called convection. Winds move across Earth as warm air rises from the tropics and cold air falls from the poles.

Warm air that rises at the equator cools as it moves up and away from the equator. At about 30° north and south of the equator, the air sinks back to Earth, causing large wind currents known as trade winds.

These arrows show the direction winds are blowing. Light winds are blue. Strong winds are orange.

Tornadoes

A tornado is a violent funnel-shaped air column that extends from a thunderstorm to the ground. It has very strong winds that can reach speeds of 419 kilometers an hour. They form from thunderstorms and come about quickly. This makes them hard to predict. The path of a tornado can change quickly. So it is also hard to predict its path.

Tornadoes can happen all over the United States. They are very common in the plains area between the Rocky Mountains and the Appalachians.

Severe-Weather Safety

Thunderstorms

- Find shelter in a building or car. Keep car windows closed.
- In the woods: Take shelter under the shorter trees. If boating or swimming, go to land and find shelter.
- Outside in an open space: Squat low to the ground. Place your hands on your knees with your head between them. Make yourself as small as possible.

Tornadoes

- Take shelter underground in a basement or storm shelter.
- If no basement or shelter: Go to an inside room, hallway, or closet on the first floor away from windows.
- Outside: Lie flat in a ditch. Lie facedown and cover your head with your hands.

Severe Weather

What should you do when you hear thunder? Thunder can't hurt you, but the lightning that goes with it can. Knowing what to do can help keep you safe during severe weather.

Thunderstorm

141

Thunderstorms

A thunderstorm is a small, powerful storm that produces strong winds, heavy rain, lightning, and thunder. They happen all the time. At any given time, about 1,800 thunderstorms are occurring around the world. They happen more in spring and summer, but they can happen in every season.

Every thunderstorm has lightning and heavy rains. This can be dangerous. Lightning can kill people. Heavy rains can cause flash floods.

Local Winds

Rising and sinking air also creates local winds. The temperature of large bodies of water does not change as quickly as land temperature. Sunlight raises the temperature of land. The air over the land gets hotter and rises. But the air over the water stays cool. The cool air from above the water flows in underneath the rising warm air above the land. At night, the land becomes cooler than the water and the flow of air reverses. The air temperature of land near water stays more even because of this pattern.

Winds and Local Weather

Water vapor in the air condenses when air rises and cools near the equator. This causes a lot of rain in this region. At 30° north or south latitude, dry air falls toward Earth. This is where some of Earth's deserts are located.

Local weather is also affected by jet streams. A jet stream is a band of wind moving at high speed in the upper troposphere and lower stratosphere. It moves from west to east. The jet stream affects local weather by moving air of different temperatures from place to place.

How do clouds and precipitation form?

Humidity

Humidity is the amount of water vapor in the air. Water enters the atmosphere as water vapor within the water cycle. Air temperature determines how much water vapor the air can hold. Warm air can hold more water vapor than cool air. Dew, fog, or clouds form as air gets cooler and water vapor condenses, or changes from a gas to a liquid.

No matter what the air temperature is, there is a limit to the amount of water that air can hold. **Relative humidity** is the amount of water the air contains compared to the amount of water the air could hold at its current temperature. One hundred percent is the highest relative humidity. It means that the air is holding as much water as it can.

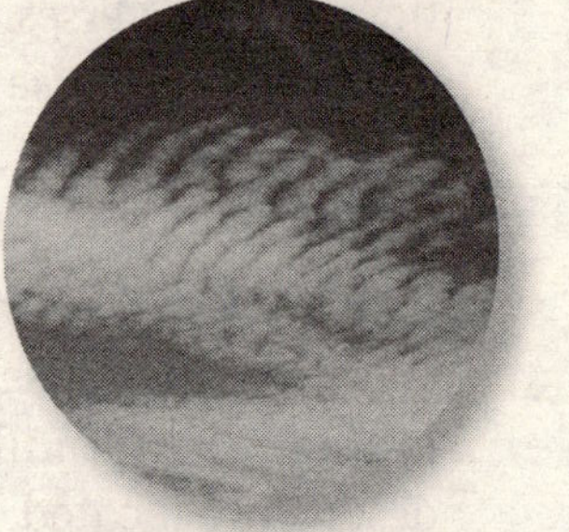

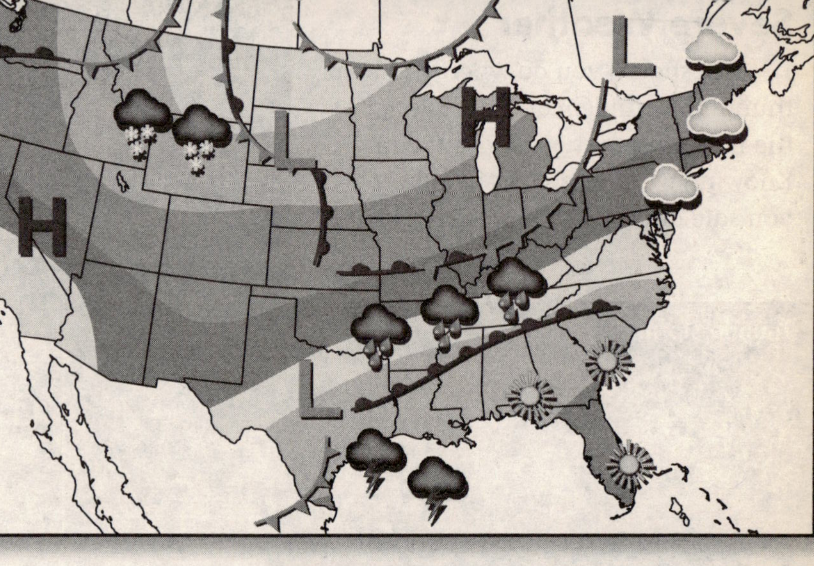

Map Key

Warm Front 
A mass of warm air runs into a mass of cooler air. The warm air is forced above the cooler air. As the warm air rises, it cools and condenses, forming clouds. Periods of steady rain or drizzle result.

What causes weather and climate?

Air Masses and Fronts

Weather is the condition of the atmosphere at a particular time and place. Air masses and fronts produce the weather. An **air mass** is a very large body of air. The whole mass has about the same temperature and humidity. The area over which it forms determines the temperature and moisture of the air mass.

Air masses of different temperatures do not mix easily. A boundary, called a **front,** forms between them. Weather at a front is usually cloudy or stormy. **Meteorologists** are scientists who study weather. They track air masses to predict weather conditions.

Cold Front

Warm Front

Cold Front

A mass of cold air runs into a mass of warm air, forcing the warm air above the cold air. As the warm air rises, it cools and condenses. Clouds form, and heavy rain or snow may follow. Cold fronts move more quickly than warm fronts.

Stationary Front

A warm air mass and a cold air mass meet, but neither one moves toward the other. As its name implies, a stationary front does not move quickly. It can stay over an area for several days. The weather produced is similar to a warm front.

Cirrus clouds are thin and look feathery. Because they form high in the atmosphere where temperatures are below 0°C.

Fluffy cirrocumulus clouds form high in the atmosphere. These clouds are made of ice crystals and do not usually result in precipitation.

Dark, heavy cumulonimbus clouds can reach high into the atmosphere. They usually result in a short, heavy rainfall or a thunderstorm.

Cumulus clouds usually form near Earth's surface. They usually form late in the day, when air warmed by land is rising into the atmosphere.

Stratus clouds form between two and six kilometers above Earth's surface. They are flat, white clouds that will produce mist or a steady drizzle.

Clouds

Clouds form when air rises and cools. Cooler air can hold less water vapor. This causes condensation of the water in air as it rises. Tiny droplets form around dust, smoke, and salt particles in air. Millions of these droplets collect and form clouds. If the temperature in the cloud is cold enough, the water droplets freeze to form ice crystals. Clouds get larger as more droplets form.

Clouds are grouped by their shape and by how high they are above Earth's surface. There are three main cloud forms. Cirrus clouds are thin and made of ice crystals. They do not result in precipitation. Cumulus clouds are puffy. They form when air warmed by land rises. Stratus clouds are flat, white clouds that may produce mist or steady drizzle.

How Precipitation Forms

Precipitation is all the forms of moisture that fall from the atmosphere to the Earth's surface. Rain, sleet, snow, and hail are common forms of precipitation. Clouds produce precipitation when they hold a lot of moisture.

Water droplets and ice crystals in clouds get larger when water clings to them. When the crystals are large enough to fall, they fall as precipitation.

Rain and Snow

Rain falls when water droplets or ice crystals fall from clouds through temperatures that are above 0°C, or freezing. Snow falls if ice crystals drop from clouds and the temperature under the clouds is below freezing. Snow crystals can be feathery and six-sided snowflakes, or flat hexagons. The shape of snowflakes depends on the temperature and the amount of moisture in a cloud.

Sleet and Hail

Sleet forms when rain falls through a large layer of freezing air. The rain freezes as it falls. It reaches the ground as raindrop-sized particles of ice. Freezing rain, called glaze, happens when air is cold but not cold enough to freeze the water. The drops freeze when they hit a freezing surface.

Hail is round hard particles of ice. Hail usually falls in warmer summer months. When winds toss ice crystals up and down inside cumulonimbus clouds, hail forms. Droplets of water attach and freeze to the crystals as they move and freeze. This happens over and over until the hailstone grows heavy enough to fall. Hailstones can be as big as baseballs.

How Precipitation Forms

144

Genre	Comprehension Skill	Text Features	Science Content
Nonfiction	Sequence	• Captions • Charts • Diagrams • Glossary	Matter

Scott Foresman Science 6.13

ISBN 0-328-14006-6

PEARSON
Scott
Foresman

scottforesman.com

145

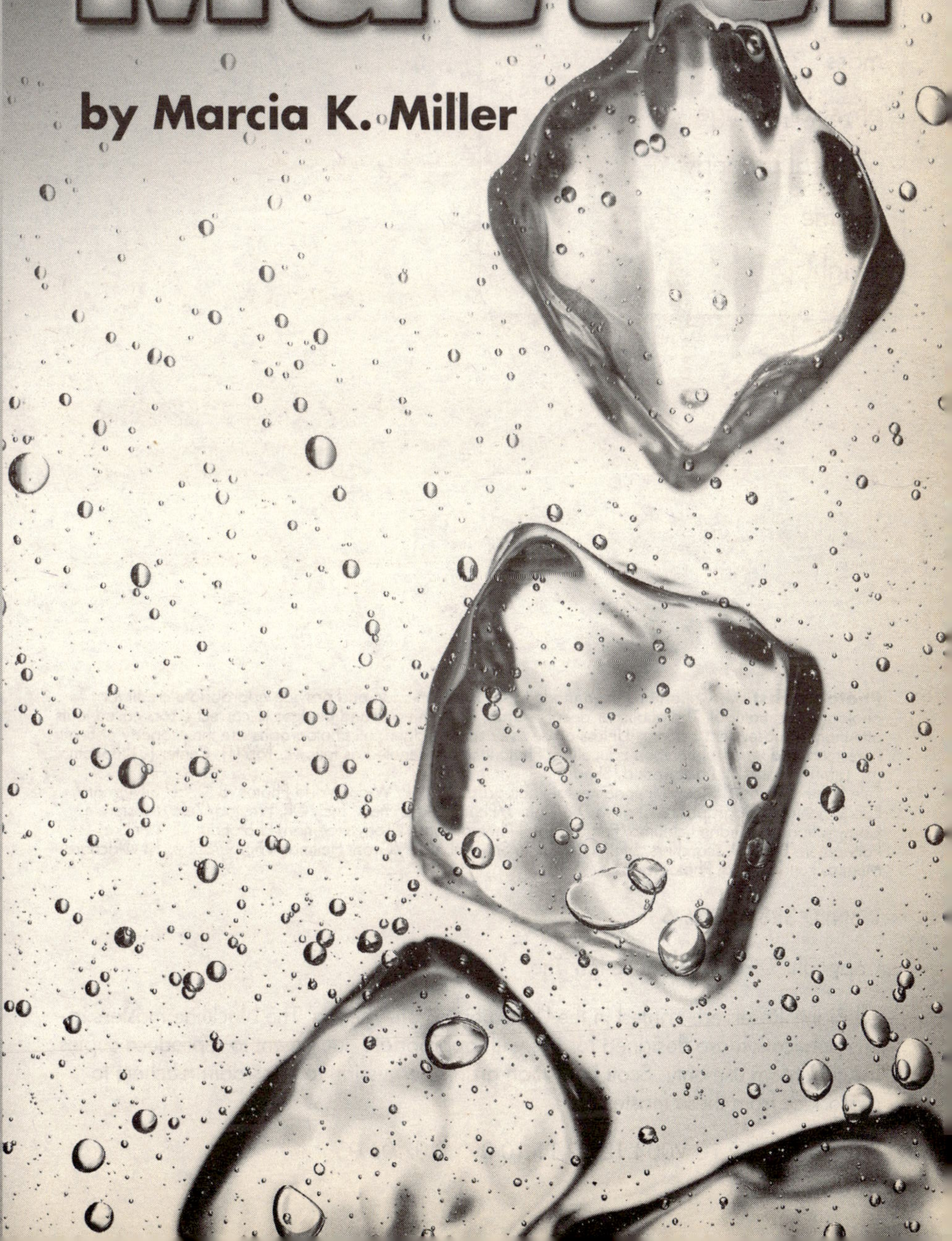

Vocabulary

chemical change

chemical property

condensation

density

mass

physical change

physical property

volume

weight

What did you learn?

1. What do you measure when you measure an object's mass?

2. How do particles differ in the four states of matter?

3. When water boils, it changes to water vapor. Is this a physical or a chemical change? Explain.

4. **Writing** in Science You drop a cork and a copper penny into a bowl of water. Write to explain what you think will happen and why. Use details from the book to support your answer.

5. **Sequence** Use the sequence words *first, next, after,* and *finally* to tell how to find the density of a substance.

Photographs: Every effort has been made to secure permission and provide appropriate credit for photographic material. The publisher deeply regrets any omission and pledges to correct errors called to its attention in subsequent editions. Unless otherwise acknowledged, all photographs are the property of Scott Foresman, a division of Pearson Education. Photo locators denoted as follows: Top (T), Center (C), Bottom (B), Left (L), Right (R), Background (Bkgd).
Title Page: ©Richard Megna/Fundamental Photographs; 6 AP/Wide World Photos; 8 ©Paul Silverman/Fundamental Photographs, ©Charles D. Winters/Photo Researchers, Inc., ©P. Freytag/Zefa/Masterfile Corporation; 9 ©Diane Schiumo/Fundamental Photographs, ©Tony Freeman/PhotoEdit; 11 ©Pekka Parviainen/Photo Researchers, Inc.; 12 ©Runk/Schoenberger/Grant Heilman Photography; 14 ©Richard Megna/Fundamental Photographs

ISBN: 0-328-14006-6

Matter

by Marcia K. Miller

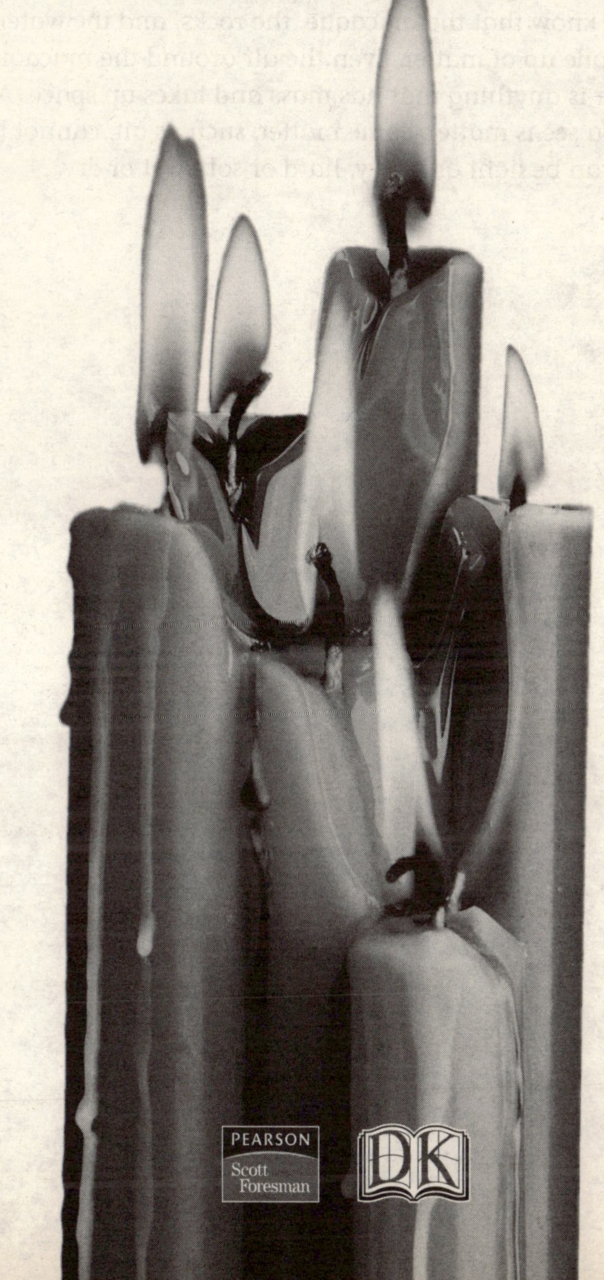

Glossary

chemical change — a change in which one or more substances change into new substances that have different properties

chemical property — a property of a substance that tells how it forms new substances when it mixes with something else

condensation — the change of state from a gas to a liquid

density — a measure of the amount of matter that fills a given space

mass — the amount of matter that makes up a substance

physical change — a change that may affect a substance's appearance without changing its physical properties

physical property — a property of a substance that can be seen or measured without changing the substance

volume — the amount of space that an object takes up

weight — a measure of the pull of gravity on an object

147

What is matter?

Measuring Matter

The animal in the picture is a macaque. This kind of monkey lives in Japan. You know that the macaque, the rocks, and the water in the picture are made up of matter. Even the air around the macaque is matter. Matter is anything that has mass and takes up space. Almost everything you see is matter. Some matter, such as air, cannot be seen. Matter can be light or heavy, hard or soft, wet or dry.

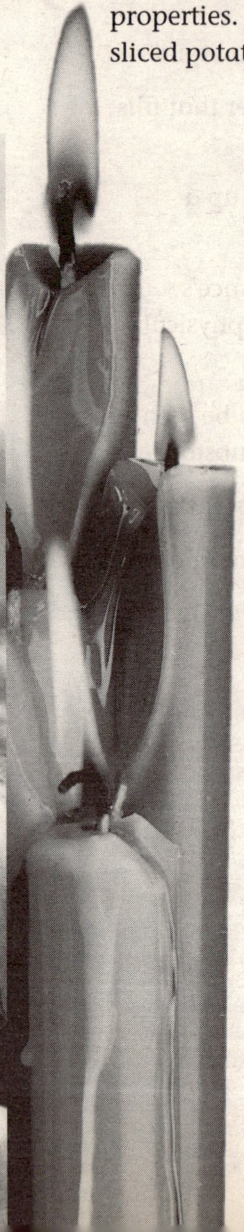

Physical Changes

The physical properties of a substance do not change when it melts, freezes, or boils. During a **physical change**, a substance may look different, but its properties stay the same. Water is water whether it is a solid, a liquid, or a gas. A change of state is not a change of properties. Sawing doesn't change wood. A sliced potato is still a potato.

Shredding the potato is a physical change. Each bit of potato is the same as the original vegetable. But cooking is a chemical change.

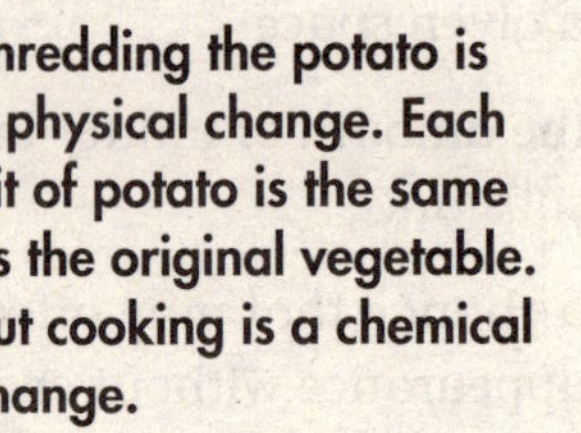

Chemical Changes

Look at the candles in the photo. Wax melting is a physical change. But what about the burning wick? It is undergoing a chemical change. In a **chemical change**, one or more substances change into new substances that have different properties.

The wick and oxygen in the air undergo a chemical change during burning. Three new substances form: ash, carbon dioxide, and water vapor. None of these has the properties of the wick or the oxygen.

There are often signs that a chemical change is occurring. Heat, light, sound, and/or color change often mean a chemical change is happening.

Mass and Weight

People often mix up mass and weight. But these are two different properties of objects. Mass is a measure of the amount of matter in an object. Mass is the same for an object wherever it is in the universe. **Weight** is a measure of the pull of gravity on an object. It is measured using a spring scale in units called newtons. Weight can change if an object moves to a place that has a different force of gravity. You have the same mass whether you are on Earth or on the Moon. But you weigh six times as much on Earth as you would on the Moon!

Density

Here's an old riddle. *Which weighs more— a pound of feathers or a pound of lead?* Do you know?

The feathers and the lead weigh the same amount. Both weigh one pound! But one pound of lead is a lot smaller than one pound of feathers. Why is this?

Spring scale

Balance

Melting and Freezing

What might happen if you heated solid iron to a high temperature? It would turn into liquid iron. This process of a solid becoming a liquid is called melting. A substance turns into a liquid when it is heated to its melting point. Lead melts at 327.5°C. This is far higher than water's melting point of 0°C.

A substance must gain heat in order to melt. But when a substance loses heat, its particles slow down. They form a solid. This process is called freezing. The temperature at which a substance freezes is its freezing point. A freezing point is the same temperature as the melting point.

A substance will melt more slowly if it is insulated. Insulation slows the movement of heat.

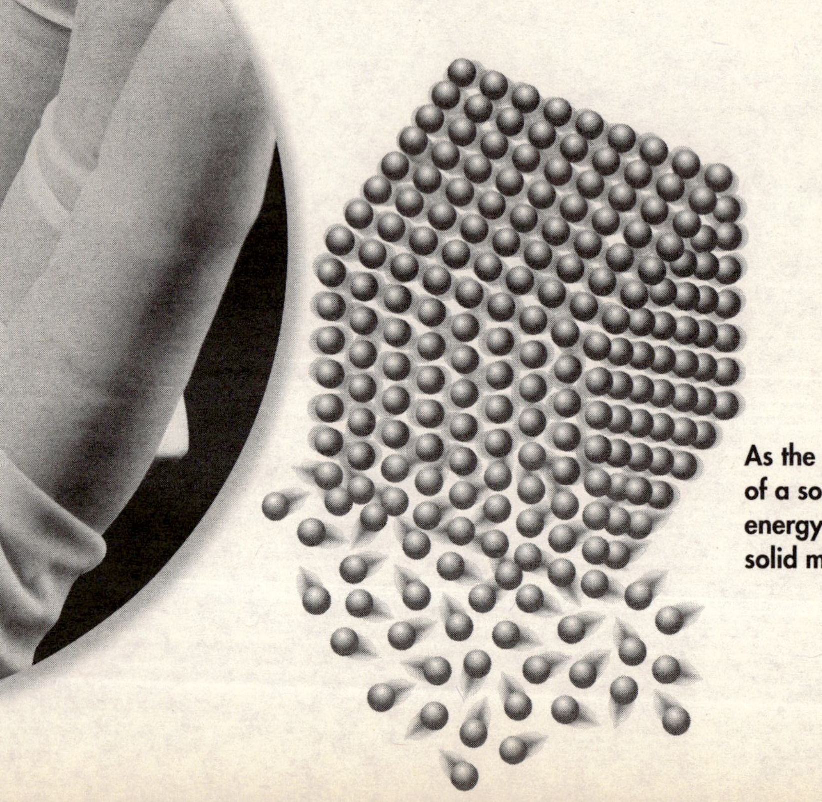
As the particles of a solid gain energy, the solid melts.

Changes of State

Look at the matter around you. Many things are solids. Some are liquids. Others are gases. We know oxygen is a gas. We are used to seeing iron as a solid and mercury as a liquid. Why does matter at the same temperature exist in different states?

You have read that the particles in matter attract one another. These attractions can be strong or weak. For example, iron particles are strongly attracted to each other. Oxygen particles in air are less strongly attracted. That is why iron is a solid and oxygen is a gas at normal temperature.

Temperature affects the force of attraction. Heating a substance causes its particles to gain energy. They move faster. With enough added heat, the particles will gain enough energy to break some of their attraction. A solid becomes a liquid. Add even more heat and the particles will break free of all their attraction. A liquid becomes a gas.

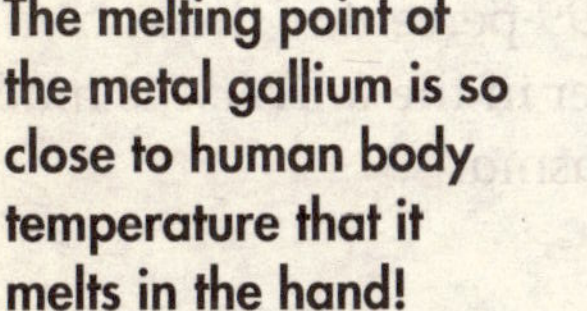

The melting point of the metal gallium is so close to human body temperature that it melts in the hand!

The matter that makes up lead is more tightly packed than the matter that makes up feathers. Lead has a greater density. **Density** is a measure of the amount of matter that fills a given space. You can also say that density is mass per unit volume.

Think of density this way. Picture a cube of lead that measures 1 centimeter on each side. Its volume would be 1 cubic centimeter. Its mass would be 11.35 grams. A cube of cork of the same size has the same volume—1 cubic centimeter. But its mass is only 0.24 grams. The particles of matter in the lead are more tightly packed than the particles of matter in the cork are. The lead cube would be heavier.

You can use a formula to find density.

$$\text{density} = \frac{\text{mass}}{\text{volume}} \text{ or } \frac{m}{v}$$

Suppose you have an object with a mass of 30 grams. Its volume is 15 cubic centimeters. What is its density? Follow the steps to find the density.

$$\text{density} = \frac{m}{v} = \frac{30g}{15cm^3} = \frac{2g}{cm^3}$$

Each cubic centimeter of the substance in that cube has a mass of 2 grams.

The liquid and solid substances in this tube have different densities. A substance with less density floats on top of a substance with more density.

Using Density To Identify Substances

How can it help to know the density of a substance? Every substance has a particular density. So you can use density to figure out what a substance is.

Picture a small cube of lead and a large lead pipe. The density of lead is always the same. It is 11.35 grams per cubic centimeter. This means the lead cube and the lead pipe have the same density even though they are different sizes. The density of one substance is usually different than the density of any other substance.

Suppose you find a piece of metal. You don't know what metal it is, but you want to find out. First, use a balance to find its mass. Then measure it to find its volume. Use those two numbers to find its density. Then look at a table similar to the one at the right. Suppose you calculated a density of 10.50 grams per cubic centimeter. Look for a material that has the same density. Which metal matches?

Oil is less dense than water. So oil floats on top of water. This is why oil spilled at sea is likely to wash up on a nearby beach.

Densities of Common Materials	
Material	**Density (g/cm³)**
Gold	19.32
Lead	11.35
Silver	10.50
Copper	8.96
Rubber	1.10
Water	1.00
Cork	0.24
Wood White oak Balsa	 0.68 0.16

This is the aurora borealis. It is also known as the northern lights. It is made of plasma formed when charged particles from the Sun mix with gases in the high atmosphere.

Liquids

Liquids have definite volume but no definite shape. The particles of a liquid move fast enough to break some of the attraction between them. They can slide past each other. So a liquid takes the shape of the container that holds it. You can pour a carton of juice into a cup. The shape of the juice changes, but its volume stays the same.

Gases

A gas has no particular shape or volume. Its particles move quickly. They break away from one another and move in many different directions. A gas takes the shape of the container it is in. The air you breathe is made up of gases that fill and take the shape of the room you are in.

Plasma

Plasma has no definite shape or volume, yet it is not a gas. Its particles have electric charges. Plasmas are not common on Earth. They are found in lightning, fire, and neon lights. Scientists think that 99 percent of the known matter in the universe is made up of plasma.

How can matter change?

States of Matter

Is your desk moving? You'll probably say no. But the matter that makes up your desk is moving.

All matter is made up of tiny particles. You cannot see them without a microscope. The particles always move and bump into each other. Their speed and how strongly they attract each other is what makes matter a solid, a liquid, a gas, or plasma. These are called the states of matter.

Solids

The shape and volume of the four states of matter show their differences. A solid has a definite shape and volume. Its particles are very close together. They don't move quickly. A strong attraction holds them together. A solid keeps its shape and volume even if you move it around. Your chair, the floor, and the hair on your head are all solids.

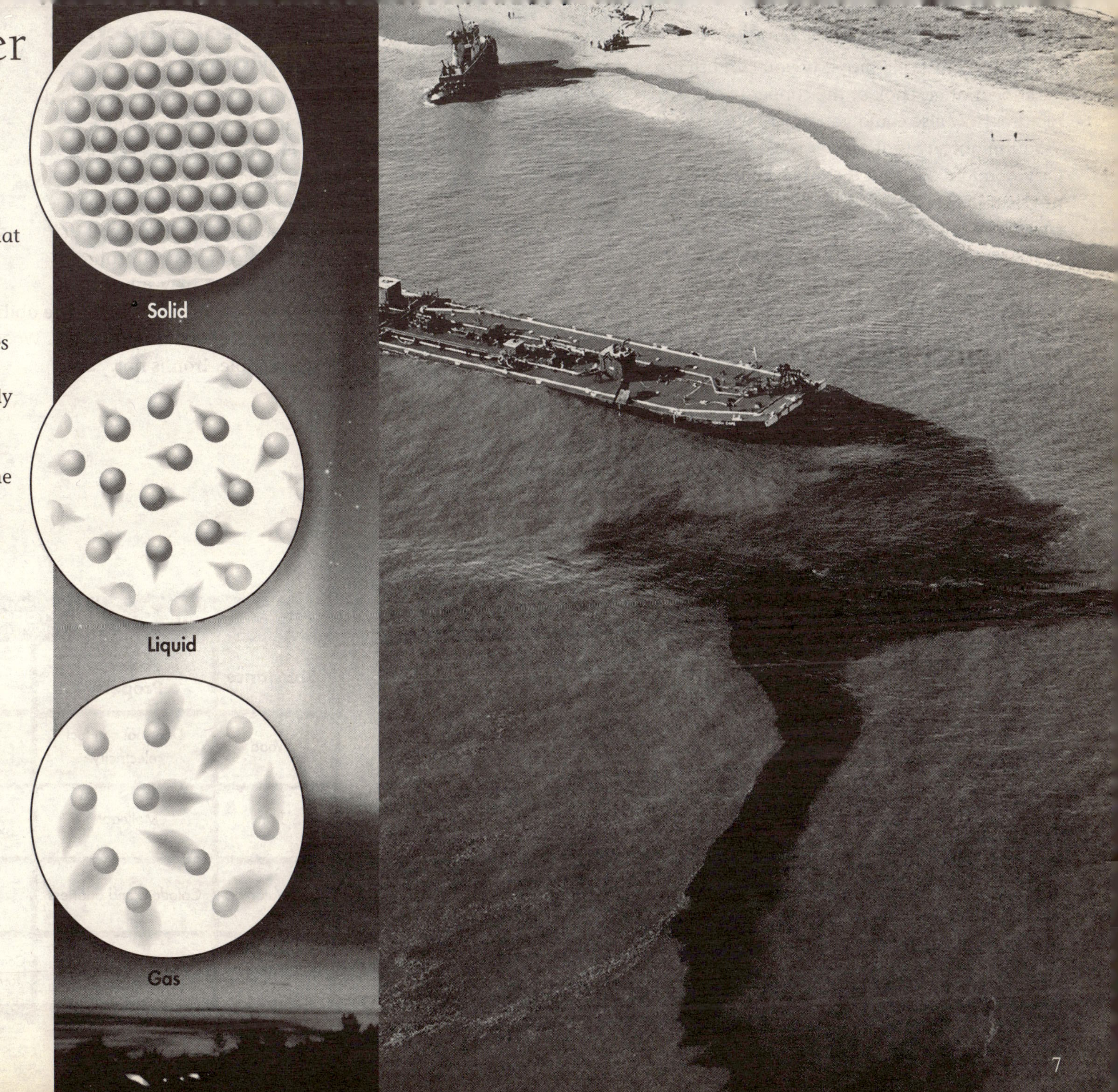

Physical Properties of Matter

Density is just one property you can use to describe matter. Look at the copper in the picture. How else could you describe it?

You might say that copper is a solid. Or you might say that it shines. These are physical properties of copper. A **physical property** of matter is anything you can see or measure without changing the substance. The physical properties of a substance are always the same.

Copper has useful physical properties. Copper is malleable. You can pound, roll, or shape it. Copper is also ductile. You can pull it into thin strips, such as wire.

Copper conducts heat and electricity very well. It is often used to make electrical wires and cooking pots. Wood does not conduct heat or electricity well. A wooden spoon lets you stir hot liquid without burning your hand.

Matter has other physical properties. It may dissolve in other substances. It may be magnetic. Different substances may freeze and boil at different temperatures.

Copper

The boiling point of a liquid is one of its physical properties.

Water freezes and melts at 0°C. The freezing point of a substance is a physical property.

Chemical Properties Of Matter

Matter can also be described by its chemical properties. A **chemical property** of a substance determines what happens when it mixes with something else. The wood in the photo below is burning. It changes into new substances, ash and gases, as it burns. The ability to burn is called flammability. Wood is flammable. Iron is not.

When placed in acid, the zinc covering the nail goes through a chemical change. The gold in the bracelet is not affected by the acid.

Wood is flammable.

Some Common Properties		
Substance	**Physical Property**	**Chemical Property**
Wood	Does not conduct electricity	Flammable
Iron	Malleable	Combines with oxygen to form rust
Water	Colorless and odorless	Does not burn
Copper	Conducts electricity	Combines with oxygen to form the mineral cuprite

Science

Science

Building Blocks of Matter

by Lillian Duggan

Genre	Comprehension Skill	Text Features	Science Content
Nonfiction	Draw Conclusions	• Captions • Charts • Diagrams • Glossary	Building Blocks of Matter

Scott Foresman Science 6.14

ISBN 0-328-14009-0

PEARSON

Scott Foresman

scottforesman.com

What did you learn?

1. What is the current atomic model called?

2. If an element has four protons, how many electrons does it have?

3. The chemical formula for water is H_2O. How many atoms of hydrogen and how many atoms of oxygen does a water molecule have?

4. **Writing** in Science Sand is a mixture. Write to explain how elements and compounds combine to form sand. Include details from the book to support your answer.

5. **Compare and Contrast** Many common products and foods are made with acids and bases. Describe the similarities and differences between acids and bases.

Photographs: Every effort has been made to secure permission and provide appropriate credit for photographic material. The publisher deeply regrets any omission and pledges to correct errors called to its attention in subsequent editions. Unless otherwise acknowledged, all photographs are the property of Scott Foresman, a division of Pearson Education. Photo locators denoted as follows: Top (T), Center (C), Bottom (B), Left (L), Right (R), Background (Bkgd).
Title Page: ©Andrew Syred/Photo Researchers, Inc.; 2 ©Danny Lehman/Corbis; 3 (CL) ©DK Images, (BR) Stephen Oliver/©DK Images; 5 (TL, TLB, CLT, CL, BL) ©Bettmann/Corbis, (CLB) ©Hulton-Deutsch Collection/Corbis, (BLT) Gary J. Shulfer/C. Marvin Lang/University of Wisconsin at Stevens Point; 6 (BC, CR) ©DK Images; 8 (BL) ©Larry Stepanowicz/Visuals Unlimited, (TR) ©Richard Megna/Fundamental Photographs; 9 (B) ©David Samuel Robbins/Corbis; 14 (TR, CC) ©Richard Megna/Fundamental Photographs; 15 (CC) ©Andrew Syred/Photo Researchers, Inc., (BC) ©Richard Megna/Fundamental Photographs; 16 Brand X Pictures; 17 Digital Vision, Andrew Jaster, Getty Images, ©G. Tompkinson/ Photo Researchers, Inc., ©Charles D. Winters/Photo Researchers, Inc., ©Mark Schneider/Visuals Unlimited, ©Adam Hart-Davis/Photo Researchers, Inc., ©Astrid & Hanns-Frieder Michler/Photo Researchers, Inc.; 18 ©Araldo de Luca/Corbis; 19 ©DK Images; 20 ©DK Images, ©P. Jude/Photo Researchers, Inc.; 22 (BL) ©Prof. P. Motta/Photo Researchers, Inc., (CC) ©Richard Megna/Fundamental Photographs, (BR) ©F. Krahmer/Zefa/Masterfile Corporation; 23 (CLB) ©Michelle Garrett/Corbis, (CCL) ©Mark A. Johnson/Corbis, (BC) ©ER Productions/Corbis, (CR) ©Scott T. Smith/Corbis

ISBN: 0-328-14009-0

Glossary

compound   a substance made up of two or more elements that are chemically combined to form a new substance with different properties

concentration   the measure of the amount of solute dissolved in a solvent

element   a substance made up of only one kind of atom

mixture   a combination of substances in which the atoms of the substances are not chemically combined

periodic table   a table in which the elements are listed in order according to their atomic number

solubility   the maximum amount of solute that can be dissolved in a solvent at a certain temperature

solute   a substance that is dissolved in another substance

solution   a mixture that forms when one substance dissolves in another

solvent   a substance in which a solute is dissolved

Building Blocks of Matter

by Lillian Duggan

How did we learn about atoms?

Structure of the Atom

Charcoal and aluminum foil look different, but both are made up of atoms joined together. The carbon in charcoal and the aluminum in aluminum foil are both pure substances. The smallest whole piece of a pure substance is an atom.

Atoms are too small to study directly. Scientists make models of atoms to help picture them. Over the years, the model of the atom has changed because scientists have learned more and more about it. The model of the atom that scientists use today is called the electron cloud model.

Scientists study atoms using machines like this.

The pH Scale

Scientists use the pH scale to describe the strength of acids and bases. The measurements of the pH scale range from 0 to 14. If a substance has a pH between 0 and 7, it is an acid. The strength of an acid decreases as pH increases. If a substance has a pH between 7 and 14, it is a base. The strength of a base increases as pH increases. A pH of 7 is neutral.

Acids
- Taste sour (Never taste a substance to test for the presence of acids.)
- React strongly with some metals to form new compounds
- Change blue litmus paper to red

Bases
- Taste bitter (Never taste a substance to test for the presence of bases.)
- Feel slippery
- Change red litmus paper to blue

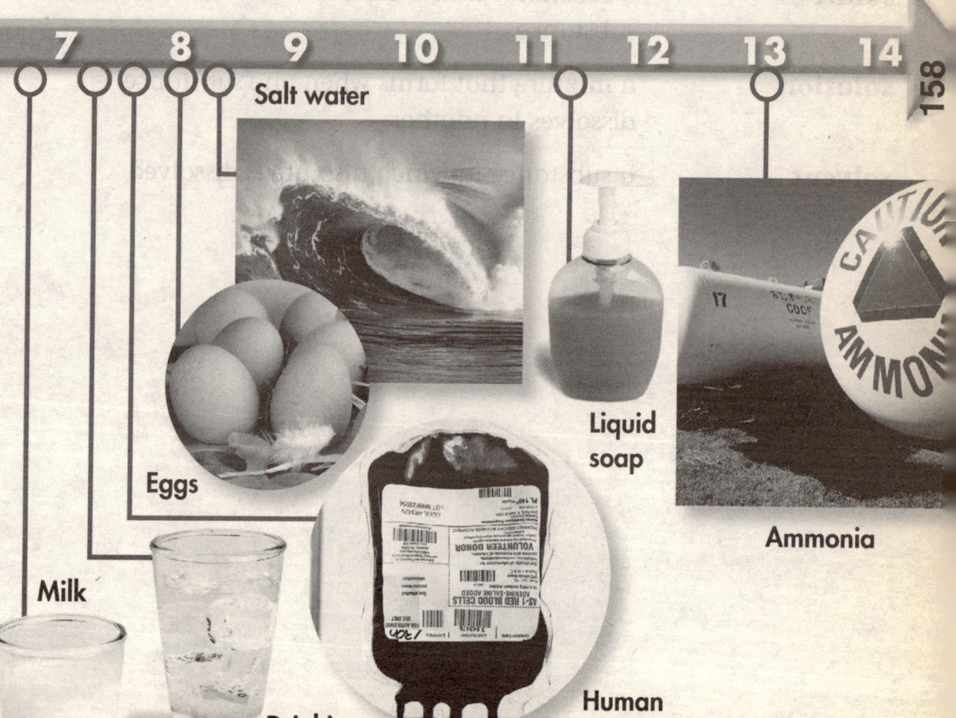

Acids and Bases

Many people think of acids as dangerous chemicals. Some acids can be strong enough to burn your skin, but many acids are weak. Some weak acids are found in foods that you eat, such as sour candy, pickles, milk, and citrus fruits. Weak acids in your body cells are important to your health.

Because some acids are dangerous, never touch an acid to identify it. Instead, use an indicator—a compound that changes color when it comes in contact with an acid. Blue litmus paper is an indicator that turns red when acid touches it.

Bases are commonly found in household products such as shampoo, oven cleaners and drain cleaners. Strong bases are just as dangerous as strong acids. Many are poisonous and can burn your skin. Red litmus paper turns blue when dipped in a base.

In the electron cloud model, the atom is divided into two main parts. These are the nucleus and the electron cloud. The nucleus is in the center of the atom and contains protons and neutrons. A proton is a particle that has a positive charge. A neutron is a particle that has no charge.

The electron cloud surrounds the nucleus. It contains electrons and a lot of empty space. An electron is a particle that has a negative charge.

Scientists have found other smaller particles. These particles make up protons and neutrons. Scientists are still learning more about these particles.

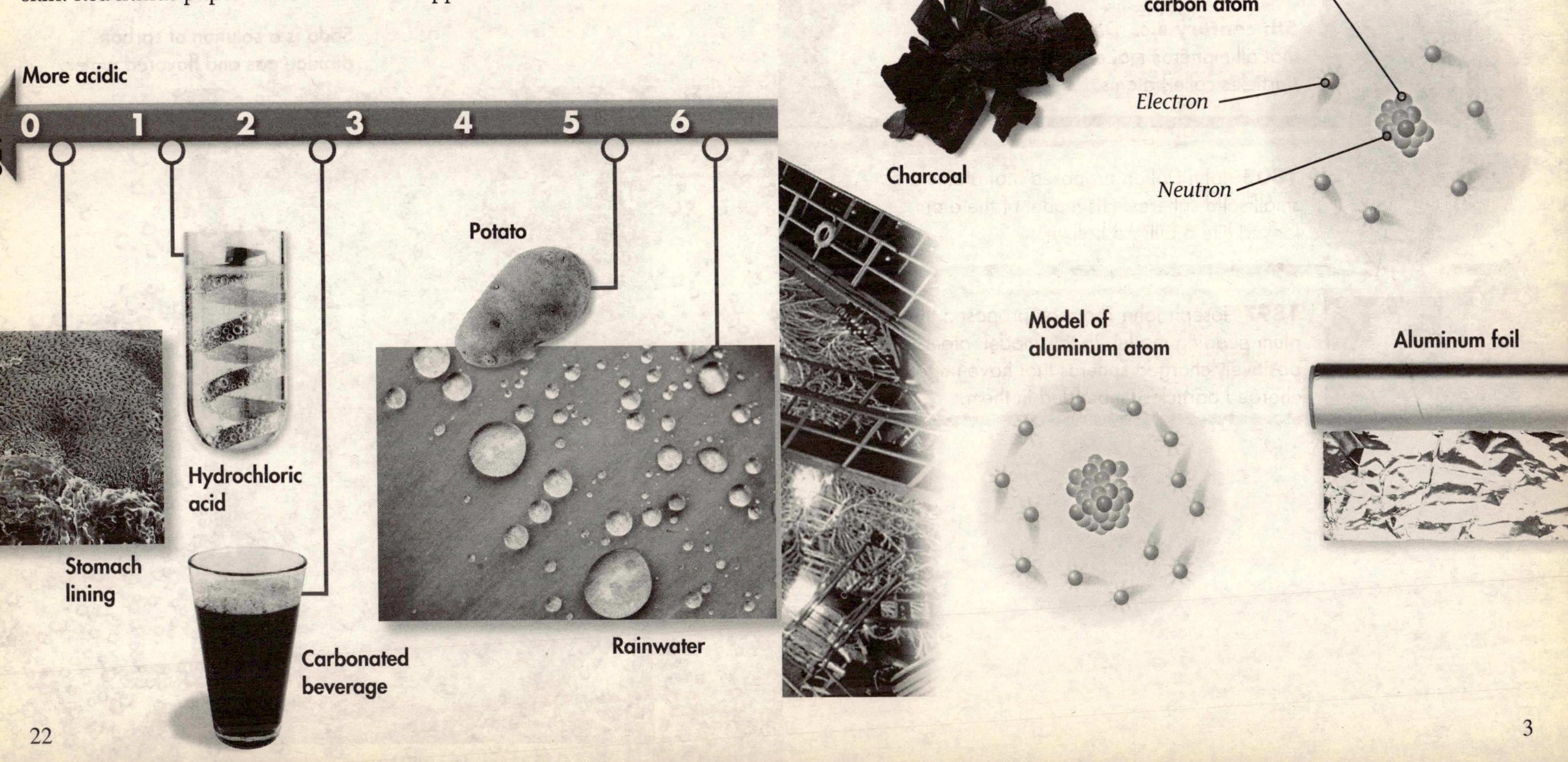

History of the Atom

The model of the atom has changed over the past two thousand years. The first person to say that matter was made up of smaller particles was probably the Greek philosopher Leucippus. Democritus, a student of Leucippus, called the particles *atomos*, which means "indivisible." Democritus believed that atoms were all hard solids in different shapes and sizes, but made of the same material. He also believed they could not be destroyed.

Aristotle, another Greek philosopher, believed that matter could be divided again and again. Many people accepted Aristotle's ideas up until the 1600s.

5th century B.C. Democritus proposed that all matter is made up of indestructible particles called atoms.

1803 John Dalton proposed that atoms are small solid spheres. His model of the atom looked like a billiard ball.

1897 Joseph John Thomson proposed the plum pudding model. In this model, atoms are positively-charged spheres that have negatively-charged particles embedded in them.

You can make a substance dissolve faster by mixing or stirring the solution. Increasing the temperature of the solvent or crushing the solute into smaller pieces also makes substances dissolve faster.

Have you ever noticed that sugar sometimes falls to the bottom of a glass of iced tea? That's because the solution has reached its saturation point. This is the point at which no more solute can be dissolved in the solvent. All solutions have a saturation point, which limits how much solute can be dissolved in the solvent.

Pressure also affects solubility. Carbon dioxide gas and flavored water form a solution when they're under pressure. When you open a soda bottle or can, the gas is no longer under pressure and is no longer soluble. The gas comes out of the solution, rises to the top of the container, and escapes into the atmosphere.

Soda is a solution of carbon dioxide gas and flavored water.

Concentration

Solutions may contain different amounts of solute and solvent. **Concentration** is the measure of the amount of solute dissolved in a solvent. A solution may be described as being either concentrated or dilute. A concentrated solution has more solute per volume of solvent than a dilute solution has. The white vinegar in your kitchen is a dilute solution of acetic acid and water. More concentrated acetic acid solutions are used in laboratories and food manufacturing facilities.

Solubility is the maximum amount of solute that can be dissolved in a solvent at a certain temperature. We express solubility as grams of solute per milliliter of solvent. The amount of solute that can dissolve in a solvent is affected by the temperature of the solvent. For example, it is more difficult to dissolve sugar in iced tea than in hot tea. Adding the ice changes the tea's temperature. This affects the sugar's solubility in the tea.

Whipped cream is a solution of a liquid and a gas. The liquid is butter fat and the gas is air.

In 1803 a British scientist named John Dalton used scientific methods to prove that atoms exist. Dalton developed an atomic theory, that stated all matter is made of atoms, which cannot be created, divided, or destroyed.

The chart below shows how the model of the atom has changed over time. Today, scientists generally agree that the electron cloud model is a good working model of the atom. As technology improves, scientists continue to learn more about the atom.

1911 Ernest Rutherford found that most of the mass of the atom is in its center. He called the center of the atom a nucleus. In his model, negatively-charged electrons orbit a dense, positively-charged nucleus. His model looks like a model of the solar system.

1913 Niels Bohr proposed that electrons travel in fixed orbits called shells. Electrons cannot move from one shell to another without gaining or losing energy.

1920s Erwin Schrodinger and Werner Heisenberg proposed the electron cloud model of the atom.

How are elements grouped?

Elements

Look around you. Everything you see is made of tiny atoms. Most matter is made of more than one kind of atom. For example, water is made of hydrogen atoms and oxygen atoms.

An **element** is a substance made up of only one kind of atom. Elements cannot be broken down into other substances, so they are also called pure substances. You are probably familiar with some elements such as carbon, aluminum, gold, silver, and copper.

Gold is an element that is often used in jewelry.

Silver and copper are elements that are used in jewelry and electrical wiring.

Chromatography

Substances in a mixture can be identified based on how soluble they are. This can be done using a process called chromatography. In this example, the mixture of color pigments found in rose petals is being separated. As the liquid moves up the paper strip, particles of the pigments dissolved in the liquid form bands. Each band is a different pigment. Many police departments use chromatography to identify all kinds of substances.

Chromography is being used to identify the pigments in these rose petals.

Yellow gold used in
jewelry is a solution
of gold and copper.

Solutions

When you look at a bowl of vegetable soup, you can see several different substances. But some mixtures look the same throughout. These are called solutions. A **solution** forms when one substance dissolves in another. Salt water is a common solution.

The two components that make up a solution are the solute and the solvent. The **solute** is the substance that is dissolved. The **solvent** is the substance in which the solute is dissolved. In salt water, the solute is salt and the solvent is water.

Whenever a solute dissolves in a solvent, the solute breaks down into very small particles and mixes evenly with the particles of the solvent. You can't see the salt particles in salt water because they are too small.

Solids and gases also form solutions. Stainless steel is a solution of three solids—chromium, nickel, and iron. Kitchen utensils such as forks are made with stainless steel. Air is a solution made up of several gases. The main gases in air are nitrogen, oxygen, and argon.

About 100 elements are found naturally on Earth. They make up everything that has been found on Earth and in space. The 26 letters of the alphabet combine to form different words. Similarly, elements combine in different ways to make different types of matter.

We identify each element by how many protons are found in its nucleus. No two elements have the same number of protons. For example, we know that any atom that has 79 protons in its nucleus is a gold atom.

The atoms of elements have an even number of protons and electrons. If an element has 79 protons in its nucleus, there must be 79 electrons in its electron cloud. With the same number of protons and electrons, atoms have no electrical charge.

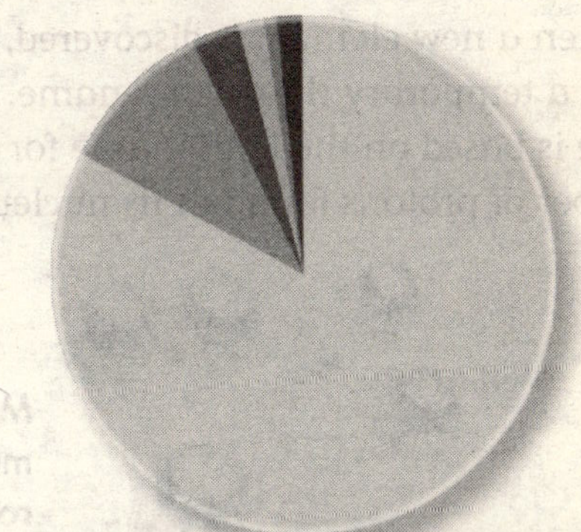

All living and nonliving things are made up of elements. This circle graph shows most of the elements that make up your body.

Symbols for Elements

Scientists use abbreviations for writing the names of the elements. These abbreviations are called chemical symbols, and they are made up of one, two, or three letters.

A chemical symbol is usually the first letter of the element's name. Another letter from the name is added if that symbol is already used by another element.

Some elements that were discovered in ancient times were given Greek or Latin names. The symbols for some of these elements were taken from their old name. For example, gold was given the symbol Au after its Latin name *aurum*.

When a new element is discovered, it's given a temporary three-letter name. The name is based on the Latin name for the number of protons found in its nucleus.

Mercury is the only metal that is liquid at room temperature.

Mixtures

If matter is not an element or a compound, it is probably a mixture. A **mixture** is a combination of substances in which the atoms of the substances are not chemically combined. Mixtures may contain elements, compounds, or both.

The substances in a mixture keep their own properties. The carrots, potatoes, and other vegetables that make up the bowl of soup below are all separate and easy to identify. Also, the components of a mixture may be present in any ratio. One bowl of soup may have more potatoes than another bowl.

Separating Mixtures

Mixtures can be separated easily. If you like, you can pick the carrots out of the soup and eat them first.

To separate other types of mixtures, you need to know the physical properties of the substances that make them up. Suppose you wanted to separate a mixture of salt, iron filings, and sand. The iron filings are magnetic, so you could use a magnet to remove them. You could then add water to the salt and sand. The salt will dissolve, enabling you to filter out the sand using filter paper. Finally, you can evaporate the water from the mixture of water and salt so that only solid salt particles remain.

This soup is a mixture. Its components are not chemically combined.

Classifying Elements

The properties of an element are determined by the number of protons and electrons in its atoms. Depending on its properties, each element is classified as a metal, a nonmetal, or a metalloid.

Metals are elements that are usually hard, conduct heat and electricity well, and can be drawn into wires and hammered into sheets. Nonmetals are elements that are usually brittle, conduct heat and electricity poorly, and cannot be formed into wires or sheets. Metalloids are elements that have some properties of both metals and nonmetals.

Silicon is an element that is used to make computer parts.

Neon is a nonmetal that is used in colorful signs.

The Periodic Table

Scientists have organized all of the known elements in the **periodic table.** The periodic table lists the elements in order according to their atomic number. An element's atomic number is the number of protons in the nucleus of its atom. The elements are listed from left to right in order from the lowest atomic number to the highest.

The metals are found on the left side of the table, and the nonmetals are found on the right side. Between the metals and nonmetals are the metalloids, which run in a zigzag line. Aluminum is an exception. Even though it is found along the zigzag line, aluminum is a metal.

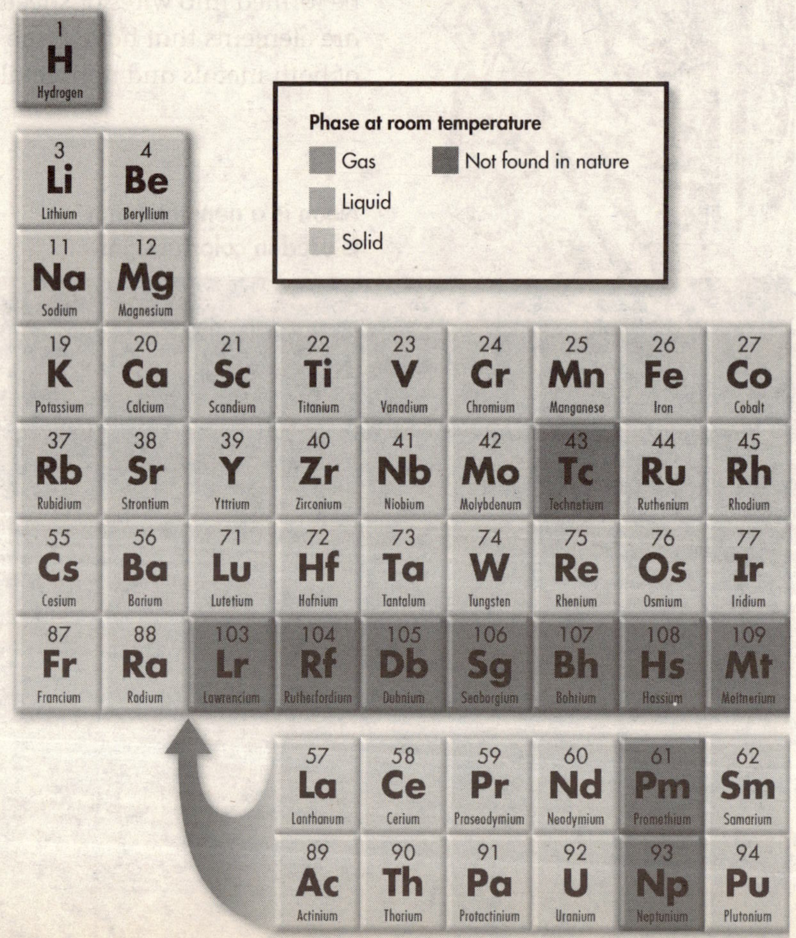

Every particle of a compound is made of the same ratio of elements. For example, in table salt there is one chlorine atom for every sodium atom.

The properties of a compound are different from the properties of the elements that make it up. For example, sodium is a silvery white metal, and chlorine is a poisonous gas. These two elements combine to form a substance you eat every day—table salt!

Chemical Formulas

Every compound has its own chemical formula. It includes a chemical symbol for every element in the compound. It also includes subscripts that tell how many atoms of each element are in the compound. If there is no subscript beside a chemical symbol, there is only one atom of that element in the compound. For example, the chemical formula for water is H_2O. This means water is made up of two hydrogen atoms and one oxygen atom.

Sodium chloride (table salt)

Sodium hydroxide and hydrogen

What are compounds and mixtures?

Atoms Together

Most atoms are found in nature as part of compounds rather than as elements. A **compound** is a substance made up of two or more elements that are chemically combined to form a new substance with different properties. Salt is a compound made of sodium and chlorine. Many substances in your body are compounds, including water, proteins, and DNA.

Compounds are formed when elements combine in exact ratios. The properties of compounds are different from those of the elements that make them up.

At the bottom of the periodic table are two rows of elements called the Lanthanide series and the Actinide series. The first element in the Lanthanide series, lanthanum, has an atomic number of 57. It should follow barium, which has an atomic number of 56. Actinium, the first element in the Actinide series, should follow radium. These rows were placed at the bottom of the table so that the table would not be too wide to fit on a page.

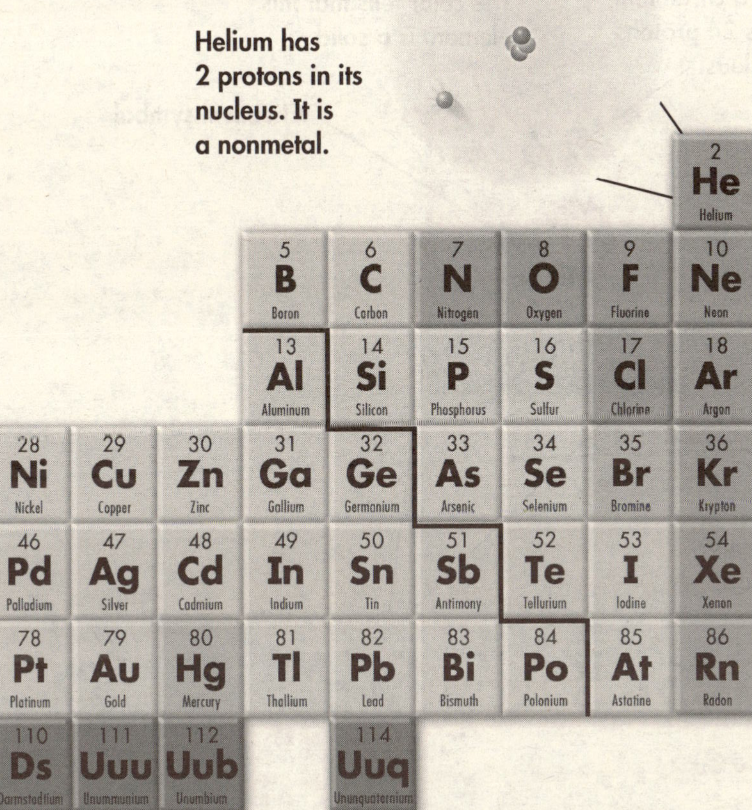

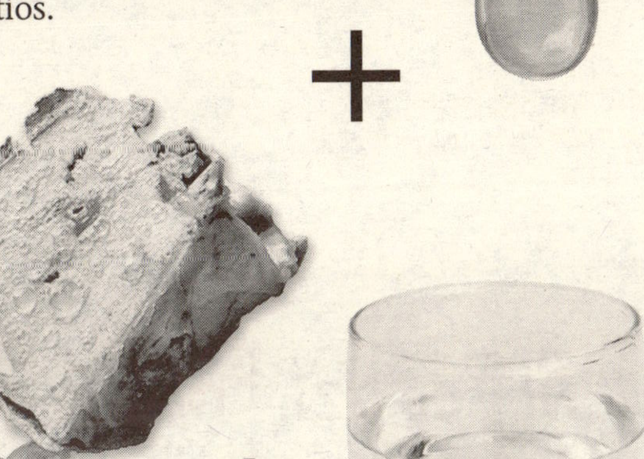

When sodium combines with chlorine, it forms sodium chloride (table salt). When sodium combines with water, it reacts violently to form hydrogen gas and sodium hydroxide.

Information on the Periodic Table

You can find a great deal of information about the elements in the periodic table. Each element has its own individual block, which contains information about that element.

Look at the block for the element chromium below. It shows the element's name, atomic number, and chemical symbol. It also tells that chromium is a metal and that it is a solid at room temperature.

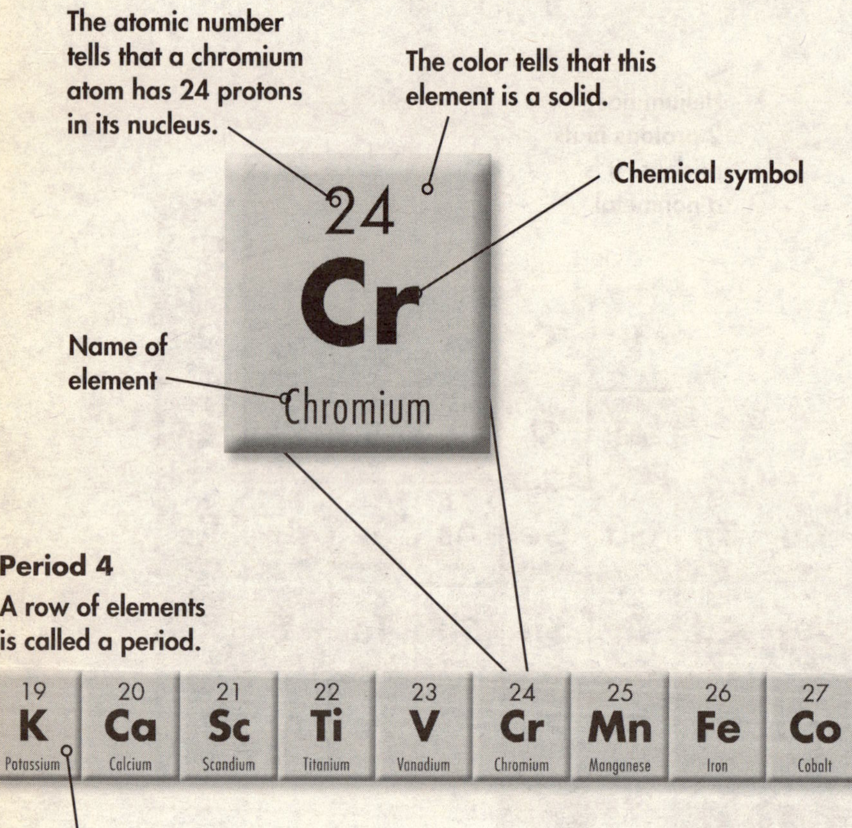

The word *periodic* means "a regular, repeated pattern." The elements in the periodic table are organized in a pattern. Their properties change in a predictable way from left to right and from top to bottom.

There are 18 columns in the periodic table. They are called groups or families. All the elements within a particular family react with other substances in similar ways. For example, all the elements in Group 1 (except for hydrogen) react strongly with water. The elements in Group 18 react very little with other elements. These are called inactive elements.

The seven rows in the periodic table are called periods. The elements in a period have very different properties from one another. The first element of each period reacts violently. The last element of each period is always inactive.

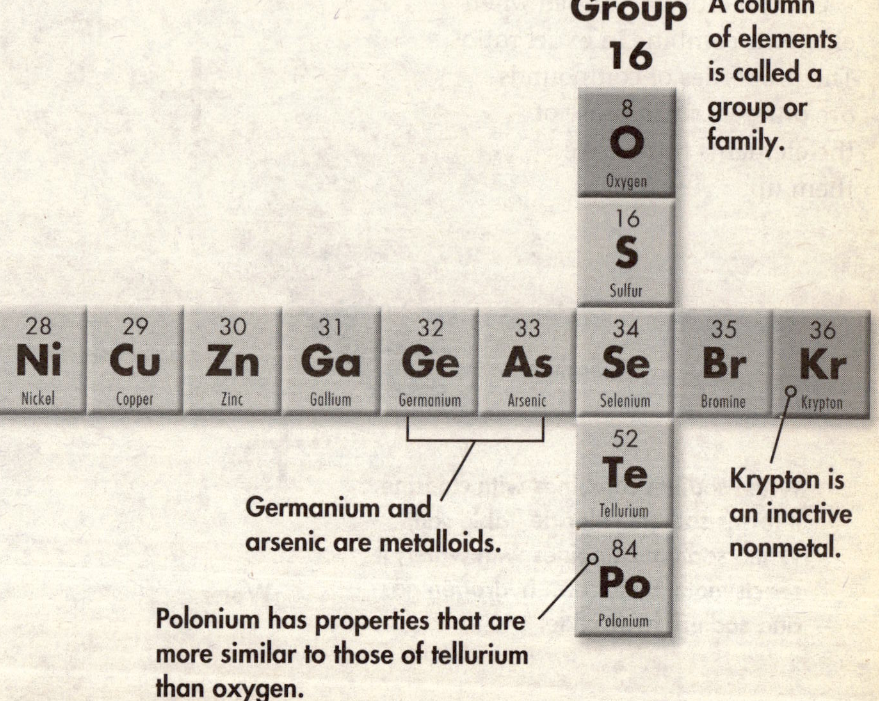

Forces and Motion

by Marcia K. Miller

Genre	Comprehension Skill	Text Features	Science Content
Nonfiction	Predict	• Captions • Charts • Diagrams • Glossary	Forces and Motion

Scott Foresman Science 6.15

ISBN 0-328-14012-0

9 780328 140121

90000

What did you learn?

1. How do balanced forces affect the motion of an object?

2. Explain how the Moon's gravitational pull can be observed on Earth.

3. How is instantaneous speed different from average speed?

4. **Writing** in Science It is necessary to have a frame of reference to describe motion. Use your own words to write a description of the motion of a bus from the frame of reference of a person riding on that bus. Include details from the book to support your answer.

5. **Predict** Suppose you are riding a bicycle. You stop to put a heavy object on the back of the bike. How will the increased mass affect the bike's acceleration if you pedal with the same force as you did before?

Illustrations: Title Page, 4, 5, 11, 13, 15, 16 Clint Hansen; 16 Peter Bollinger
Photographs: Every effort has been made to secure permission and provide appropriate credit for photographic material. The publisher deeply regrets any omission and pledges to correct errors called to its attention in subsequent editions. Unless otherwise acknowledged, all photographs are the property of Scott Foresman, a division of Pearson Education. Photo locators denoted as follows: Top (T), Center (C), Bottom (B), Left (L), Right (R), Background (Bkgd).
2 ©Fabio Muzzi/Age Fotostock; 4 (BC) ©Herman Eisenbeiss/Photo Researchers, Inc.; 7 ©Michael Newman/PhotoEdit; 8 (CC) ©Hackenberg/Zefa/Masterfile Corporation, (B) ©Dr. Jeremy Burgess/Photo Researchers, Inc.; 10 (CL) ©DK Images, (BL) Getty Images; 11 (CR) ©DK Images, (BR) Getty Images; 14 ©Lester Lefkowitz/Corbis; 18 ©Bettmann/Corbis; 19 ©David Woods/Corbis; 22 (TR) ©Nigel J. Dennis; Gallo Images/Corbis, (BL) ©W. Wisniewski/Zefa/Masterfile Corporation; 23 ©Patrick Bennett/Corbis

ISBN: 0-328-14012-0

Forces and Motion

by Marcia K. Miller

Glossary

acceleration	the rate at which velocity changes
force	a push or pull that has both size and direction
friction	the force that resists the movement of one surface past another
gravitational force	the force of attraction between any object and every other object in the universe
inertia	the tendency of an object to stay at rest or in motion unless a force acts on it
momentum	a measure of the force needed to stop a moving object
speed	a measure of how fast an object is moving
velocity	the speed of an object in a particular direction

What happens when forces act on objects?

Forces

How can a big elephant balance on a small ball? The elephant stays up because of forces acting on the animal and on the ball. A **force** is a push or pull. Forces have both size and direction.

Some forces act only if objects are touching each other. Suppose you use your hands to push a heavy box. Your hands and the box touch. The elephant in the picture touches the ball, pushing down on it.

Momentum

Momentum is a measure of the force needed to stop a moving object. It depends on mass and velocity. Momentum from one object can be transferred to another object when they collide. The total momentum *before* a collision equals the total momentum *after* the collision. This is known as the law of conservation of momentum.

The momentum of the basketball before it hits the bowling ball must equal the momentum of the basketball plus the momentum of the bowling ball after the collision. The basketball slows down because it gives part of its momentum to the bowling ball.

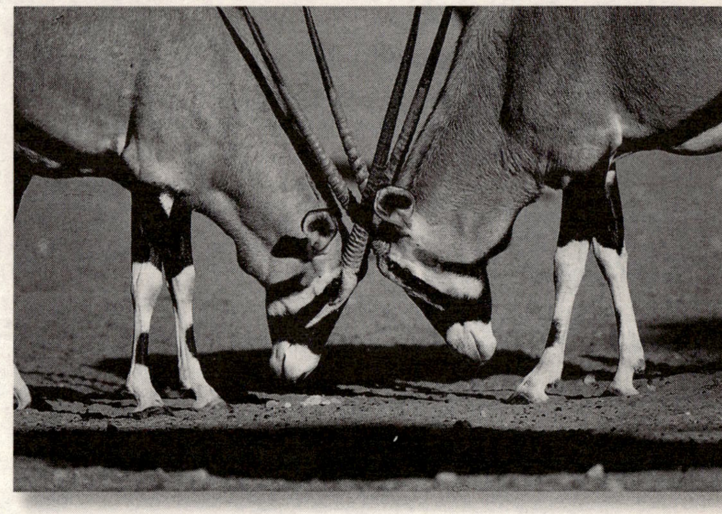

These oryx are applying equal but opposite force.

Third Law of Motion

When you throw a ball on the ground, it bounces upward. But the force of your throw was downward. Newton's third law of motion explains how this happens.

When a force is applied to an object, the object applies an equal force in the opposite direction. The ball you threw on the ground exerts a downward force on the ground. The ground exerts an equal but upward force on the ball.

Newton's third law of motion is sometimes called the law of action and reaction. For every action, there is an equal and opposite reaction. Before a leopard jumps, it bends its legs and pushes very hard against the rock. The rock exerts an equal force, pushing the leopard into the air. The leopard's push is the action force. The rock's equal but opposite push is the reaction force.

Newton's third law of motion explains what happens when two objects collide, or hit each other. Think of a basketball rolling along the floor. It hits a bowling ball that is sitting still. The bowling ball has greater mass than the basketball does. The basketball rolls back away from the bowling ball. The bowling ball only moves a short distance.

Other forces act between objects that aren't touching. When you jump up, Earth's gravity pulls you down. Objects with an electrical charge can attract or repel each other even when they are far apart. Hold two magnets close together. They push and pull on each other, even though they are not touching.

Scientists measure forces in units called newtons (N). One newton is the force needed to change the speed of a one-kilogram object by one meter per second each second. It takes about one newton to lift a small apple.

You can use a spring scale to measure force. You attach an object to one end of the scale and hold the other end. A spring inside the scale stretches. This shows the force needed to support the object.

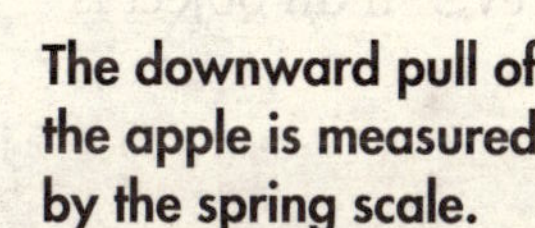

Why does this leopard move upward when it pushes downward on the rock?

The downward pull of the apple is measured by the spring scale.

Forces on Objects

A kite flies through the air. It dips and glides. Different forces act on the kite. The weight of the kite pulls it down. The force of the wind pushes it up. You can change the direction of the kite by applying force to the string.

Most objects have more than one force acting on them. Some forces act in the same direction. Other forces act in different directions. The effect of the forces on an object is found by adding together all the forces acting on the object.

The forces acting on an object are similar to a game of tug-of-war. One team pulls the rope one way. The other team pulls the rope the other way. If one team pulls with more force than the other team, the rope moves toward the stronger team. If both teams apply the same amount of force, the rope doesn't move.

Unbalanced forces on an object at rest can make it move. They can cause the speed or direction of a moving object to change. Balanced forces do not cause any change in motion. This is true even if an object is already moving.

The downward force of a water strider on the water is balanced by the upward force of the water.

The force of the wind against the sail causes a sailboat to move through water.

sing an Equation

This equation shows the second law of motion:

$$acceleration = force \div mass$$

Only unbalanced forces accelerate an object. Suppose you and a friend push on opposite sides of a box. You use the same force. The box won't move. But if one of you pushes with more force than the other, the box moves. It accelerates in the direction of the greater force.

Second Law of Motion

According to Newton's second law of motion, a force causes an object to accelerate. The acceleration of an object depends on the mass of the object and the strength of the net force applied.

An unbalanced force makes an object accelerate. Look at the dogs in the wagons. The large dog has greater mass than the small dog. Only a small force is needed to pull the wagon with the small dog. The wagon with the large dog will not accelerate as much if the same force is applied. When equal force is applied, an object with greater mass will accelerate less.

Suppose you push the wagon with the small dog. It rolls. If you push the same wagon harder, it rolls faster. An object's acceleration increases as the net force increases. The acceleration decreases as the net force decreases.

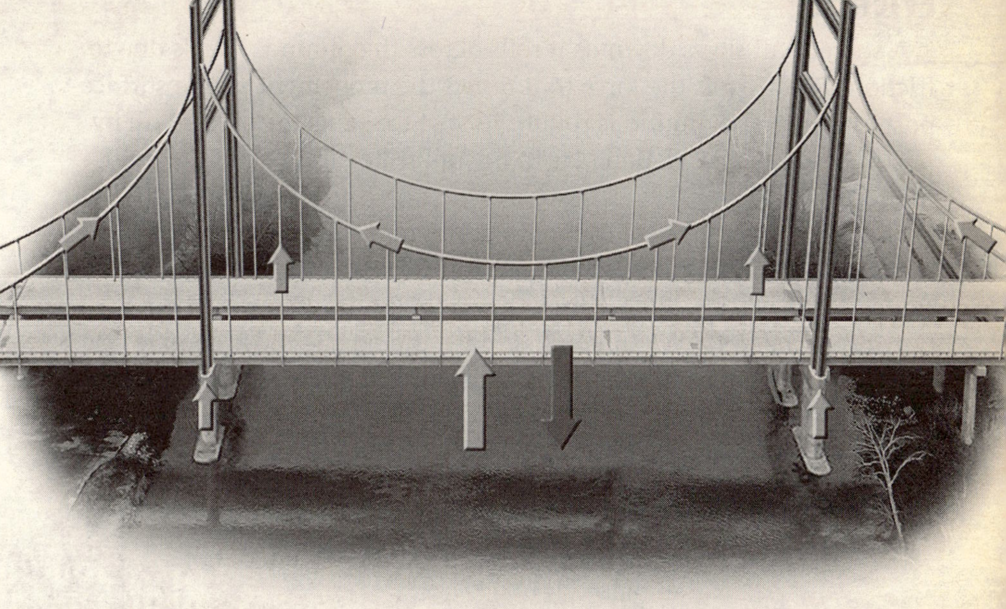

The arrows show the directions of forces that allow the strong wire cables to support the weight of the road and the automobiles that cross it.

You add the forces together to find the overall effect of forces acting on an object. The result is called the net force. Here's how it works. Suppose a 5 N force pulls an object to the right. A 3 N force pulls it to the left. The effect is the same as a 2 N force pulling to the right. The net force is 2 N to the right.

The net force on an object may not always determine the direction the object moves. But it determines the change in an object's motion. Suppose you are riding your bike on a flat sidewalk. You lightly apply the brakes. What happens? The bike continues along the sidewalk as the force of the brakes acts against the bike's forward motion. The bike keeps going, but more slowly. A stronger force could stop the bicycle.

Friction

A soccer ball slows down as it rolls across the ground. This is due to friction. **Friction** is the force that resists the movement of one surface past another. The ground is rough. Its surface stops the soccer ball by pushing against it. Friction acts in the opposite direction of the ball's motion.

There are three types of friction. Rolling and sliding friction act on objects in motion. Rolling friction slows the spinning of a skateboard's wheels. Sliding friction makes it hard to push a heavy box along the floor. When you first push the box, static friction resists its movement. The box is easier to push once it starts moving. Static friction is usually stronger than sliding friction.

Inertia

Newton's first law of motion is often called the law of inertia. **Inertia** is the tendency of an object to stay at rest or in motion unless a force acts on it. Inertia lets an ice skater glide a long way. Ice has little friction to slow the skater down. Inertia keeps a rock on the ground still.

Suppose you have two jars that are the same size. One is full of feathers. The other is full of coins. The jar with the coins is harder to move. Why? The jar of coins has more mass. The amount of inertia an object has depends on its mass. The greater an object's mass, the greater its inertia.

This crash-test dummy shows the effect of inertia. When the car stops suddenly, the forward motion of the dummy continues. The force that stopped the car does not stop the dummy. The force of the seat belt and air bag stops the dummy's forward motion.

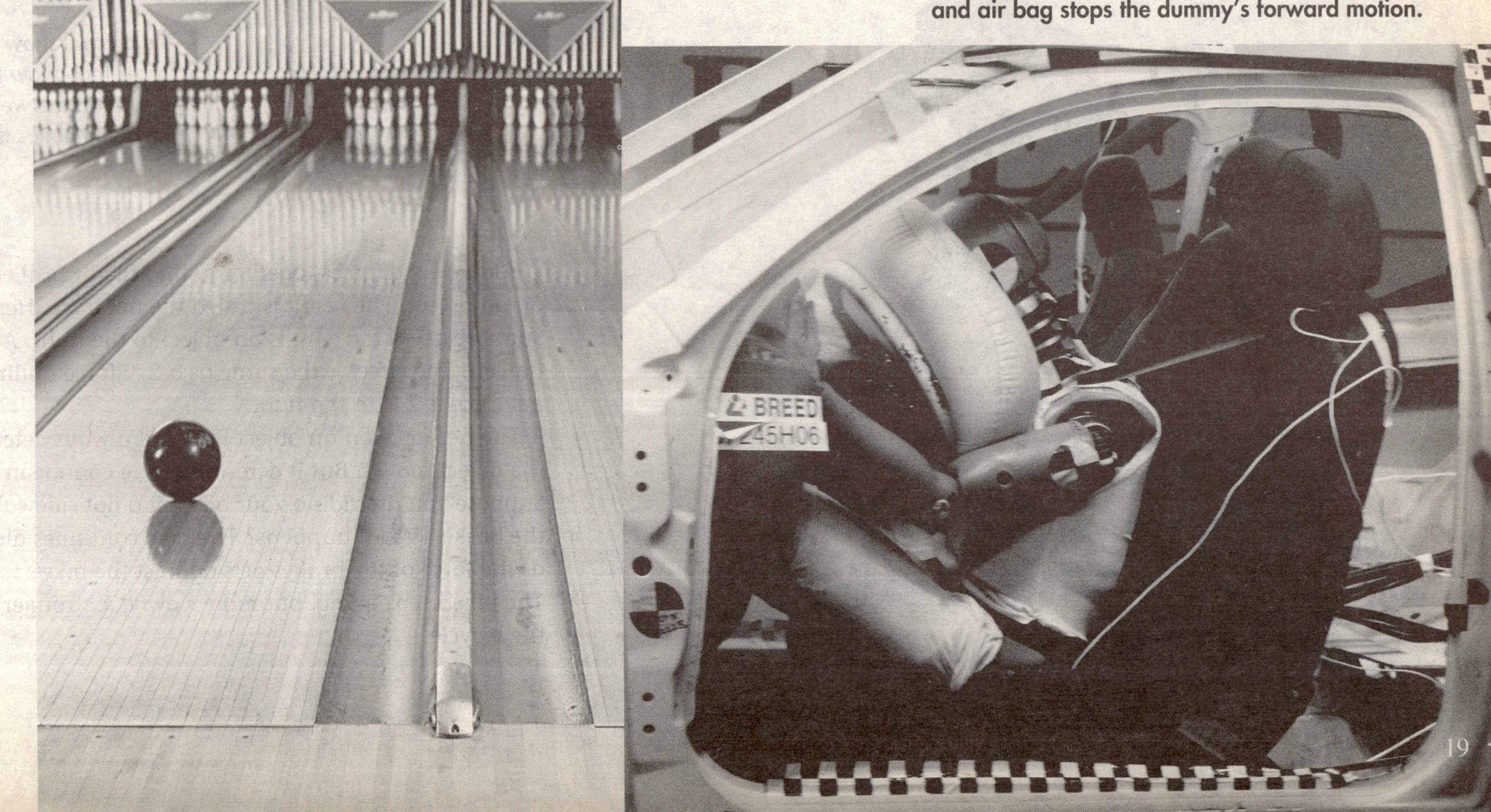

What are the laws of motion?

Studying Motion

People have wondered about motion for thousands of years. They have tried in many ways to explain it. In the 1600s Italian scientist Galileo Galilei studied falling objects. People then thought that objects slowed down and stopped on their own. They did not know about friction.

Isaac Newton published his book *Principia* in 1686. He linked forces to the motion of objects. Newton didn't discover all the laws of motion. But his book put together many important ideas in a way that people could understand.

First Law of Motion

Newton's first law states that an object at rest remains at rest. An object in motion remains in motion at constant speed and in a straight line unless acted upon by an unbalanced force.

You already know the first part of this law. Put a book on your desk. The book stays in place until you pick it up or another force acts on it.

The law also says that objects stay in motion. But motion in daily life doesn't seem to follow this law. If you kick a soccer ball, it moves for a while. But it will slow down and stop. You have to keep pedaling to keep your bicycle moving. Why?

One reason is friction. Friction can slow or stop objects in motion. The ground applies a frictional force on the bicycle wheels. Air friction slows motion as air pushes against the bicycle. Gravity and other forces may also slow an object's motion.

The bowling pins stay at rest until acted upon by the bowling ball.

Friction varies with the kinds of surfaces that are rubbing against each other. It also varies with how strongly they push together. Even smooth surfaces have tiny rough spots. Most surfaces have tiny bumps and holes on them. These rough spots catch on each other and cause the surfaces to move more slowly. Movement also slows when the particles from the two surfaces attract. The attraction causes the surfaces to stick together.

There is usually more friction with rougher surfaces. A soft or rubbery surface also has more friction because it bends. But even very smooth and flat surfaces have friction between them. Their particles attract, causing friction.

Type of Friction	Description
Rolling	Resists the motion of a rolling object
Sliding	Resists the motion of a sliding object
Static	Resists the motion of an object just as it begins to move

The floor of a bowling lane is very smooth. This reduces the rolling friction between the wood and the ball.

Helpful and Harmful Friction

Friction can be useful. Suppose you were walking across a room without friction. It would be like walking on ice! You need friction between your feet and the floor so you won't slip. Drivers use friction all the time. When a driver steps on the brakes, the brake pads press against the brake drum. This friction slows the car.

Friction can wear out engine parts and reduce efficiency.

Velocity

The distance the bus travels on the return trip is the same. So is the travel time. But the direction of motion is different. **Velocity** is the speed of an object in a particular direction. The velocity of the bus on the first trip was 54 km/h east. On the return trip, the velocity would be 54 km/h west.

The velocity of an object changes constantly as it moves along a curved path, even if its speed stays the same. Velocity changes because the direction of the object changes.

Acceleration

Moving objects often change their speed and direction. The rate at which velocity changes is called **acceleration.** Acceleration doesn't happen only when an object speeds up. It also happens when an object slows down or when it changes direction.

A force must act on an object for the velocity to change. So acceleration takes place when unbalanced forces act on the object.

Calculating Speed

Speed is a measure of how fast an object is moving. You can find speed by dividing the distance traveled by the time needed to go that distance. Suppose the bus in the picture takes 10 minutes to travel between points that are 9 kilometers apart. Use this equation to find its average speed:

$$\text{average speed} = \frac{\text{distance}}{\text{time}} = \frac{9 \text{ km}}{10 \text{ min}} \times \frac{60 \text{ min}}{1 \text{ h}} = 54 \frac{\text{km}}{\text{h}}$$

The speed of 54 kilometers per hour is the average for the whole trip. But the bus probably didn't travel at exactly that speed for the whole time. Speed at any moment is called instantaneous speed. This is the speed shown on the speedometer.

Sometimes friction is harmful. Think about what happens when objects rub together. Heat is produced. How do your hands feel when you rub them together quickly? They start to feel warm. Energy from your hands is converted into thermal energy because of the friction. Engines may not run well because of heat produced by friction. Friction between wind and soil can cause erosion. Friction from the road wears away the rubber on car tires.

The metal surface of a car's engine looks and feels smooth. But this photo taken with a microscope shows tiny bumps that cause friction.

How does gravity affect objects?

Gravitational Force

Life on Earth depends on gravity. Throw a ball into the air. You know it will fall back down. Earth's gravity pulls all objects on Earth toward its center. **Gravitational force** is the force of attraction between any object and every other object in the universe. This force keeps the water in the oceans. It keeps the air near Earth. It affects how plants grow. It affects how your bones develop.

Isaac Newton was an English scientist in the 1600s. He realized that gravity depends on the masses of the objects that apply forces on each other. An object with greater mass has stronger gravitational pull than an object with less mass. Hold this book in your hand. It pulls on you with a gravitational attraction. You pull on it too. You don't feel the pull of the book because both you and the book have low mass. But Earth has great mass. That is why you feel Earth's gravity. The Moon has less mass than Earth, so its gravitational force is weaker.

The Moon's gravity is about one-sixth the gravity on Earth. An object with a mass of 100 kg weighs 980 N on Earth, but only 160 N on the Moon.

Kinds of Motion

Circular motion is movement around a central point. A seat on a Ferris wheel has circular motion. The central point for the seat's motion is the axle of the ride. A looping roller coaster also has circular motion. So do planets in orbit and the wheels of a bicycle.

As the bicycle wheels turn, the bicycle itself moves in a straight line. You can see straight-line motion as you watch a parade move down the street.

Vibrational motion is harder to observe. A vibration is a rapid back-and-forth movement. The strings on a guitar vibrate to make sounds. Your vocal cords vibrate when you speak.

With the ground as your frame of reference, you would say that the seats of the Ferris wheel are moving.

When you ride a Ferris wheel, the seat is your frame of reference. The ground appears to move.

How can you describe motion?

Observing Motion

Riding a roller coaster can feel similar to flying. You rise up, swoop down, and turn over and under. What do you see as the roller coaster moves? When you move closer to the ground, objects seem to be moving toward you. When you move higher, the objects seem to be moving away from you. How is this possible?

The way to describe motion depends on a frame of reference. A frame of reference is any object that can be used to detect motion.

On a roller coaster, your seat may be a frame of reference. You are not moving compared to the seat. You and the seat move together. What if you use the ground as your frame of reference? It seems perfectly still. Your seat moves in reference to the ground.

When describing motion, Earth is usually a frame of reference. If you are sitting still, you aren't moving relative to Earth. But Earth is moving relative to the Sun, and so are you. Earth moves through space. It also rotates on its axis. Yet you aren't aware of these motions, because the objects around you are also motionless when Earth is the frame of reference.

14

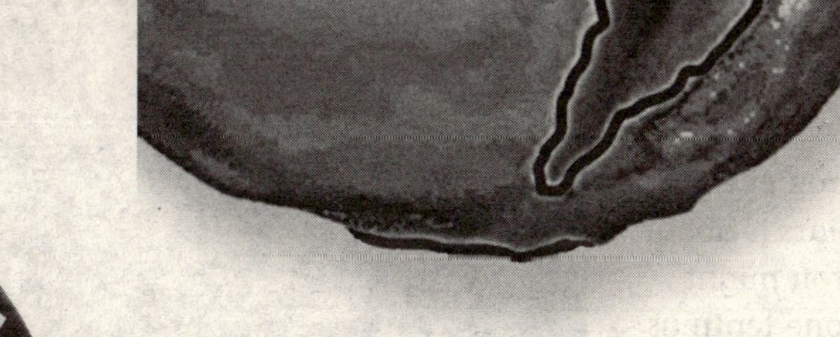

Newton also found that gravitational force changes with the distance between two objects. Objects farther apart have less pull on each other than objects that are close together. Earth's gravitational pull is slightly less when you are in an airplane than it is when you are on Earth's surface.

You can measure Earth's gravitational pull on your body. How? Just weigh yourself! Remember, an object's mass is the amount of matter it contains. Mass is the same wherever you are in the universe. But weight changes depending on where you are. You weigh more on Earth than you would on the Moon. Weight is another force that can be measured in newtons.

11

Gravity and the Universe

Newton's theories showed that gravity is what makes the planets and the stars move. The Moon revolves around Earth because of the gravitational pull between them. What keeps Earth and the planets in orbit around the Sun? It is the gravitational pull of the Sun. The Moon and planets would fly off into outer space without that pull.

Earth and the other planets have much less mass than our Sun. So the pull of the planets does not have much effect on the movement of the Sun. Some planets in other solar systems have masses much closer to the masses of their stars. In those cases, the gravity of a planet can make a star wobble. Astronomers use this wobble to find distant planets.

The force of gravity is different on every planet and moon. The mass of Mars is about one-tenth the mass of Earth. So you might think gravity on Mars would be one-tenth as strong as Earth's gravity. But because Mars is smaller than Earth, the gravity on Mars is about one-half the gravity on Earth. The gravitational pull of a planet depends on the distance from its surface to its center.

This is also why you can't feel the Sun's gravity here on Earth. The Sun is much larger than Earth, but it is also extremely far away. Because you are so far from the Sun, you feel only Earth's gravity.

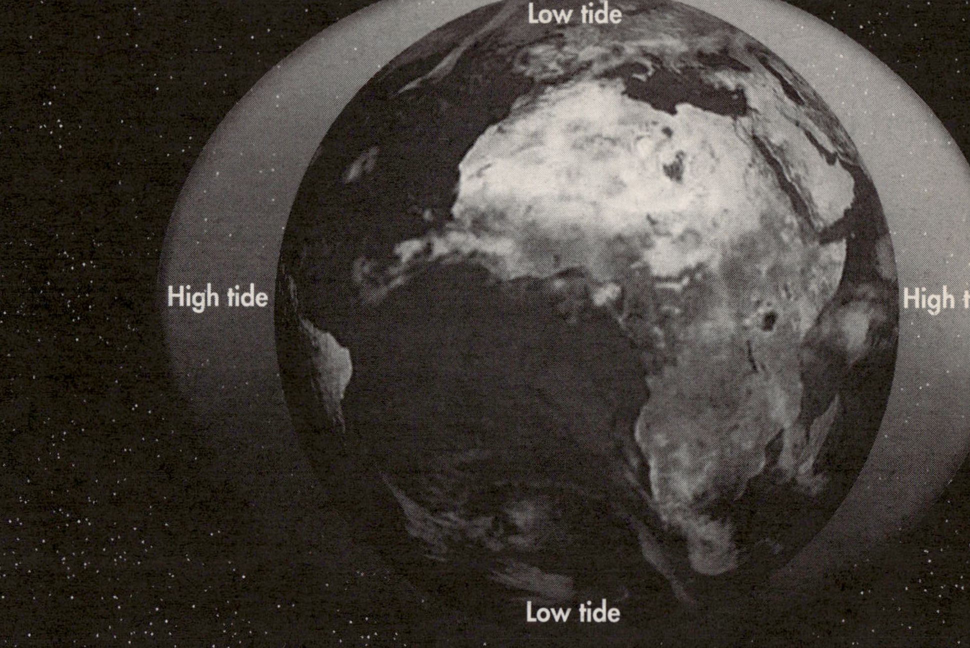

Tides

Water levels rise and fall near the ocean's shores. These events are called tides. Each day, coastal areas around the world have two high tides and two low tides.

The Moon's gravitational attraction pulls on everything on Earth, including water. When this happens, we experience high tide on that side of Earth. At the same time, the side of Earth opposite the Moon also experiences high tide. While the sides toward the Moon and opposite the Moon are experiencing high tide, the two sides in between are experiencing low tide. The Sun also pulls on Earth's water, but because the Sun is farther away, the effect is smaller.

Machines

by Lillian Duggan

Genre	Comprehension Skill	Text Features	Science Content
Nonfiction	Cause and Effect	• Captions • Charts • Diagrams • Glossary	Simple Machines

Scott Foresman Science 6.16

PEARSON
Scott Foresman

scottforesman.com

Vocabulary

compound machine

effort force

fulcrum

load

machine

simple machine

work

What did you learn?

1. A machine used 2 newtons of force to push a box 100 meters. Calculate how much work the machine did.

2. How do simple machines allow people to do work using an effort force that is less than the load?

3. Suppose you have to move a heavy box up a flight of stairs. How would a ramp make your job easier?

4. **Writing** in Science   Some of the effort that goes into a machine gets wasted. Write to explain what happens to this effort and how the loss can be reduced. Include details from the book to support your answer.

5. **Cause and Effect** Cars are too heavy for people to lift. What is the effect of using a car jack to lift a car?

Illustrations: 11–13 Peter Bollinger
Photographs: Every effort has been made to secure permission and provide appropriate credit for photographic material. The publisher deeply regrets any omission and pledges to correct errors called to its attention in subsequent editions. Unless otherwise acknowledged, all photographs are the property of Scott Foresman, a division of Pearson Education. Photo locators denoted as follows: Top (T), Center (C), Bottom (B), Left (L), Right (R), Background (Bkgd).
2 ©Mark Moffett/Minden Pictures; 3 Corbis, ©DK Images; 4 ©D. Rose/Zefa/Masterfile Corporation; 7 (TL, BR) ©DK Images, (BL) ©Royalty-Free/Corbis; 8 ©Conrad Zobel/Corbis; 9 ©Jeremy Horner/Corbis, ©DK Images; 10 ©Gail Mooney/Masterfile Corporation

ISBN: 0-328-14015-5

Glossary

compound machine	a machine that contains one or more simple machines
effort force	the force applied to a lever to lift a load
fulcrum	the supporting part of a lever
load	an object's weight that applies a force on a lever
machine	any device that helps people do work
simple machine	a machine made up of one or two parts
work	using force to move an object a certain distance

Machines

by Lillian Duggan

How do machines help people work?

Measuring Work

When you think about work, you might think of washing the dishes or doing your homework. But scientists think of work differently. **Work** means using force to move an object a certain distance. The force comes from pushing or pulling. If an object does not move when you push it, you haven't done any work.

Use this equation to find how much work is done:

work = force × distance

Work is measured in a unit called the joule. Joule is abbreviated as J.

1 joule (J) = 1 newton (N) × 1 meter (m)

Let's say you push a box using a force of 200 newtons. The box moves 1 meter. You can find the work done by multiplying the force by the distance: 200 N × 1 m = 200 J.

These leafcutter ants are doing work. They're moving leaves across a distance.

A Winch
The winch crank is a wheel and axle. It cranks the rope in or out to raise or lower the sail. The rope end is used to lift weights.

Mast

E Wheel
The steering wheel is a wheel and axle that changes the direction of the rudder.

F Block and Tackle
This pulley system is used to move the large main sail.

Mainsail

C Propeller
The propeller is a type of screw. When it spins, it pushes the boat through the water.

B Keel
The keel is a wedge that helps keep the boat stable and moving straight.

15

Compound Machines

Most of the machines that people use every day are compound machines. You probably know that the cars, buses, and airplanes that we use for transportation are compound machines.

Many compound machines have hundreds or thousands of parts. These parts form the simple machines that combine to make a compound machine. The sailboat on this page is a compound machine. It has many parts and combines many simple machines.

Work and Machines

In science, a **machine** is any device that helps people do work. A machine does not have to be large and complicated. Many machines are very simple and have few parts. A **simple machine** is a tool made up of one or two parts.

Have you ever used chopsticks to pick up food? You hold them in the middle and squeeze the ends together. Then you move the food to your mouth. A pair of chopsticks is a simple machine. They help you do work by using force to move food to your mouth.

Bigger machines that have many parts are called compound machines. A **compound machine** is made up of one or more simple machines. Cars, trucks, and airplanes are compound machines that have many parts.

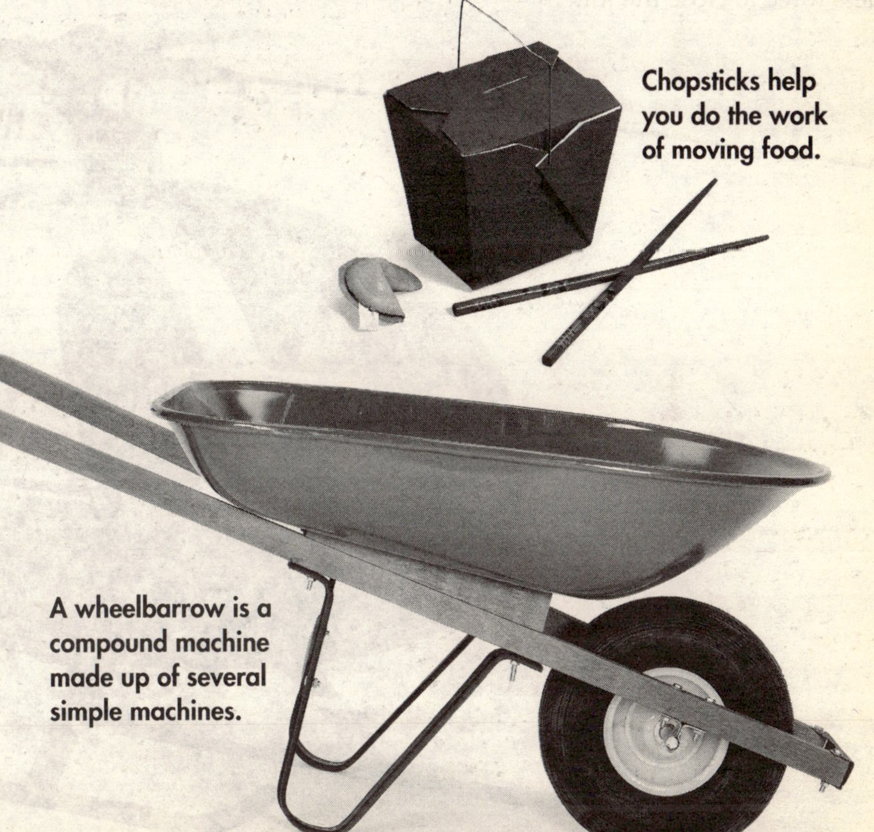

Chopsticks help you do the work of moving food.

A wheelbarrow is a compound machine made up of several simple machines.

How Machines Help

Machines do not change the amount of work that is done. Remember, work is equal to force multiplied by distance. Machines make work easier by changing the distance over which the force is applied. Spreading the force required over a longer distance decreases the amount of force you need to apply at one time.

A car jack is a machine that helps you lift a car. Cars are too heavy for people to lift. A jack decreases the force that's needed to lift such a heavy object by applying force over a longer distance.

A screw-top lid works the same way. Without the screw top, you would have to slam down the lid hard to cover a jar. With a screw top you must move the lid a longer distance, but you use less force to close the jar.

A moveable pulley is a pulley that is attached to the load. When you apply a force to the load, the pulley moves along with it. The pulley decreases the effort force, so that you don't have to pull as hard. However, you have to apply the force over a greater distance. This is because you must make both sides of the rope move in order to move the load.

A system called a block and tackle combines several pulleys. All the pulleys in the system are attached to the same rope. The more pulleys in the system, the less effort is required to lift the load. A block and tackle with a lot of pulleys can lift a very heavy object, such as a piano.

A moveable pulley moves with the load.

Several pulleys are combined in a block and tackle.

Pulley

A pulley is a wheel with a groove along its edge. A rope or chain runs through the groove. A load is attached to one end of the rope. The load is lifted when an effort force is applied to the other end of the rope.

The two types of pulleys are fixed pulleys and moveable pulleys. A fixed pulley stays in one place. When you pull the rope down on one end, the load is lifted on the other end. The fixed pulley does not change the amount of force you have to use to lift the load, but it makes lifting easier by changing the direction of the force.

In a fixed pulley, the load is lifted when an effort force pulls down on the other end.

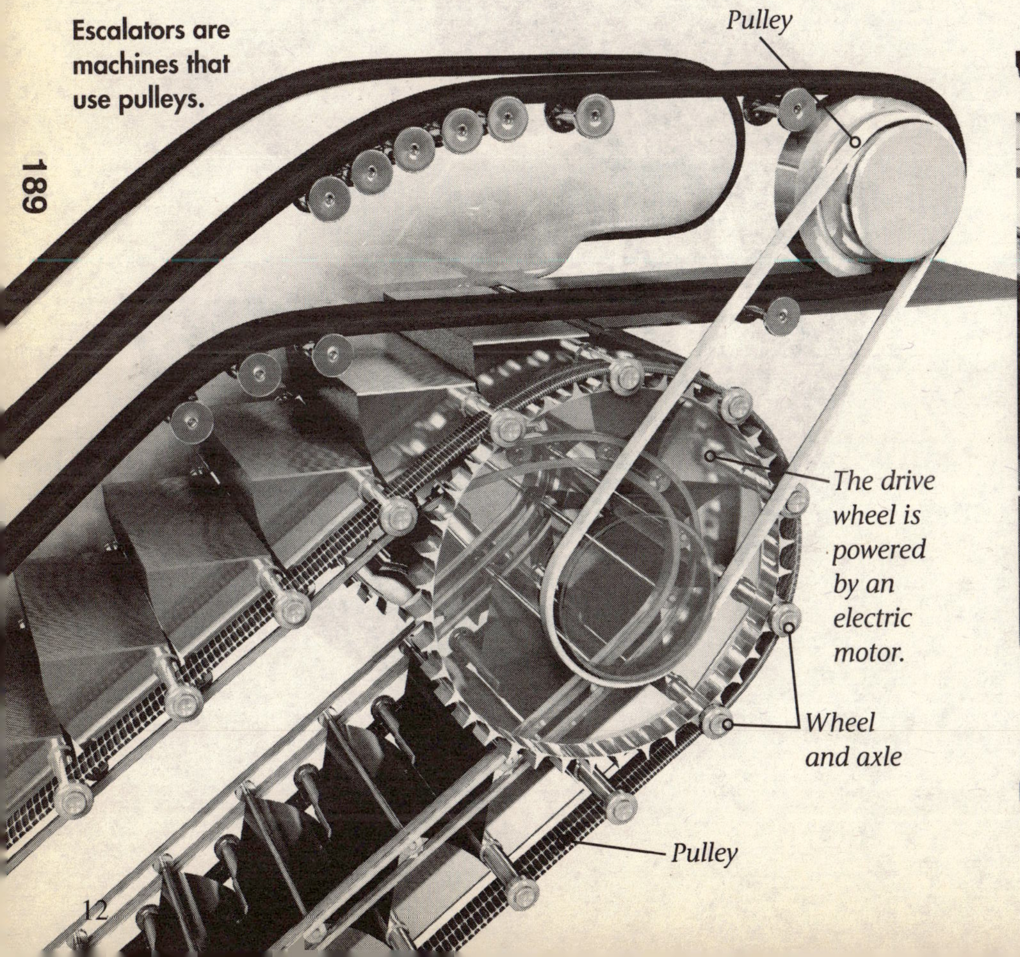

Escalators are machines that use pulleys.

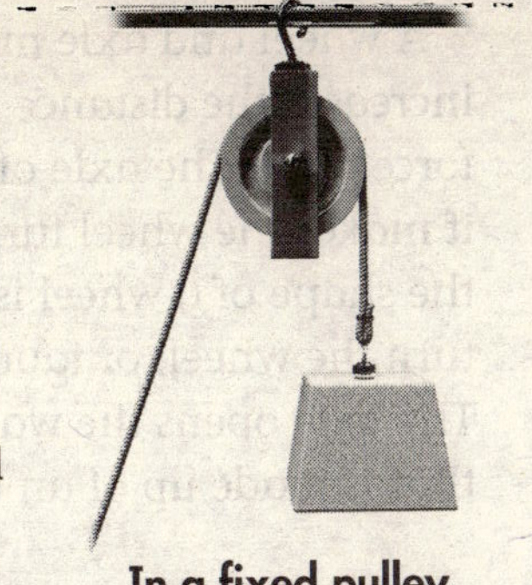

12

Machines and Friction

When you use a machine to do a job, you put work into it. You supply a force as a push or pull. Sometimes the work can come from another energy source, such as a battery.

The amount of work a machine does is always less than the amount of work put into it. Some of the work is lost to friction. Friction between the moving parts of a machine gives off heat. The more moving parts a machine has, the more work is lost to friction.

Lubricants such as oil, wax, and grease can help reduce friction, as can wheels, rollers, and balls. The wheels on inline skates have ball bearings inside that reduce friction.

This helicopter has many moving parts, which produce heat.

What are types of simple machines?

Types of Simple Machines

There are six types of simple machines: the lever, inclined plane, wedge, screw, wheel and axle, and pulley.

Lever

A lever is a simple machine made of one or more bars resting on a support. The support is called the **fulcrum.** One example of a lever is a crowbar. In the crowbar on this page, the fulcrum is at the bottom. The cinder block that the crowbar is lifting is the **load.** The load applies a force on the crowbar. To lift the load, you must apply a force to the opposite end of the crowbar. This force is called the **effort force.** Using a crowbar, you could lift a heavy cinder block with much less effort than you would need to lift it without one. But you have to apply the force over a greater distance.

If the fulcrum is closer to the load, less force is needed to move the load, but the load will not be lifted as high. If the fulcrum is closer to the effort force, more force is needed to move the load, but the load will be lifted higher. There is always a trade-off between force and distance.

Key

E   Effort force

F   Fulcrum

L   Load

A wheel and axle makes work easier in one of two ways. It either increases the distance through which a force acts, or increases the force itself. The axle of a Ferris wheel turns only a small distance, but it makes the wheel turn a much greater distance. A water faucet in the shape of a wheel is another type of wheel and axle. When you turn the wheel, or faucet, the force you use is increased in the axle. The axle opens the water valve. Think about trying to turn a faucet that is made up of an axle without a wheel.

Wheel and Axle

If you've ever ridden on a Ferris wheel, then you've seen a wheel and axle at work. A wheel and axle is a simple machine made of a wheel with a rod running through the middle. The diameter of the rod is much smaller than the diameter of the wheel. When the wheel turns, it moves a much greater distance than the axle. However, the axle's smaller turns are much more powerful.

The small rod in the center of the Ferris wheel makes the large wheel turn.

Types of Levers

The location of the fulcrum, load, and effort force is different in different types of levers.

First-Class Lever In a pair of pliers, the fulcrum is between the effort force and the load. You apply the effort force when you squeeze the handles.

Second-Class Lever In a nutcracker, the effort force is at one end, the fulcrum is at the other end, and the load is in the middle. You apply the effort force when you squeeze the handles.

Third-Class Lever In a crab's claw, the fulcrum is at one end, the load is at the other end, and the effort force is in the middle. The fulcrum is a joint that connects the claw with the crab's arm. The crab applies the effort force using muscles in the middle of its claw.

Inclined Plane

Another type of simple machine is the inclined plane. An inclined plane is a slanted surface. A ramp is an inclined plane that people often use to make lifting easier.

Suppose you have to move a heavy box up a flight of stairs. As the diagram shows, moving the box up a ramp requires less force than moving it up the stairs. However, the load must travel a greater distance up the ramp. The amount of work is the same in both cases.

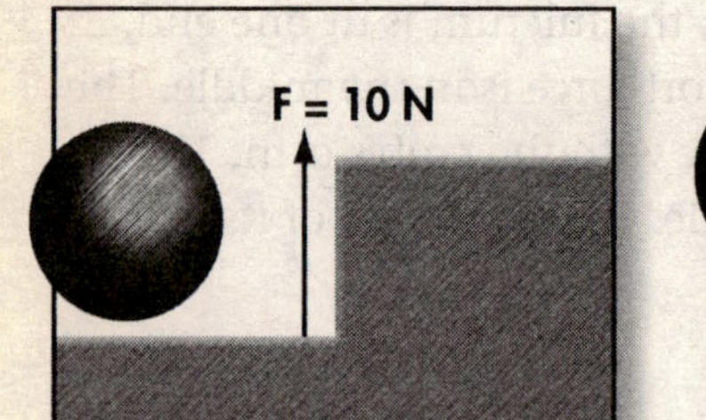

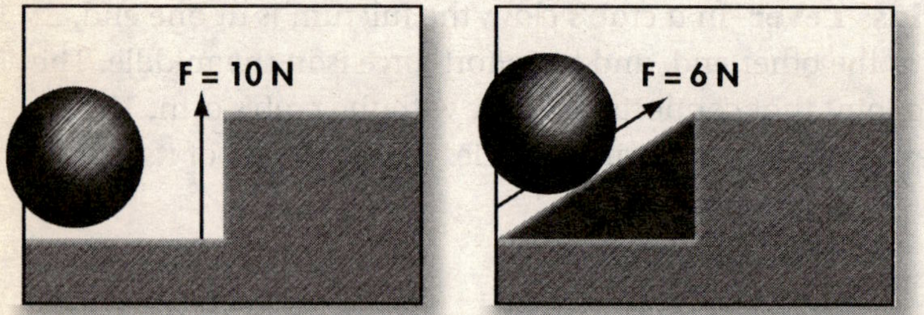

This winding road is an inclined plane. Cars must travel a greater distance, but it is easier than driving straight up.

The Wedge

A wedge is a simple machine made of one or two inclined planes. In a wedge, the edges of the inclined planes come to a point. A wedge cannot do work unless it is moving. A force applied to the flat end of the wedge moves it forward. The inclined planes change the direction of that force. Wedges are useful for cutting objects or digging into the ground.

The Screw

A screw is an inclined plane wrapped in a spiral. The ridges on a screw are called threads. If unwound, the threads of a screw would form an inclined plane. Screws are often used to fasten things together. Like other inclined planes, a screw decreases the force needed to do work, but it increases the distance.

The pointed front of a ship, called the prow, is a wedge. It helps the ship move through the water more easily.

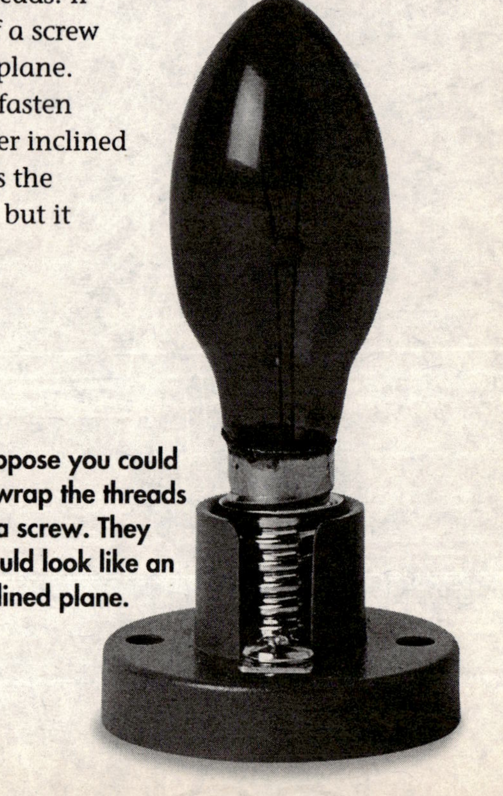
Suppose you could unwrap the threads of a screw. They would look like an inclined plane.

Changing Energy Forms

by Lillian Duggan

Genre	Comprehension Skill	Text Features	Science Content
Nonfiction	Sequence	• Captions • Charts • Diagrams • Glossary	Forms of Energy

Scott Foresman Science 6.17

PEARSON
Scott Foresman

ISBN 0-328-14018-X

scottforesman.com

What did you learn?

1. What causes an electric charge to move along atoms?

2. What is the difference between a series circuit and a parallel circuit?

3. How can you make an electromagnet stronger?

4. **Writing** in Science The law of conservation of energy states that whenever energy changes from one form to another, the total amount of energy does not change. Explain how this law is related to a bouncing ball. Include details from the book to support your answer.

5. Sequence Describe in order the energy changes that are involved in drinking a glass of orange juice, starting with the Sun.

Illustrations: 12–15 Tony Randazzo
Photographs: Every effort has been made to secure permission and provide appropriate credit for photographic material. The publisher deeply regrets any omission and pledges to correct errors called to its attention in subsequent editions. Unless otherwise acknowledged, all photographs are the property of Scott Foresman, a division of Pearson Education. Photo locators denoted as follows: Top (T), Center (C), Bottom (B), Left (L), Right (R), Background (Bkgd).
2 ©Norbert Wu/Minden Pictures; 3 (TR) ©Rosenfeld Images Ltd./Photo Researchers, Inc., (B) ©Bruce H. Frisch/Photo Researchers, Inc.; 5 ©Simon Fraser/Photo Researchers, Inc.; 6 (BC) ©Dr. Paul A. Zahl/Photo Researchers, Inc.; 10 (TR, BL) ©Doug Martin/Photo Researchers, Inc.

ISBN: 0-328-14018-X

Glossary

electric circuit	a closed path along which current can flow
electric current	a flow of electric charge in a material
electric motor	a device that changes electrical energy to kinetic energy
energy	the ability to cause change or to do work
generator	a device that changes mechanical energy into electrical energy
kinetic energy	the energy of a moving object
magnetic domain	a large number of atoms with their magnetic fields pointing in the same direction
potential energy	mechanical energy due to an object's position

Changing Energy Forms

by Lillian Duggan

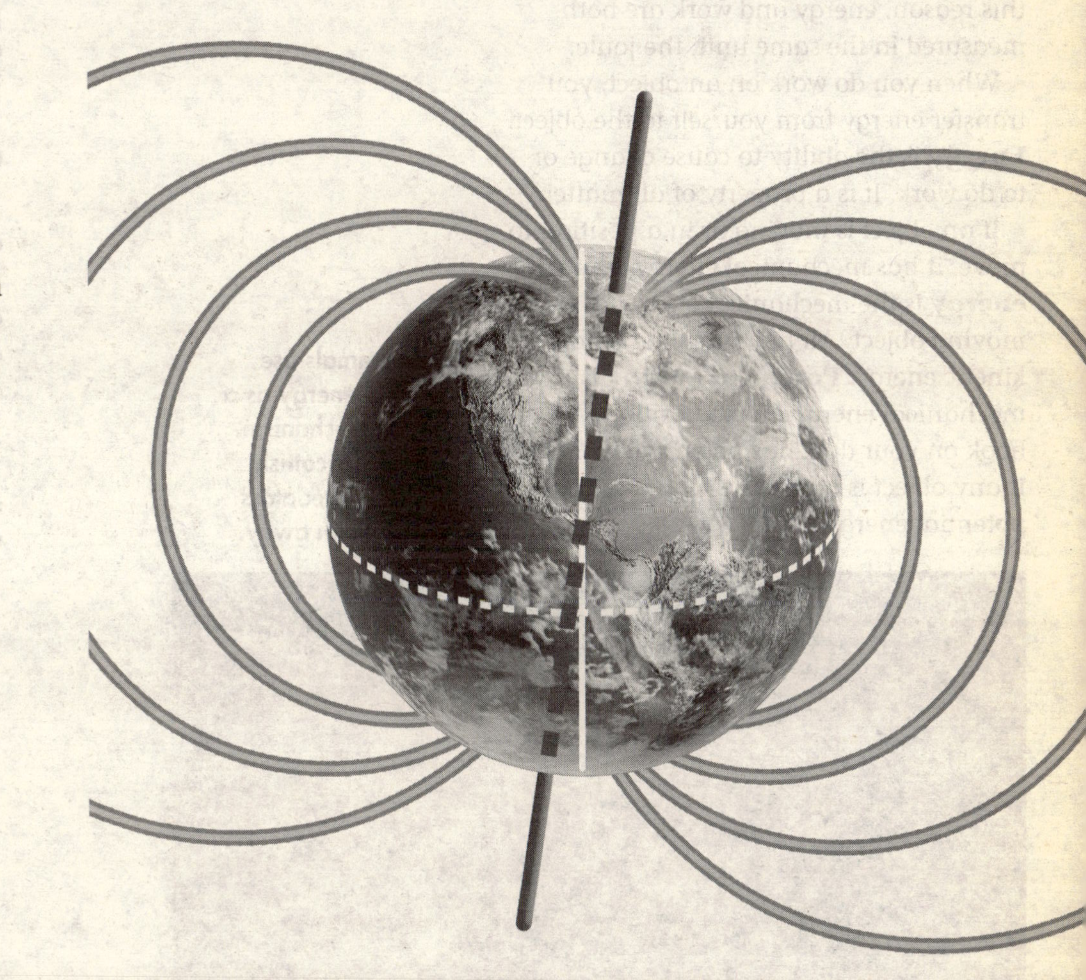

How can energy change?

Forms of Energy

Every change, from cutting an apple to flipping a switch, involves energy. This is because energy is needed to do work. For this reason, energy and work are both measured in the same unit, the joule.

When you do work on an object, you transfer energy from yourself to the object. **Energy** is the ability to cause change or to do work. It is a property of all matter.

If an object is moving or in a position to move, it has mechanical energy. **Kinetic energy** is the mechanical energy of a moving object. All moving objects have kinetic energy. **Potential energy** is mechanical energy due to position. A book on your desk has potential energy. If any object is above the ground, it has potential energy.

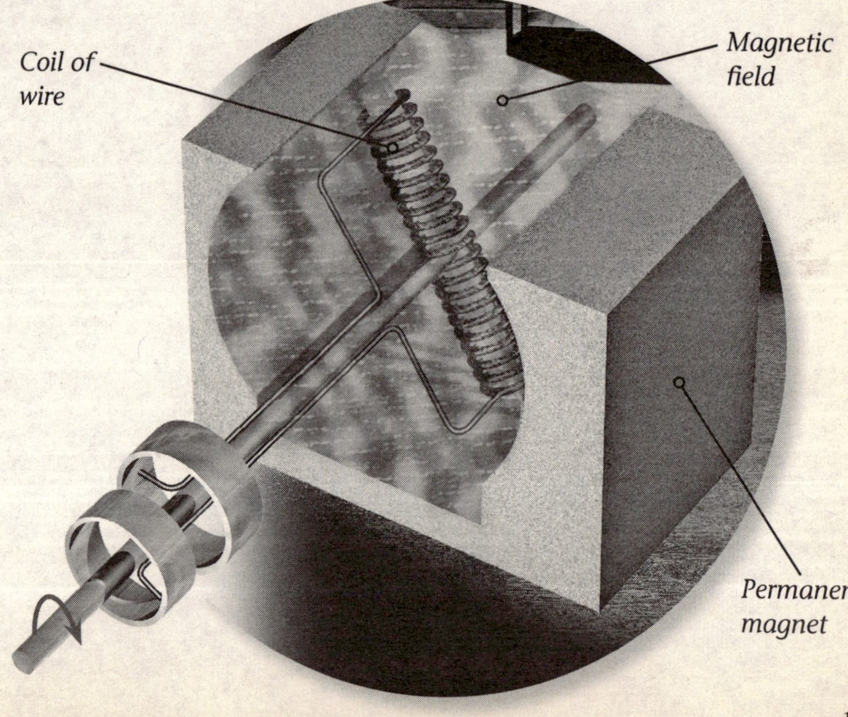

Some animals use electrical energy as a defense mechanism. This electric catfish shocks its predators to keep them away.

Changing Magnetism into Electricity

Oersted proved that moving electric charges could produce a magnetic field. In 1831, an English scientist named Michael Faraday proved that a magnetic field could produce an electric current. This process is called electromagnetic induction. You can make a changing magnetic field by moving a bar magnet through a wire coil. This causes a current to flow in the wire. The current that is produced gets stronger when you move the magnet faster. Most of the electrical energy we use in our homes, schools, and other buildings is produced by electromagnetic induction.

Generators

A **generator** is a device that changes mechanical energy into electrical energy. A generator has two main parts: a permanent magnet and a wire coil. A source of mechanical energy causes the coil to spin within the field of the magnet. The spinning produces an electric current that changes direction again and again. This type of current is called an alternating current.

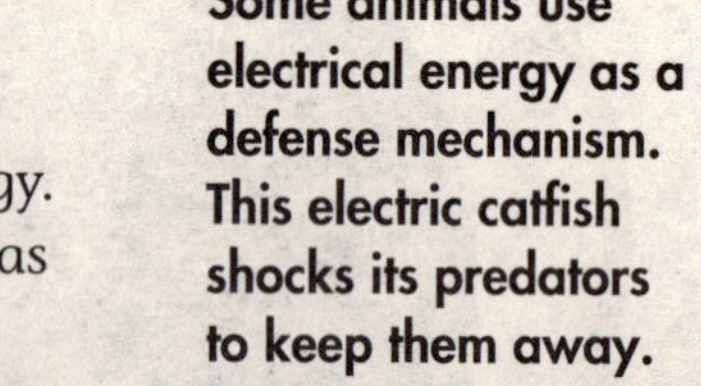

Electric Motor

An **electric motor** is a device that changes electrical energy to kinetic energy. It has three parts: a permanent magnet, an electromagnet, and a device that changes the direction of the electric current flowing through the electromagnet.

When current passes through the electromagnet, each pole is attracted to the opposite pole of the permanent magnet. This causes the electromagnet to turn. As the opposite poles line up, the current reverses direction. This causes the electromagnet's poles to switch, so that two like poles are now near each other. These poles push each other away, causing the electromagnet to keep turning. The current on the electromagnet constantly changes direction, which keeps the electromagnet spinning.

Electric Motor

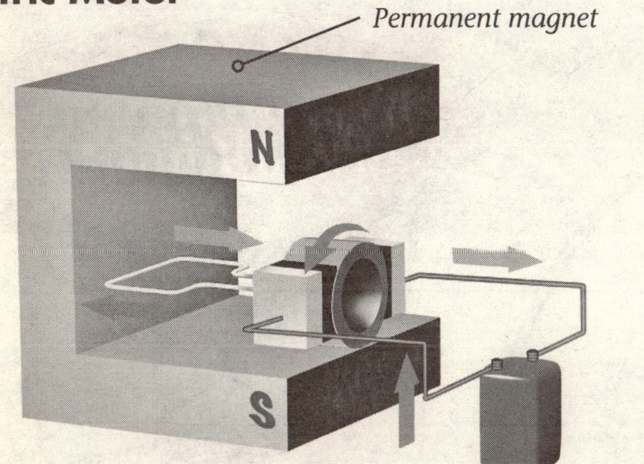

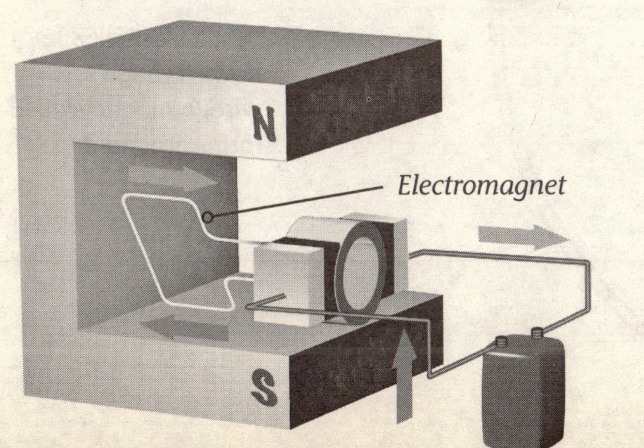

There are many forms of energy. Chemical energy is stored in the bonds that hold atoms together. Food has chemical energy that is transferred to your body when you eat it. Gasoline has chemical energy that cars use. Nuclear energy is stored inside the nucleus of an atom. At nuclear power plants, reactions take place that cause atoms to break apart, releasing this energy.

Thermal energy is energy in the form of heat. Thermal energy moves from one object to another. Electrical energy powers televisions and lights. It comes from the movement of electrons.

The light beam from this high-powered laser changes to thermal energy. It cuts through metal by melting it.

Energy Changes

Energy changes happen around you and inside you all the time. Drinking a glass of orange juice involves many energy changes, starting with the Sun. The Sun's nuclear energy changes to radiant energy, which travels to Earth. On Earth the leaves of an orange tree take in this energy. They change it into chemical energy. The chemical energy is stored in the plant's cells.

When you drink a glass of orange juice, you take in this stored chemical energy. Some chemical energy is changed to thermal energy to keep you warm. Some chemical energy is changed to kinetic energy when you move.

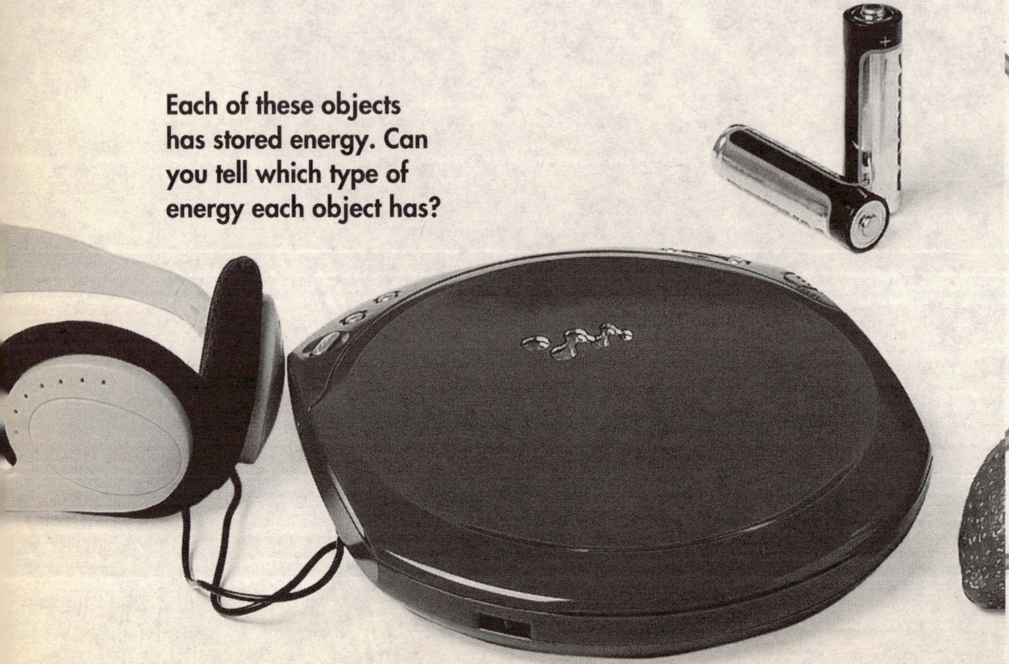

Each of these objects has stored energy. Can you tell which type of energy each object has?

Electromagnets

In 1820, Hans Christian Oersted, a physicist and a teacher, found that electric currents produce magnetic fields. The relationship between electric currents and magnetism is called electromagnetism.

When a wire is carrying a current, a magnetic field circles the wire. Shaping the wire into a coil makes the magnetic field similar to the field around a bar magnet. If you add more coils to the wire or put iron into the coil, you make the magnetic field stronger. Iron in the coil is magnetized as current flows through the wire. This adds to the magnetic field.

Electromagnets are useful because they can be turned on and off. When an electromagnet on a crane is turned on, it attracts magnetic objects. When it's turned off, it releases the objects.

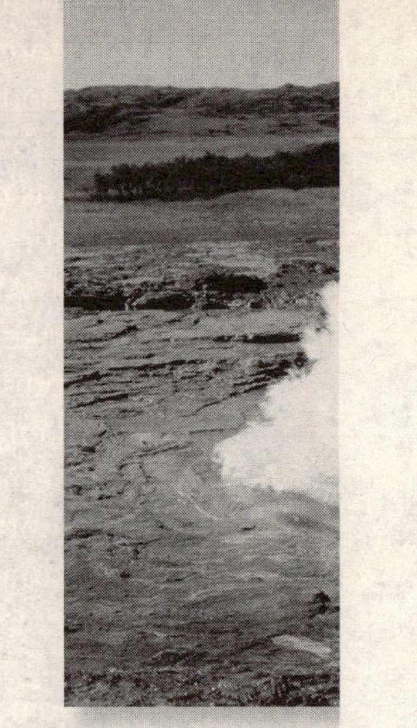

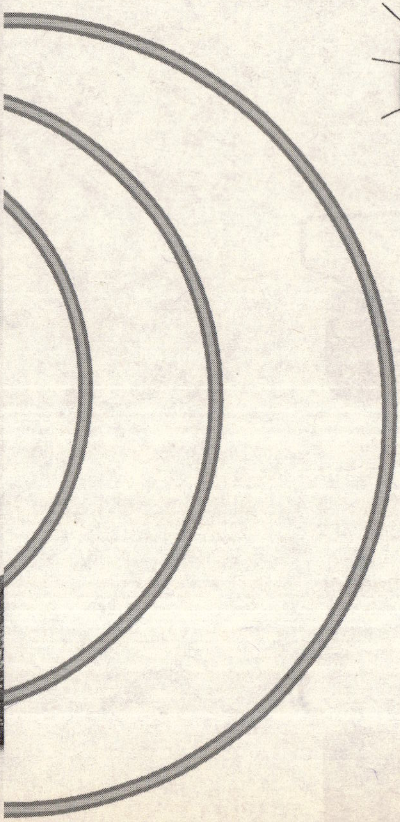

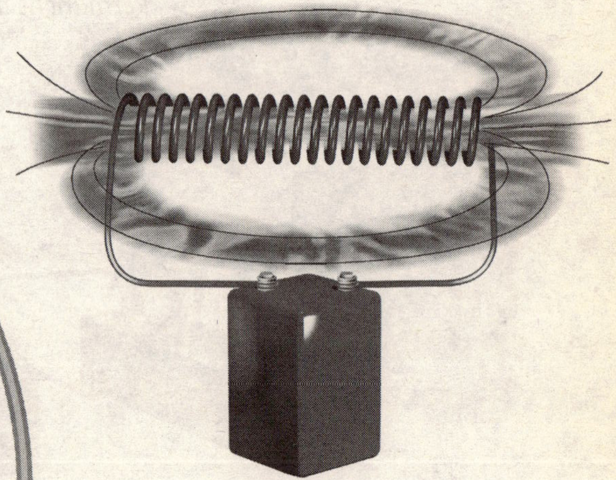

When electricity flows through this wire, a magnetic field forms around it.

Earth as a Magnet

Earth is similar to a giant bar magnet. It is surrounded by a magnetic field. The poles of this imaginary magnet are close to Earth's geographic poles—the North Pole and the South Pole. The lines of magnetic force start inside Earth, push out from one pole, and circle around to the other pole. Scientists think Earth's magnetic field is caused by its spinning and the movement of hot liquid metal deep inside Earth.

A compass needle lines up with Earth's magnetic field. It points to Earth's magnetic north.

Earth acts like a giant magnet.

Every energy form can be used to do work. When wind or moving water knock down trees or move rocks, they use kinetic energy as a force to do work. Hot underground springs have geothermal energy. They can release a lot of stored energy through geysers.

All forms of energy can be changed into thermal energy. When you rub your hands together, they get warm. The mechanical energy you use to rub your hands together changes to thermal energy. This energy change is caused by friction.

Thermal energy is also released when an object burns. When wood burns, some of the chemical energy stored in the wood changes to thermal energy.

Geothermal energy is released by geysers.

Conservation of Mass and Energy

When energy changes from one form to another, the amount of total energy does not change. Only the form of the energy changes. Think about what happens when you let a rubber ball drop onto a hard floor. The ball bounces lower and lower until it stops. With each bounce, some kinetic energy is changed into heat and sound energy. The kinetic energy lost by the ball is transferred to the air and the floor.

These light wands and the firefly convert chemical energy into light energy.

Magnetic domains are like small magnets. They each have a north pole and a south pole. If the domains in a material are pointing in different directions, it is not a magnet. Some materials can be made into magnets when placed inside a magnetic field. Their domains will line up with the field. Then the materials will be magnets.

What happens when you break a magnet in half? Do you get a north-pole magnet and a south-pole magnet? No, because the magnetic domains are still pointing in the same direction as the original magnet. So, you get two smaller magnets that each have their own north and south poles.

This iron in this frying pan is not magnetized. The magnetic domains of its atoms point in different directions.

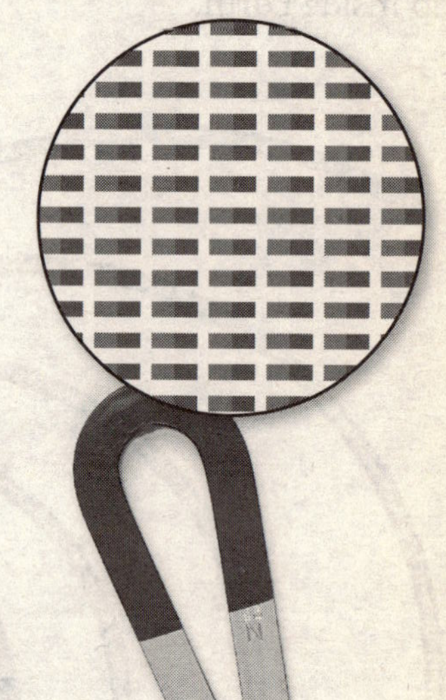

Most magnetic domains in a magnet point in the same direction.

Magnetic Fields

If you have ever played with magnets, you may have noticed that every magnet has a north pole and a south pole. If you put the opposite poles of two magnets together, they will attract, or pull toward each other. But similar poles of magnets will repel, or push away from each other when you try to bring them together. Magnets behave in this way because of their magnetic fields. A magnetic field is the area around a magnet in which it can exert force on another magnet. This field is strongest at the poles.

The electrons moving around the nucleus of an atom cause it to be slightly magnetic. But not every material can be magnetic. In most materials the magnetic fields of the atoms face in all different directions and cancel each other out. In some materials, however, the magnetism of the atoms is stronger. In materials such as iron, cobalt, and nickel, the atoms line up in groups called domains. A **magnetic domain** is a large number of atoms with their magnetic fields pointing in the same direction.

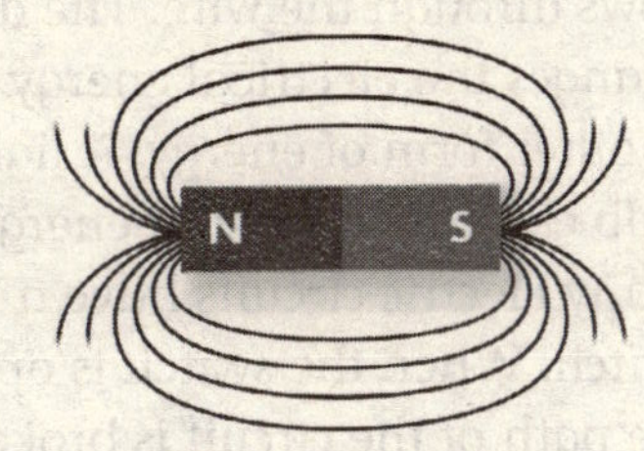

Magnetic field

If you break a magnet, each piece will have a north and a south pole.

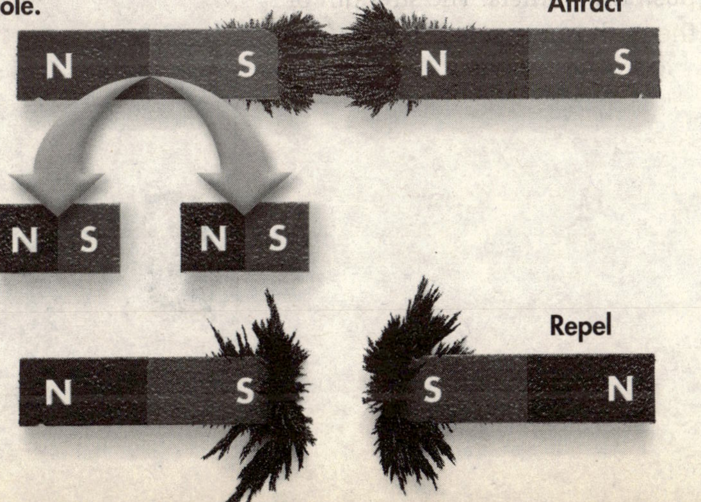

Scientists used to call the idea that energy is never lost the *law of conservation of energy*. They had a similar law about matter, called the law of conservation of mass. This law was discovered in 1784 by Antoine Lavoisier. It stated that matter cannot be created or destroyed.

Recently, scientists discovered that under rare conditions, energy and matter can be changed into one another. One example of this is nuclear energy, which is a result of matter changing into energy. Due to this discovery, scientists now use the name *law of conservation of mass and energy*. It states that the total amount of matter and energy does not change.

How are electricity and magnetism related?

Electric Current

Atoms have a nucleus of protons and neutrons surrounded by a cloud of electrons. The number of protons inside the nucleus is the same as the number of electrons surrounding it. Protons have a positive charge and electrons have a negative charge. The positive and negative charges cancel each other out. Because of this, atoms do not usually have a charge.

The electrons in some materials can move from atom to atom. This flow of electrons causes an electric charge to move along the atoms. Because the electrons all have negative charges, they push away from each other. The pushing keeps the electrons flowing and creates an electric current. An **electric current** is a flow of electric charge in a material.

A material in which electrons flow easily is a good electrical conductor. Copper is a good conductor. That is why copper is used to make electrical wires. In some materials, electrons do not flow easily. These are called insulators. Rubber is a good insulator.

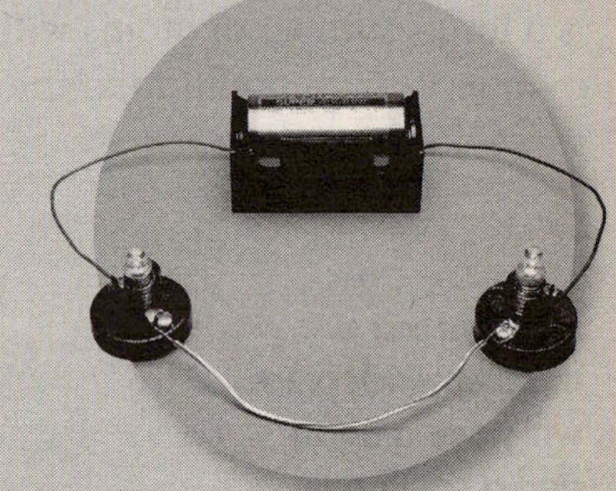

Electric Circuit

An electric current can only flow in a path that leads back to its starting point. An **electric circuit** is a closed path along which current can flow.

A simple electric circuit is made up of several parts. First, it has a source of electrical energy, such as a battery. Second, it has a wire through which the current flows. Third, a circuit has a device that uses the electrical energy that flows through the wire. The device changes the electrical energy into another form of energy. A light bulb changes it to light energy. Many electric circuits have a switch. When the switch is open, the path of the circuit is broken. Current cannot flow because the circuit is no longer complete.

The energy source in the circuit pushes electrons along. Some energy sources provide a stronger push than others. The strength of the push is measured in volts.

Series and Parallel Circuits

Circuits can be set up in series and parallel circuits. In a series circuit, there is only one path for the flow of electrons. The current flows through each light bulb. If you remove one of the light bulbs, the current will no longer flow.

In a parallel circuit, the current can flow along more than one path. If one bulb is removed, the current can still flow. The other bulb will continue to glow.

Series circuit

Parallel circuit

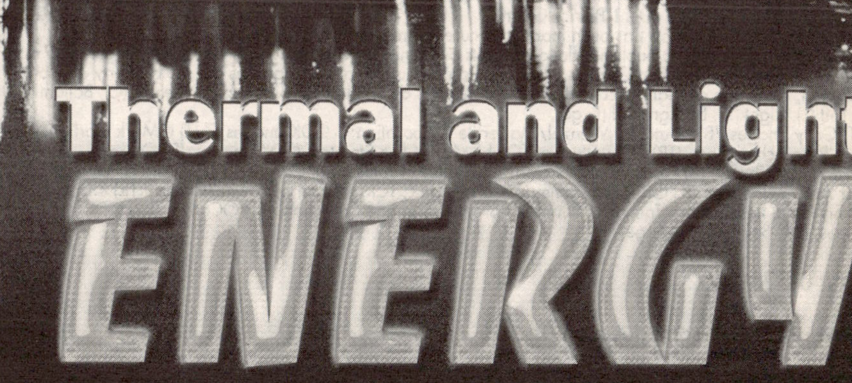

Genre	Comprehension Skill	Text Features	Science Content
Nonfiction	Compare and Contrast	• Captions • Labels • Diagrams • Glossary	Light and Heat

Scott Foresman Science 6.18

203

What did you learn?

1. What are the three types of heat transfer?

2. What causes the greenhouse effect?

3. How does dressing in layers keep you warm?

4. **Writing** in Science Hang gliders use convection currents to stay in the air. Write to explain how convection currents work in the atmosphere. Use details from the book to support your answer.

5. **Compare and Contrast** How are transverse and compressional waves similar? How are they different?

Illustrations: Title Page, 10-11 Patrick Gnan
Photographs: Every effort has been made to secure permission and provide appropriate credit for photographic material. The publisher deeply regrets any omission and pledges to correct errors called to its attention in subsequent editions. Unless otherwise acknowledged, all photographs are the property of Scott Foresman, a division of Pearson Education. Photo locators denoted as follows: Top (T), Center (C), Bottom (B), Left (L), Right (R), Background (Bkgd).
4 (T) Getty Images, (B) ©Andrew Wenzel/Masterfile Corporation; 6 ©DK Images; 7 (T) ©Mark Garlick/ Photo Researchers, Inc., (TR) ©Royalty-Free/Corbis, (CR) Clive Streeter/© DK Images, (R) ©Carroll Claver/PhotoLibrary, (B) Fundamental Photographs; 8 ©Kevin Fleming/Corbis; 11 (T) ©Alfred Pasieka/ Peter Arnold, Inc.; 13 (TL) ©Roger Ressmeyer/Corbis, (TCL, TCR) ©Lester Lefkowitz/Corbis, (TR) ©David Parker/Photo Researchers, Inc., (CL) ©Joel Sartore/NGS Image Collection, (BL) ©Corbis, (BR) ©DK Images, (BR) Sony/©DK Images

ISBN: 0-328-14021-X

Thermal and Light Energy

by Kim Calamia

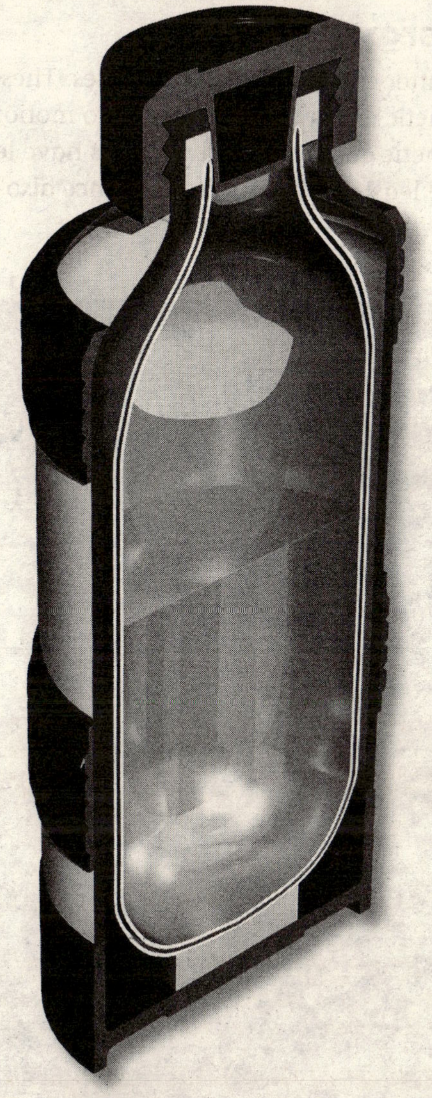

Glossary

conduction	the transfer of thermal energy between two objects that touch
conductor	a material that easily transfers thermal energy
convection	the transfer of thermal energy by the movement of the particles of a fluid
heat	the movement of thermal energy from one substance to another
insulator	a material that does not easily transfer thermal energy
radiation	the transfer of thermal energy as waves
reflection	the bouncing of light rays off the surface of a material
refraction	the change in the direction of light when it moves from one material to another
thermal energy	the total kinetic and potential energy of the particles in a substance

16

How is thermal energy transferred?

Thermal Energy

All forms of matter contain moving particles. These moving particles have kinetic energy, or energy due to motion. Gas particles have the most kinetic energy. Liquid particles have less, and solid particles have the least. Particles in a substance also have potential energy. This is energy due to position.

Particles in this molten glass are constantly flowing around each other.

Refraction and Reflection

Light can change speed as it moves from one material to another. This change in speed changes the direction. **Refraction** is the change in direction of light when it moves from one material to another. You can see this by placing a spoon in a glass of water. When you look at it from the side, the spoon seems to bend at the water's surface. This is because the light changes direction when it enters the water.

Light is reflected when it is not absorbed and does not pass through a material. The light is simply bounced back. **Reflection** happens when light bounces off the surface of a material.

Very smooth materials, such as mirrors, can reflect an image. Some surfaces, such as books, are not very smooth. Because of their roughness, light bounces off the surface in many directions at different angles. The surface is not smooth enough for you to see a clear reflection.

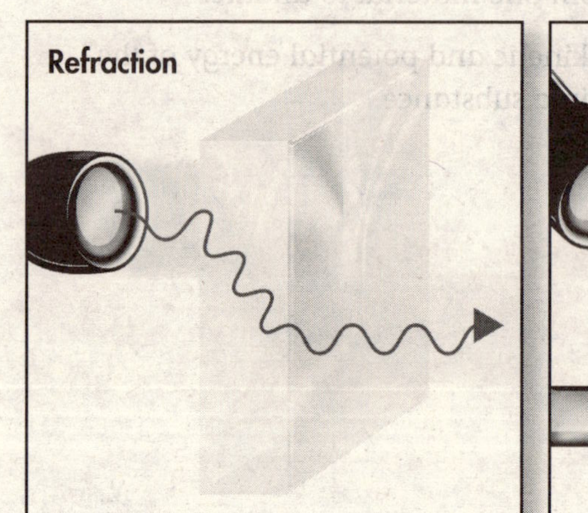

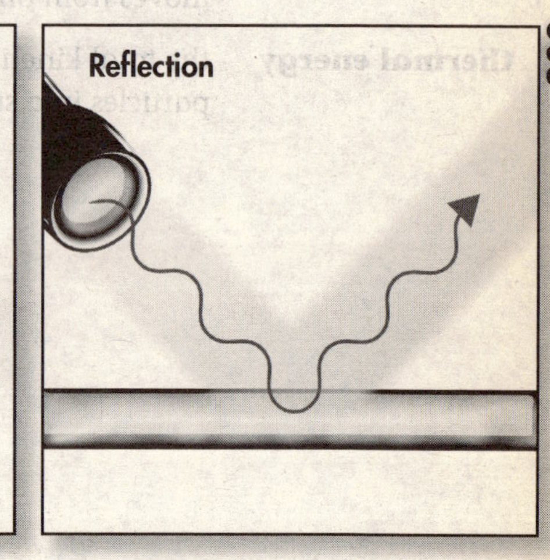

Absorption of Light

Some colors and materials absorb, or take in, more light than others. When objects absorb light, some of the light energy changes to heat energy. If you wear dark colors on a sunny day, you might get warmer than if you wear light colors.

Light can also pass through materials. Transparent materials, such as clear glass, allow almost all light to pass through them. Materials that allow some light to pass through are called translucent. Wax paper is a translucent material. Opaque materials, such as wood or metal, do not allow any light to pass through.

Electromagnetic waves travel through empty space at 300,000 kilometers per second. This is the speed of light. Light travels through different materials at different speeds. It travels quickly through gases because of their low density. Light travels more slowly through liquids. It travels most slowly through solids because of their high density.

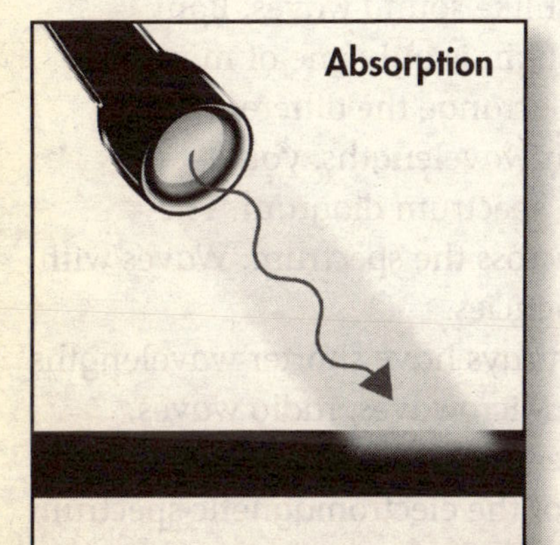

Seeing Color

The wavelengths of light that an object absorbs and reflects determine its color.

 Black objects absorb almost all light that strikes them.

White objects reflect almost all of the light that strikes them. White is a combination of all wavelengths of light.

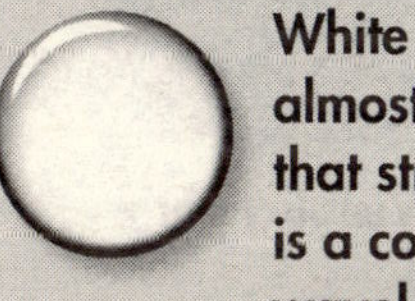 An object appears red if it absorbs all wavelengths of light except red.

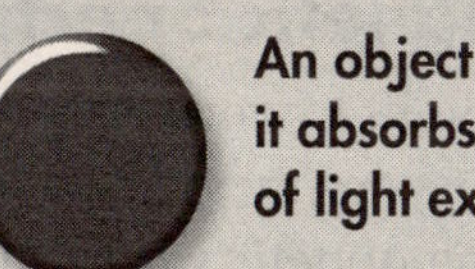 Grass is green because it absorbs all wavelengths of light except green.

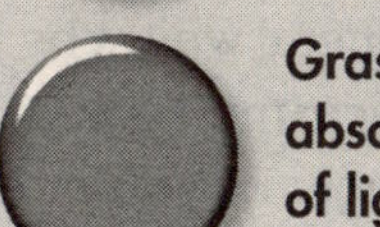 A blue object reflects only blue wavelengths of light.

Thermal energy is the total kinetic and potential energy of the particles in a substance. Substances with more particles have more thermal energy. A full cup of water has twice as many particles as half a cup of water. It also has twice as much thermal energy.

A warm cup of water has more thermal energy than a cold one. Both cups of water have the same numbers of particles. But the warm water particles are moving faster. The more thermal energy something has, the more its particles move. They have more kinetic energy. More moving particles make substances feel warmer.

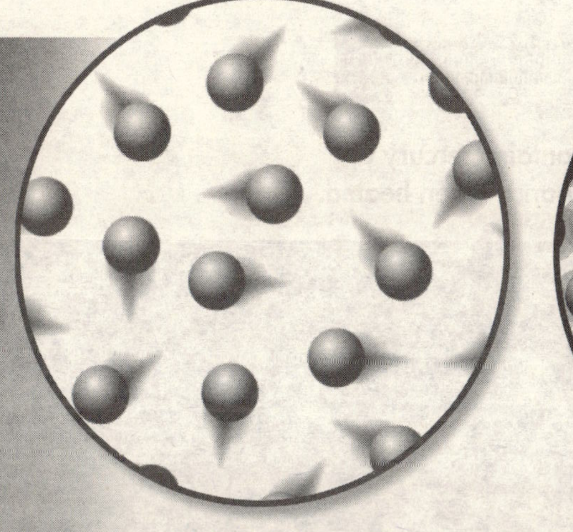

Particles in a liquid

Particles in a solid

Heat

Temperature is the average kinetic energy of a substance. When you are sick, you probably have your temperature taken with a thermometer. A thermometer measures your body's average kinetic energy.

Temperature is different from thermal energy. Remember, thermal energy is the total kinetic and potential energy in the particles of a substance. Temperature is an average.

If you had a full cup of water and poured half of it out, its amount of thermal energy would be half as much. Its temperature, however, would remain the same.

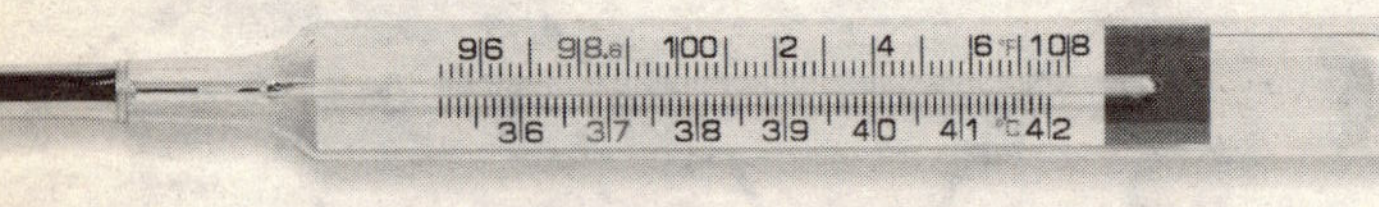

Many thermometers contain mercury or another liquid that expands when heated.

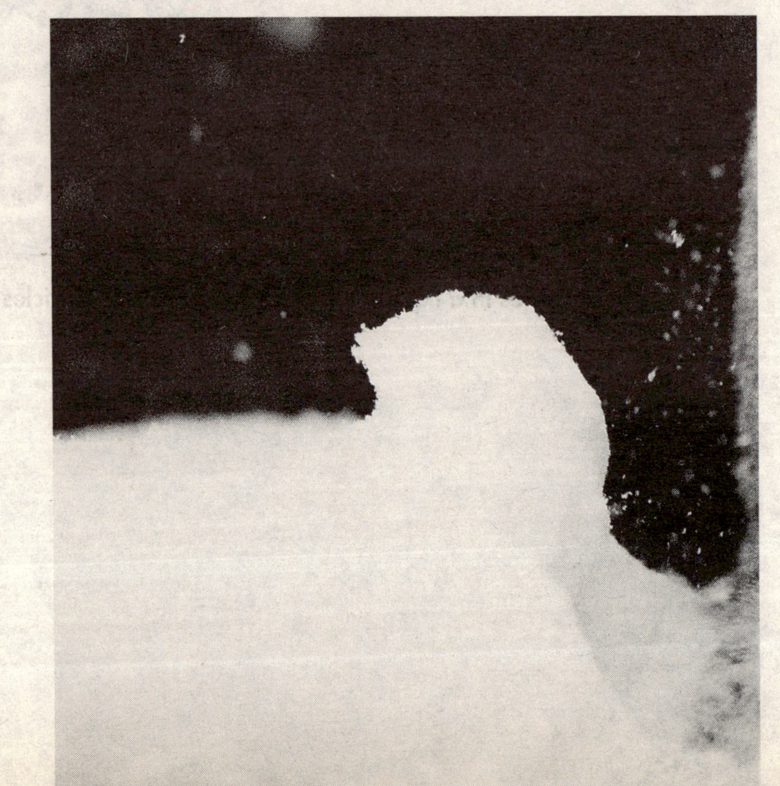

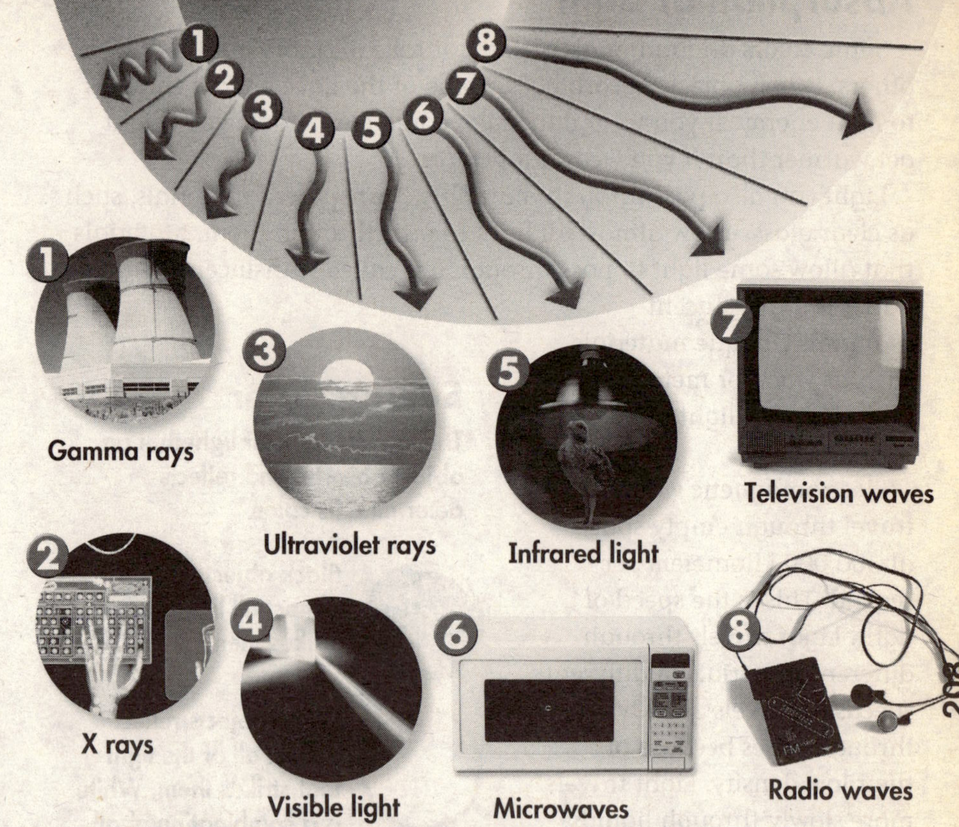

Electromagnetic Spectrum

Like sound, light travels as waves. Unlike sound waves, light can travel across empty space. Visible light is only one of many types of electromagnetic waves. If you arrange the different types of electromagnetic waves by their wavelengths, you get the electromagnetic spectrum. Look at the spectrum diagram. The wavelengths get longer as you move across the spectrum. Waves with longer wavelengths have shorter frequencies.

Gamma rays, X rays, and ultraviolet rays have shorter wavelengths of higher frequency than visible light. Microwaves, radio waves, television rays, and infrared light have longer wavelengths of lower frequency than visible light. All parts of the electromagnetic spectrum carry energy. Waves with shorter wavelengths have more energy.

How do waves carry energy?

Types of Waves

If you throw a rock into a pond, you can see waves moving. Waves are a movement of energy through matter. As a wave moves through a material, the material does not move along with the wave. The particles of the material vibrate, or move back and forth slightly. The direction of their movement depends on the type of wave.

There are two main types of waves. The waves in the pond are transverse waves. When these waves move in one direction, the particles of matter move in another. The wave travels forward, but the particles move up and down. Compressional waves work differently. Their particles move in the same direction as the wave. As the wave travels forward, the particles move back and forth. Sound waves are compressional waves. As they move through the air, they cause the air particles to move. They strike the particles next to them, causing them to move as well. In this way, the waves travel through the air to your ears. Sound waves can travel through matter but not empty space. Empty space contains no particles to carry sound waves.

Transverse wave

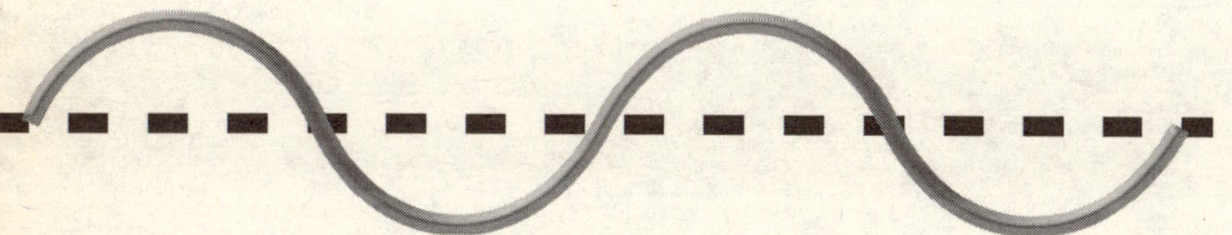

Compressional wave

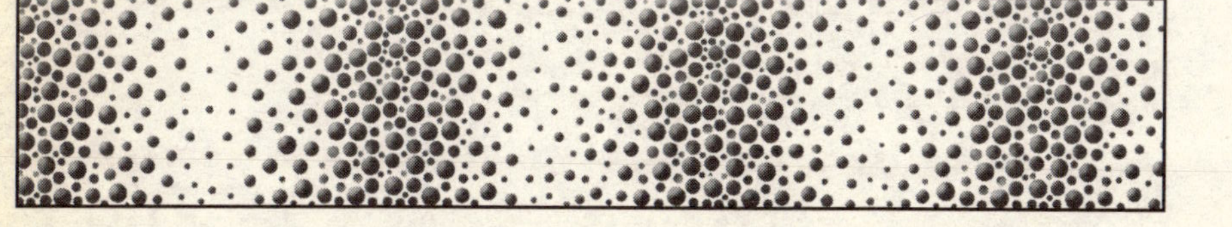

Heat is the movement of thermal energy from one substance to another. A warmer object can transfer some of its heat to a colder object. As an object takes in heat, its temperature rises. The particles in the colder object begin to move faster. Their kinetic energy increases.

Heat can move between objects that touch and between objects that do not touch. Heat is transferred in three ways: conduction, convection, and radiation.

Thermal energy is transferred from the body of the lynx to the particles in the snow.

Insulation

An **insulator** is a material that does not easily transfer heat. A **conductor** transfers heat easily. It is the opposite of an insulator.

Particles in a warmer object move faster than in a cooler object. When warm and cool objects touch, the particles in the warmer object bump into those in the cooler object. The kinetic energy of the cooler object's particles rises. Conduction causes the cooler object's temperature to rise.

Some materials have particles that vibrate easily. They are good conductors. Many metals are good conductors because their electrons are not held together tightly. The electrons carry energy as they move. Liquids and gases often are better insulators than solids. This is because their particles are more spread out. Empty space is also a good insulator. Heat cannot move through it by conduction or convection, because there are no particles to vibrate.

The particles in the warm lemonade are moving more quickly than the particles in the ice. The lemonade particles bump into the ice particles. This speeds up the ice particles and slows down the lemonade particles. The ice cubes become warmer.

The particles of lemonade do not travel into the ice. Instead, they vibrate and bump into the ice particles. Energy moves from one particle to another. Energy can move from a warmer substance to a cooler one. It can also move from a warm part of an object to a cooler part of the same object.

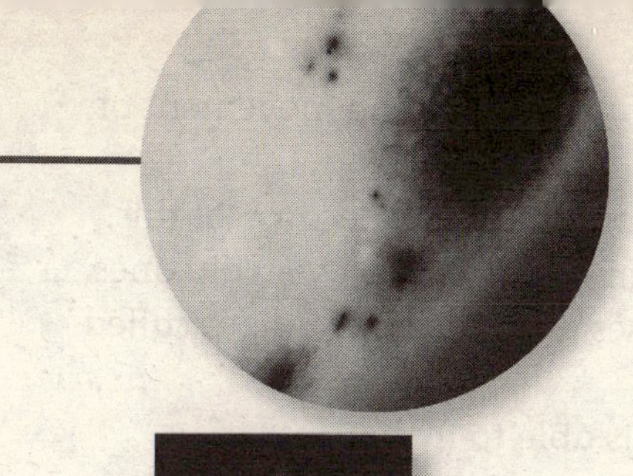

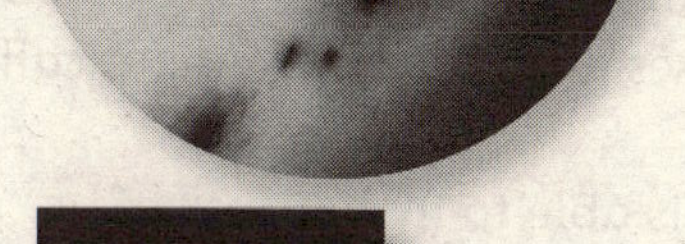

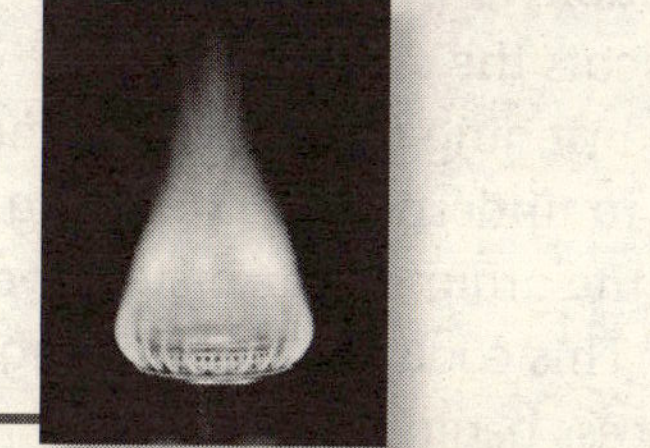

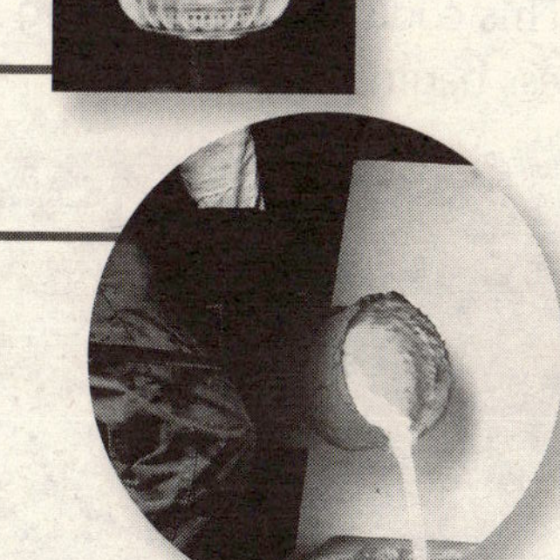

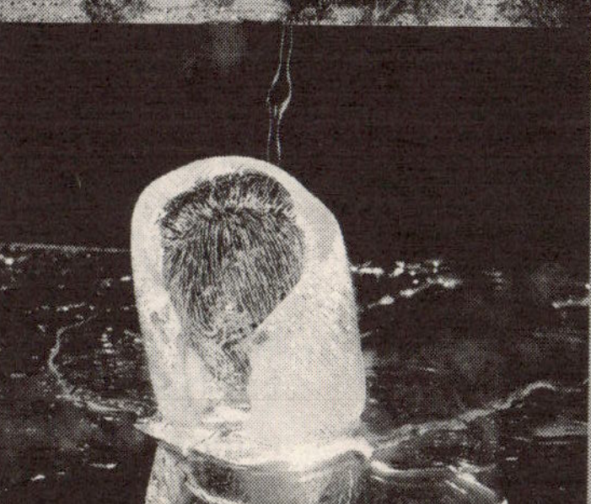

A shiny surface on the thermos slows heat transfer by radiation.

This layer of empty space contains almost no air. It slows the conduction of heat.

Convection

Convection is the transfer of thermal energy by the movement of a fluid. A fluid is any liquid or gas.

Warm fluids have lower densities than cold fluids. Because of this, cold fluids sink below warm ones. Warm fluids rise up over cold ones. This sinking and rising sometimes causes a circular movement called a convection current.

The hang glider shown on this page is able to fly because of convection currents. The warm ground heats the air it touches by convection. This warm air begins to rise, bringing the land's thermal energy with it. Cool air sinks and rushes in underneath, producing wind. When the warm air is high above the ground, it transfers the thermal energy to the cold air around it. This cools the air, causing it to sink back to the ground. Then the process begins again.

Hang gliders are able to stay up in the air due to convection currents.

Radiation

Radiation is the transfer of thermal energy as waves. It can occur through matter or empty space. The Sun gives off thermal energy as waves. This energy travels through empty space to Earth. The surface of Earth reflects some radiation back into the atmosphere. It absorbs the rest of the radiation.

Without the atmosphere to trap some of this thermal energy, Earth would become very cold. However, if the atmosphere trapped too much energy, Earth would become too warm. The trapping and holding of thermal energy by the atmosphere is called the greenhouse effect. Scientists are worried that an increase of certain gases in the atmosphere is warming Earth too much.

Earth, Sun, and Moon

by Carol Levine

Genre	Comprehension Skill	Text Features	Science Content
Nonfiction	Main Idea and Details	• Captions • Labels • Diagrams • Glossary	Earth and Space

Scott Foresman Science 6.19

What did you learn?

1. Why does the Sun look like the largest star in the sky?

2. Does the Moon give off light? Why does the Moon seem to be lit?

3. What causes the Moon to appear to be different shapes during a month?

4. **Writing** in Science The tilt of Earth on its axis causes the seasons. Write to explain how seasons change because of Earth's tilt. Use details from the book to support your answer.

5. **Main Idea and Details** Reread page 7. Write a sentence that gives the main idea of the page. Under that sentence, list two supporting details.

Illustrations: Title Page, 10 Bob Kayganich; 14 Peter Bollinger
Photographs: Every effort has been made to secure permission and provide appropriate credit for photographic material. The publisher deeply regrets any omission and pledges to correct errors called to its attention in subsequent editions. Unless otherwise acknowledged, all photographs are the property of Scott Foresman, a division of Pearson Education. Photo locators denoted as follows: Top (T), Center (C), Bottom (B), Left (L), Right (R), Background (Bkgd).
2 ©GSFC/NASA; 3 ©John Sanford/Photo Researchers, Inc.; 4 ©John Sanford/Photo Researchers, Inc., (BC) ©GRIN/NASA; 10 (CR) ©Jan Halaska/Photo Researchers, Inc.; 11 (T, BC, CR) ©Jan Halaska/Photo Researchers, Inc.; 12 ©Roger Ressmeyer/Corbis

ISBN: 0-328-14024-4

Glossary

lunar eclipse — the passing of the Moon through Earth's shadow, causing Earth's shadow to fall on the Moon

orbit — the path of an object as it revolves around another object

revolve — to move in a path around another object

rotate — to spin on an axis

solar eclipse — the passing of the Moon between the Sun and Earth causing the Moon to cast its shadow on Earth

Earth, Sun, and Moon

by Carol Levine

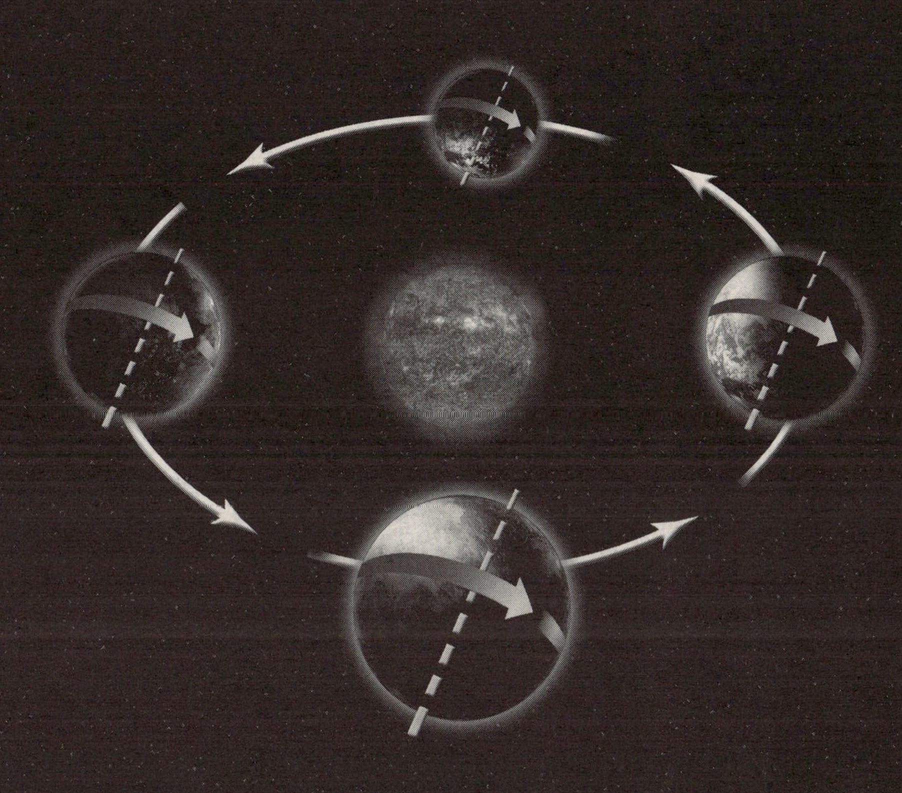

What are the characteristics of Earth's Sun and Moon?

Our Sun

Our Sun is a star. It only appears to be larger than other stars because it is much closer to Earth than the stars we see at night. It is made of hot gases called plasma. The Sun does not burn; it glows similar to a light bulb.

A heavy core makes up the inner part of the Sun. Its temperature is about 15 million degrees Celsius. Particles react in the core and release large amounts of energy. This provides light and heat that living things on Earth need to live. Without the Sun, Earth would be cold and could not support life.

The Sun has no solid surface. Swirling layers of plasma surround the core. Prominences are large loops of gases that extend thousands of kilometers from the Sun. Some stay in place for weeks. Others explode into space. Solar flares are temporary releases of energy from the Sun's surface. Energy from these flares can reach Earth. This energy causes auroras, which are light displays usually seen near Earth's poles.

A lunar eclipse occurs when the orbit of Earth places it between the Sun and the Moon. This casts a shadow on the Moon, which we see on Earth as an eclipse.

As you can see, we have learned a lot about the motions of Earth, the Sun, and the Moon since humans first started studying the sky. Night and day, the seasons, and solar and lunar eclipses are all caused by the motions of our planet and the Moon as they orbit the Sun.

Earth's Moon

The Moon has no light of its own. Sunlight reflects off the Moon's surface. This is what makes it appears lit. The Moon is like a giant rock in space. It has almost no atmosphere.

The Moon **revolves,** or moves in a path, around Earth. The Moon also spins on its axis, or **rotates,** as it revolves. The same side of the Moon always faces Earth. This is because the time it takes the Moon to revolve and the time it takes to rotate are the same.

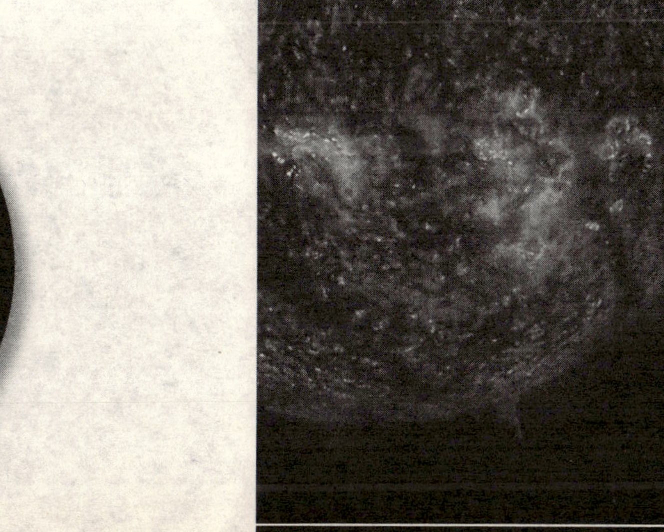

Lunar Eclipses

A solar eclipse is not the only kind of eclipse that Earth can experience. Sometimes Earth is between the Sun and the Moon during a full moon. This causes Earth's shadow to fall on the Moon. A **lunar eclipse** takes place when the Moon passes through Earth's shadow. During a total eclipse, it may take almost two hours for the Moon to completely pass through Earth's shadow. Partial eclipses, last for a shorter period of time. Lunar eclipses can be seen from all parts of Earth where it is nighttime. Lunar and solar eclipses happen about twice a year, but because a lunar eclipse can be seen from half of Earth, there is a better chance that you will see one when it happens.

Time-lapse
photo of a
lunar eclipse

Phases of the Moon

The Moon appears to change shape each night of the month. But it does not actually change. The different shapes are called the phases of the Moon. We see these changes because of changes in the size of the lighted part of the Moon we can see. Only the half of the Moon that faces the Sun is lighted. The positions of the Moon, Earth, and the Sun determine how the Moon will look from Earth at any given time. A complete cycle of the Moon happens every 29.5 days.

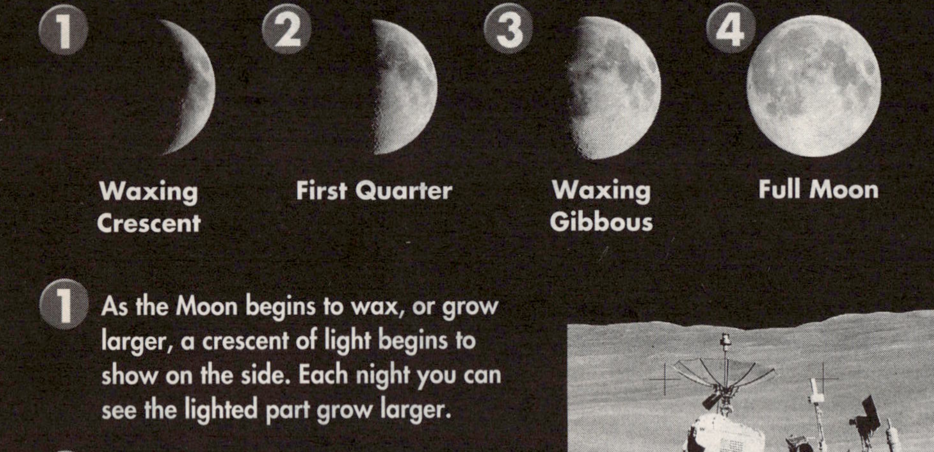

1 As the Moon begins to wax, or grow larger, a crescent of light begins to show on the side. Each night you can see the lighted part grow larger.

2 As the Moon begins to wax, you can see half of its lighted side.

3 The Moon continues to wax. The shape of the Moon we now see is called gibbous.

4 About two weeks after a new moon, the Moon appears fully lighted. It has revolved halfway around Earth.

Astronauts on the *Apollo 16* mission to the Moon in 1972 collected samples, performed experiments, and took photographs.

A solar eclipse can be total or partial. When the umbra passes over an area, the eclipse is total. The Sun is completely blocked, the sky is dark, and the stars are visible. This can last several minutes. Only a small area of Earth sees the total eclipse because the Moon's shadow is small. Areas that are close enough will experience a partial eclipse because the penumbra is passing over. A partial eclipse can also happen when the umbra misses Earth and only the penumbra passes over.

Never look directly at the Sun. To view an eclipse, use two pieces of white cardboard. Place one piece of the cardboard on the ground. Poke a small pinhole through the other piece and hold it so the Sun shines through the hole onto the cardboard on the ground. The round spot you see is an image of the Sun.

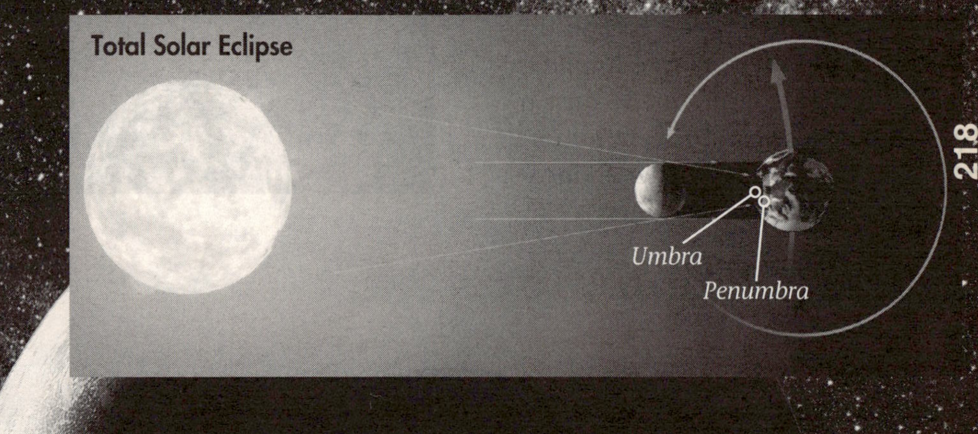

Solar Eclipses

Most of the time, the Moon's orbit is tilted at a slight angle from Earth's orbit around the Sun. This slight tilt causes the Moon to be a little above or below the Sun. There are times, however, when the tilt of the Moon's orbit around Earth causes the Moon to cross exactly between the Sun and Earth. This causes a **solar eclipse.** When this happens, the Moon blocks the light of the Sun.

During an eclipse, the Moon makes two kinds of shadows on Earth. The umbra is the darker, inner part of an eclipse shadow. The penumbra is the lighter, outer part of an eclipse shadow. Solar eclipses happen several times a year. But each place on Earth can only see one every few hundred years.

Learning About the Moon

The first visit to the Moon happened in 1959. An unmanned Soviet spacecraft called *Luna 2* landed on the Moon's surface. In 1969, *Apollo 11* carried astronauts Edwin "Buzz" Aldrin and Neil Armstrong, the first humans to land on the Moon. There were five more Moon landings. The last one was in 1972.

Information collected during the Moon landings has helped us learn about the Moon, Earth, and the rest of the solar system. The craters and other features of the Moon's surface have been examined. This helps scientists find out the ages of the Moon and of Earth.

What are the effects
of the movements
# of Earth and the Moon?

Earth on Its Axis

In the past, many people thought that the Sun moved around Earth. They thought this because they watched the Sun appear to rise in the east and set in the west every day.

Now we know that the Sun is the center of the solar system. We also know that Earth and the other planets revolve around it. Earth rotates on its axis, the imaginary line between the poles. One complete rotation takes a day. The rotation of Earth makes it seem as though the Sun is moving around our planet.

The Sun appears to rise in the east because Earth spins from west to east, and we spin with it. Daytime lasts as long as the Sun is visible. As Earth turns, the Sun seems to set in the west. Then it is nighttime.

This changes when the South Pole is tilted toward the Sun. Then the Northern Hemisphere has winter and the Southern Hemisphere has summer. Neither pole is tilted toward the Sun in spring and fall. This causes milder temperatures for both hemispheres.

During the summer, the Sun's direct light causes warm days. Your shadow at noon is very small. As the days go by, the Sun's rays reach you at a greater and greater angle. Your shadow at noon gets longer and longer. The days are not as warm. It is fall. More days pass by, and the angle of the Sun's rays is now very large. Your shadow is long because the Sun is lower in the sky. Now it is winter. Eventually, the Sun's rays strike you at a smaller angle. The days are warmer. Your shadow at noontime starts to shorten again. It is spring!

In the evening, the Sun appears to sink below the western horizon.

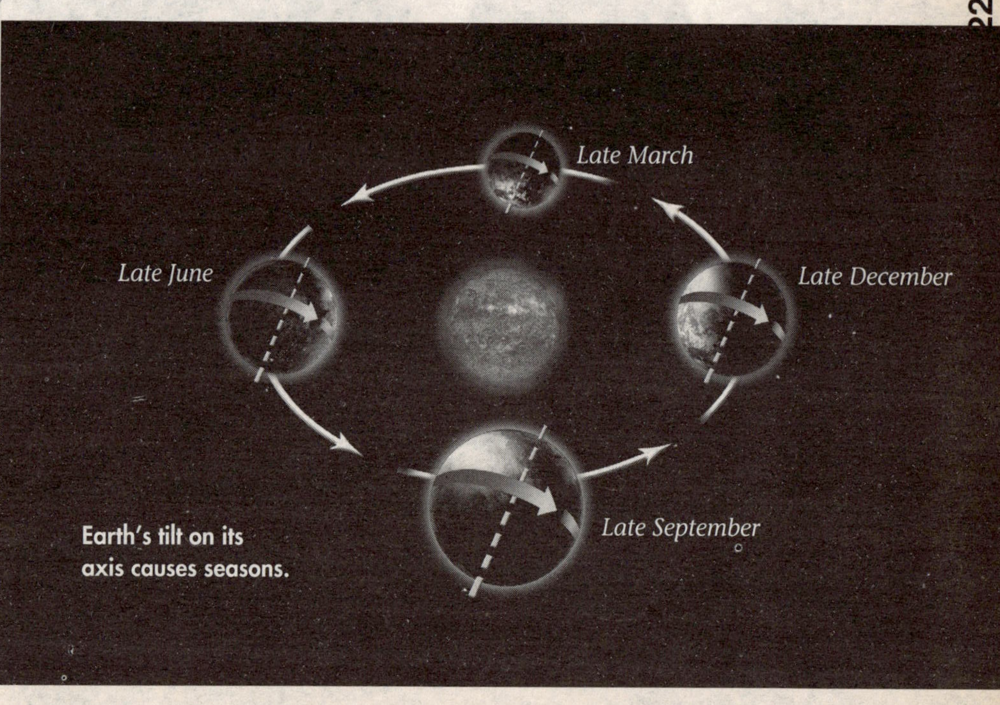

Earth's Orbit and Seasons

Earth tends to move in a straight line. But the force of the Sun's gravity pulls Earth out of its path. This causes Earth to revolve around the Sun. An **orbit** is the path of an object as it revolves around another object. Earth's orbit around the Sun is a slightly flattened and circular ellipse. One orbit takes one year, or 365 days.

Earth's elliptical orbit causes it to be closer to the Sun at some times than it is at other times. The difference in distance does not cause the seasons. In fact, Earth is closest to the Sun when the Northern Hemisphere has winter.

The tilt of Earth on its axis causes the seasons. The Northern Hemisphere of Earth has summer when the North Pole is tilted toward the Sun. During this time the Southern Hemisphere has winter.

The number of daylight hours changes throughout the year. That is because Earth is tilted on its axis. One half of Earth is always tilted a little bit toward the Sun. That side has more hours of daylight and fewer hours of nighttime. The opposite is true on the side tilted away from the Sun. The effect of Earth's tilt is greatest at the poles. When the northern part of Earth is tilted toward the Sun, the Sun never completely sets at the North Pole. When the southern part of Earth is tilted toward the Sun, the Sun never completely sets at the South Pole. Day and night at the poles each last for six months.

The Moon is usually visible at night, but sometimes it can be seen during the day. The Moon can be visible whenever it is on your side of Earth.

Earth's axis is tilted. This affects how the Sun shines on Earth.

The North Pole tilts away from the Sun. The Sun's rays are spread over a wide area. Temperatures are cooler.

At the Equator, the Sun's rays strike Earth more directly. The concentrated energy makes this area warmer.

Comparing Sizes

Earth feels very large to the humans living on it. But Earth is small compared to the Sun. They are so different in size that it is impossible to picture them to scale in a book. The Sun is more than two hundred times wider than Earth. More than one million Earths could fit inside the Sun if it were hollow. The Sun has about 330,000 times the mass of Earth. Its gravitational pull is nearly 30 times stronger.

Earth and the Moon are not nearly so different from each other. Earth is four times wider than the Moon. 50 moons could fit inside Earth if it were hollow. Earth has 80 times more mass than the Moon. It has six times the gravitational pull. Things weigh less on the Moon than they do on Earth. For instance, an object that weighs 60 newtons on Earth weighs only 10 newtons on the Moon.

Moon

Earth

Sun

Science

Space and Technology

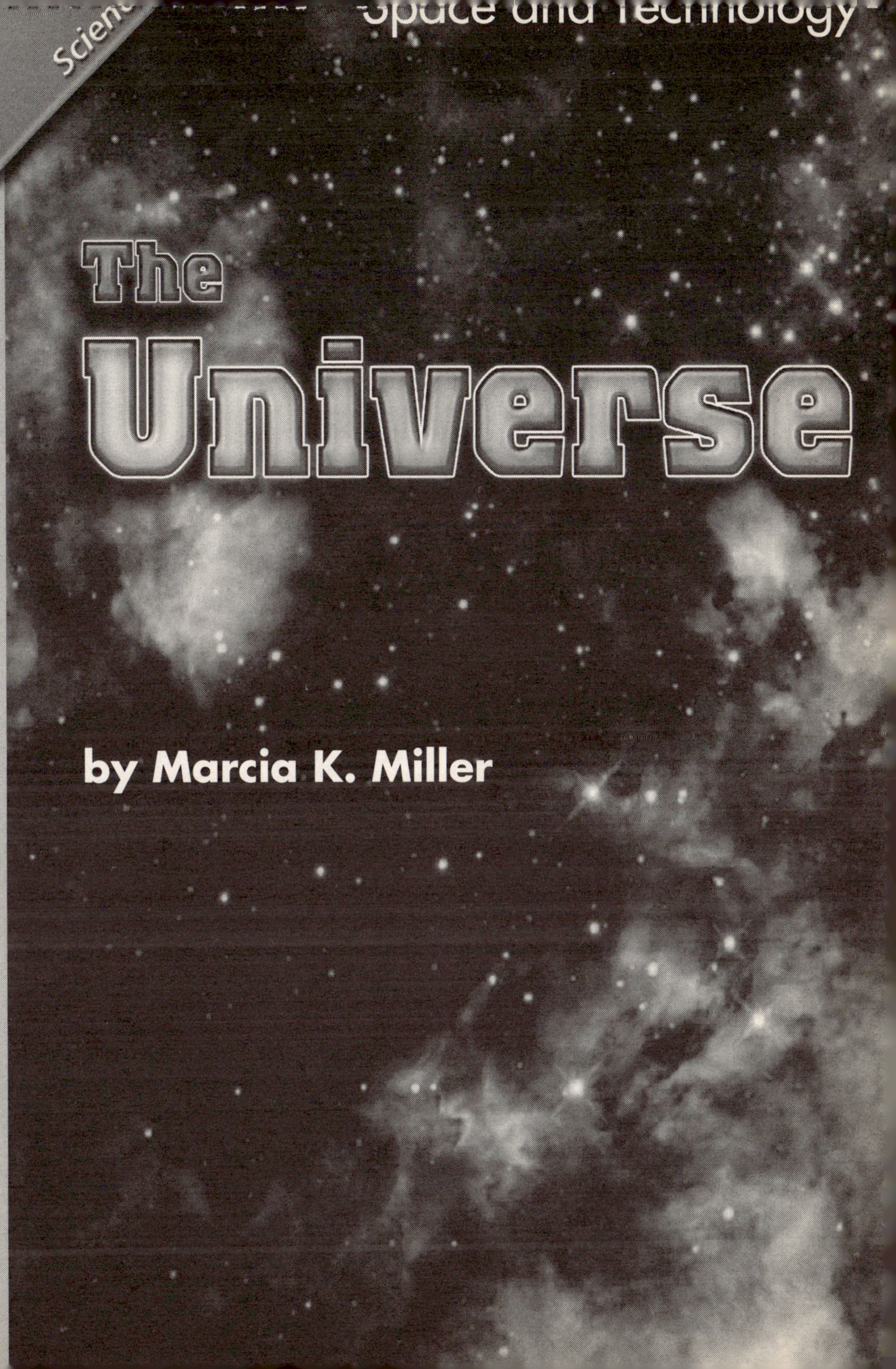

The Universe

by Marcia K. Miller

Genre	Comprehension Skill	Text Features	Science Content
Nonfiction	Draw Conclusions	• Captions • Charts • Diagrams • Glossary	Stars and Solar System

Scott Foresman Science 6.20

PEARSON Scott Foresman

scottforesman.com

ISBN 0-328-14027-9

9 780328 140275 90000

Vocabulary

astronomical unit

constellation

galaxy

light-year

magnitude

nuclear fusion

solar system

star

What did you learn?

1. What galaxy does our solar system belong to? What type of galaxy is it?

2. List the planets of our solar system in order from the Sun.

3. What does a star's color tell you about it?

4. **Writing** in Science Planets vary in many ways. For instance, they vary in how long it takes them to make one complete revolution around the Sun. Is there a link between the size of a planet's orbit and how long it takes the planet to make one revolution around the Sun? Use your own words to write about this question. Use facts given in the charts on page 5 to support your answer.

5. **Draw Conclusions** The star Antares is about 620 light-years from Earth. The star Betelgeuse is about 430 light-years away. With this data, can you tell which star is brighter in the night sky? Explain.

Illustrations: Title Page, 15 Peter Bollinger
Photographs: Every effort has been made to secure permission and provide appropriate credit for photographic material. The publisher deeply regrets any omission and pledges to correct errors called to its attention in subsequent editions. Unless otherwise acknowledged, all photographs are the property of Scott Foresman, a division of Pearson Education. Photo locators denoted as follows: Top (T), Center (C), Bottom (B), Left (L), Right (R), Background (Bkgd)
2 © Royalty-Free/Corbis; 3 ©Myron Jay Dorf/Corbis; 11 (CR) G. Li Causi/A. Ricciardi/A.Garatti/ Alessandro Vannini-Rome, Italy, (B) ©NOAO/Gatley Merrill/Ressmeyer/Corbis; 14 (T) ©Roger Ressmeyer/Corbis

ISBN: 0-328-14027-9

Glossary

astronomical unit	the average distance of Earth from the Sun, about 149.6 million kilometers
constellation	one of eighty-eight named star groups visible from Earth at night
galaxy	a huge grouping of stars
light-year	the distance light can travel in one year
magnitude	the term scientists use to describe star brightness
nuclear fusion	the process in which the nuclei of two or more atoms join, or fuse, into one larger nucleus, giving off energy
solar system	the Sun and the nine planets and other bodies that orbit around it
star	a huge, hot, glowing ball of gas

The Universe

by Marcia K. Miller

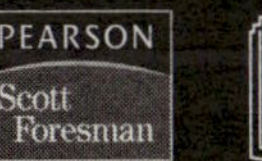

What is Earth's place in the universe?

The Universe

Astronomy is the study of space and the objects in it. It is one of the oldest sciences. We know that people have been studying the sky as far back as 3500 B.C. Early astronomers could see only small dots of light above them. In 1609 the scientist Galileo was the first person to use a telescope to look at the sky. What he found changed the way people think about space.

Scientists today use very powerful telescopes to look into the sky. We are not sure how far in any direction the universe goes. But each year scientists can see deeper and deeper into space. They study the energy, matter, and empty space that make up the universe.

Constellation Movement

Do you watch the stars? If so, then you know that patterns in the night sky change from hour to hour. A starry sky looks different in the early evening than it does in the early morning. Star patterns also change with the seasons. In the Northern Hemisphere, we see Orion high in the winter sky. But in summer we lose part or all of Orion as it dips below the horizon.

Changes like these should not surprise you. You know that the Sun appears to move across the sky during the day. Stars appear to move in the night sky. Both changes are actually due to the movements of Earth. Earth rotates on its axis as it orbits the Sun. These movements affect the star patterns we see.

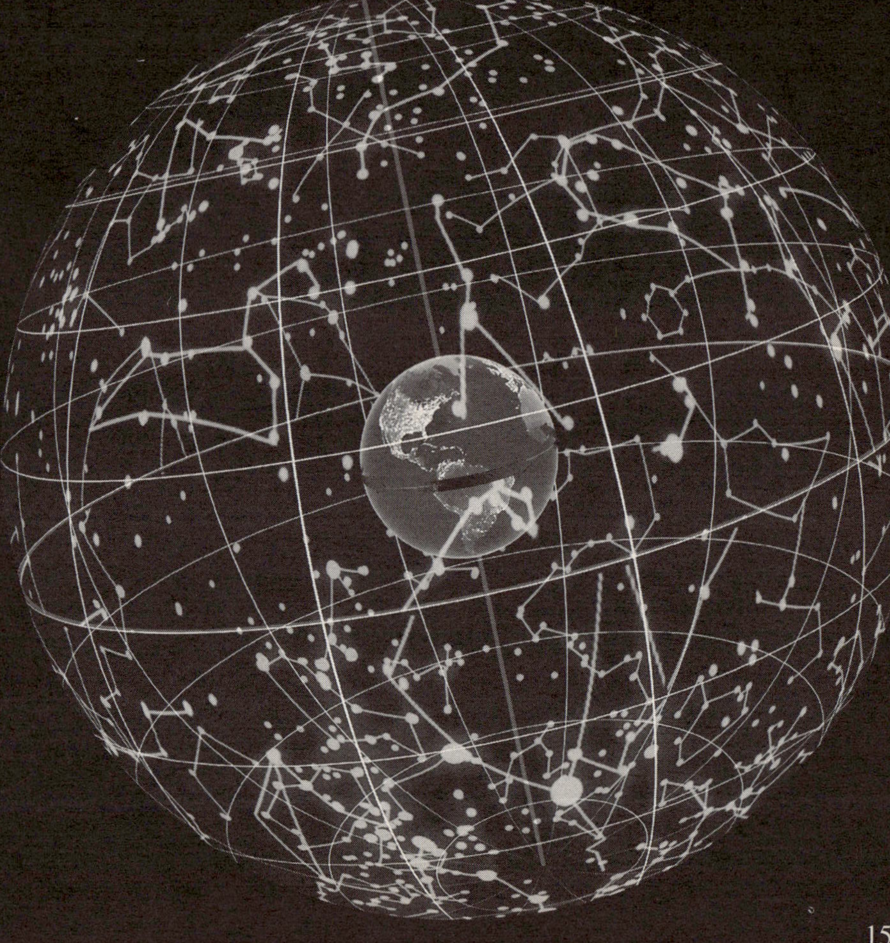

Constellations

Have you heard of Gemini, Orion, or Leo? The ancient Greeks first gave these names to groups of stars. They named a total of 48 star groups. The Greeks linked the star patterns with their myths and gods. One example is the story of Orion the hunter. He fell in love with the goddess Artemis, who placed Orion in the night sky after killing him by accident.

Scientists today divide the sky into 88 star groups called **constellations.** Every star is part of a constellation. But stars in the same constellation may not be related in any other way.

Ursa Major means "big bear." It is one of the best-known constellations. The Big Dipper is part of Ursa Major. The two stars at the end of the bowl of the Big Dipper always point to the North Star, which is always over the North Pole.

The constellation Orion

Earth is part of the Milky Way Galaxy. A **galaxy** is a huge grouping of stars. The universe is made up of clusters of billions of galaxies. Each galaxy has billions of stars.

You can see part of the Milky Way Galaxy in the night sky. It looks like a pale white stripe or band across the sky. If you were far away from the Milky Way, you would see that it forms a flat pinwheel. Our Sun is one of the stars in the Milky Way. It is located in one of the "arms" of the pinwheel. Our Sun looks brighter and bigger than other stars because it is much closer to Earth.

There are three types of galaxies. The Milky Way is a spiral galaxy. Elliptical galaxies are shaped like an ellipse, or oval. Irregular galaxies have no regular shape at all.

The Milky Way Galaxy is a spiral galaxy.

The Planets

The Sun and the bodies around it make up our **solar system.**
Earth and eight other planets orbit the Sun in our solar system.

All the planets have orbits that look almost circular, except for
Pluto, which has a more elliptical orbit. The Sun's gravity holds all of
the planets in their orbits.

A moon is a natural body that orbits a planet. Most planets have
one or more moons; only Mercury and Venus have none.

Asteroids are small bodies made of rock and metal. Over 100,000
of them orbit the Sun. Comets orbit the Sun as well They are small
bodies of ice, which orbit in long, narrow ellipses. A comet may pass
close to the Sun in part of its orbit, which causes the comet to heat
up. Then, it forms a stream of gas and dust that trails it as it moves
through space. The far end of a comet's orbit is deep in space.

Objects in our solar system are very far apart. Scientists use
a special unit to measure these great distances. It is called an
astronomical unit (AU). An **astronomical unit** is the
average distance Earth is from the Sun. One AU is equal to
149.6 million kilometers.

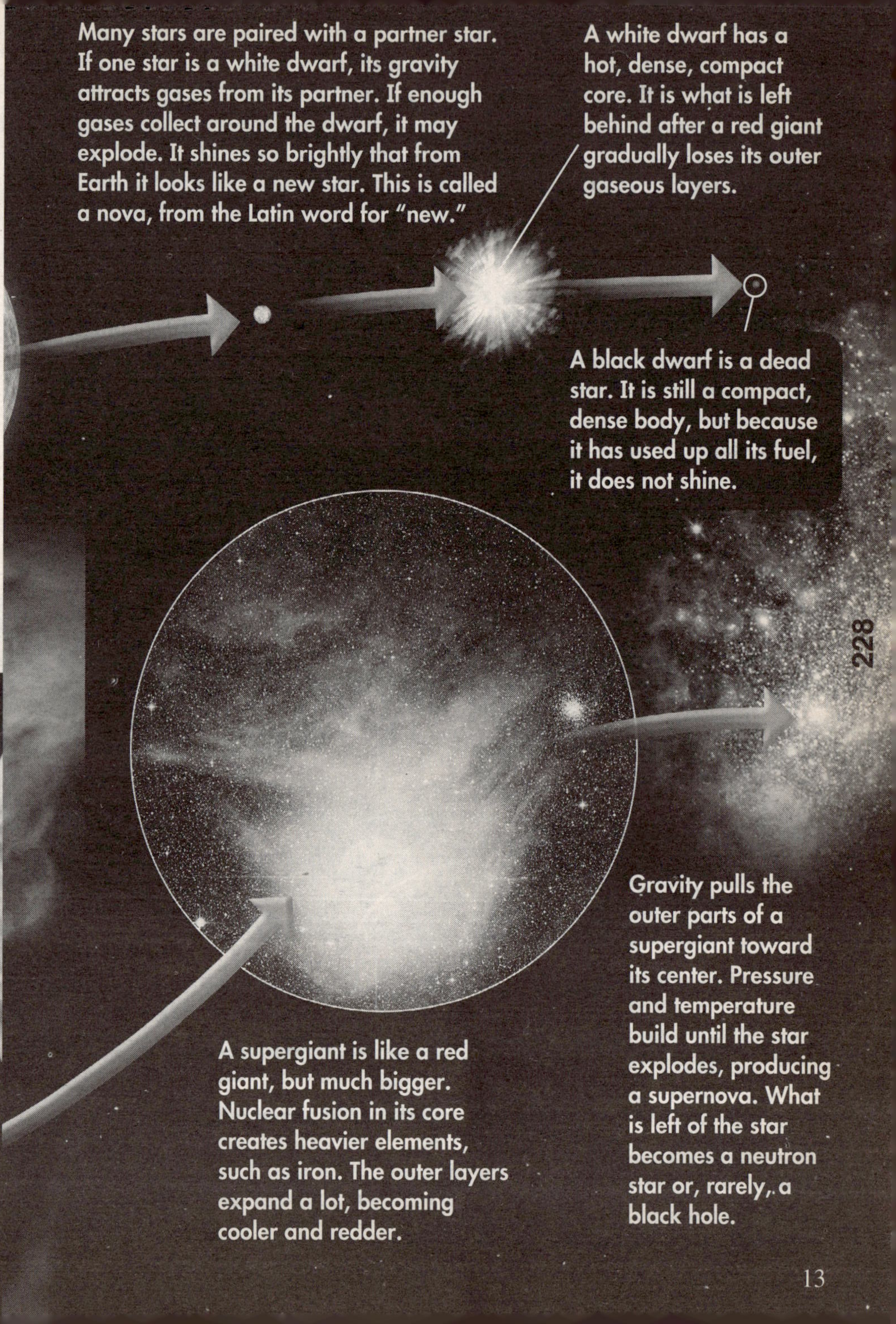

Star Life Cycle

Stars shine for billions of years, but they do not shine forever. Like living things, stars change as they age, and eventually they die. A star changes in the size, color, and brightness as it goes through its life cycle.

A star begins in a nebula. This is a huge cloud of hydrogen and other gases. Gravity pulls these gas particles together. A clump of gases is formed. The clump heats up as it pulls in more particles. Nuclear fusion begins when the star's core reaches 10,000,000°C. Energy made by fusion heats gases which then push out as gravity pulls in. When the push of gases becomes greater than the pull of gravity, fusion energy reaches the surface and a star is born!

The Inner Planets

	Mercury	Venus	Earth	Mars
Diameter (km)	4,879	12,104	12,756	6,794
Mass (compared to Earth)	0.055	0.82	1.0	0.107
Average distance from the Sun (AU)	0.39	0.72	1	1.52
Time of 1 rotation (Earth hours/days)	58.7 days	243 days	1 day	24.6 hours
Time for 1 revolution (Earth days)	88 days	224.7 days	365.2 days	687 days

The Outer Planets

	Jupiter	Saturn	Uranus	Neptune	Pluto
Diameter (km)	142,984	120,536	51,118	49,528	2,390
Mass (compared to Earth)	318	95	14.5	17.1	0.002
Average distance from the Sun (AU)	5.2	9.58	19.20	30.05	39.24
Time of 1 rotation (Earth hours/days)	9.9 hours	10.7 hours	17.2 hours	16.1 hours	6.4 days
Time for 1 revolution (Earth years)	11.9 years	29.4 years	83.7 years	163.7 years	248.0 years

A Model of the Solar System

The model here shows how the planets are arranged, but it cannot show the relative distances between them.

The solar system covers a huge distance. It is impossible to make a scale drawing of it on regular paper. Look at the table on the next page. The small units of measure help you to understand how the planets compare in size and distance.

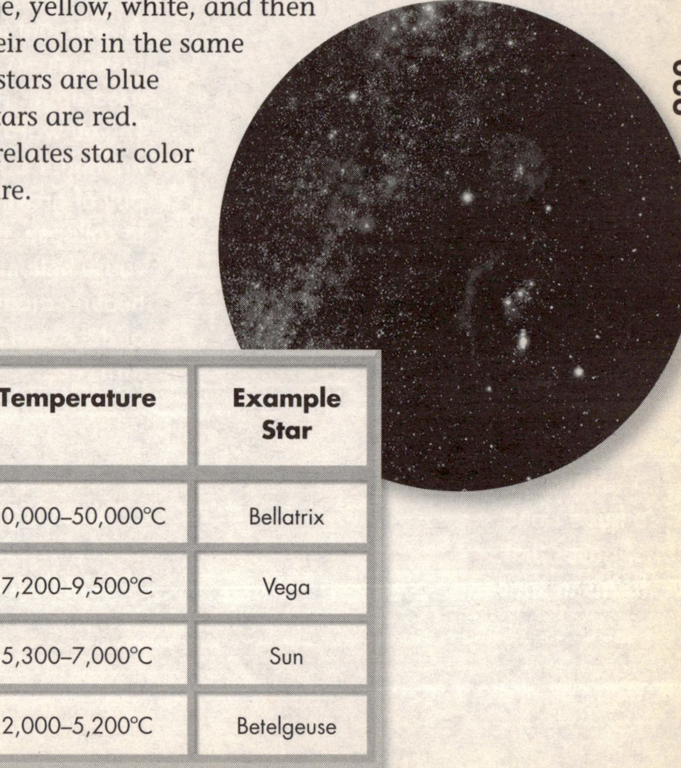

Star Brightness

Some stars appear bright because they are much closer than other stars. However, there are other reasons why stars vary in brightness.

Scientists use the term **magnitude** to describe a star's brightness. The brightness we see from Earth is called apparent magnitude. The brightest star we see is our Sun. It has the greatest apparent magnitude. No other star looks brighter to us. Absolute magnitude measures how bright stars would look if they were all exactly the same distance from Earth. Some stars are as much as 156,250 times brighter than the Sun!

Star Color

Stars appear in different colors. Some stars appear blue, while others seem white or yellow, and a few look red. Star color depends on surface temperature. Think about heating a steel bar. At first it glows red. As it gets hotter, its color changes to orange, yellow, white, and then blue. Stars get their color in the same way. The hottest stars are blue and the coolest stars are red. The chart below relates star color to star temperature.

Star Color	Temperature	Example Star
Blue	10,000–50,000°C	Bellatrix
White	7,200–9,500°C	Vega
Yellow	5,300–7,000°C	Sun
Red	2,000–5,200°C	Betelgeuse

What do we know about stars?

What Stars Are

A **star** is a huge, hot, glowing ball of gas. Stars shine because they produce huge amounts of energy. There is great heat and pressure in the center of a star. This causes the atoms there to bump into each other at very fast speeds. When this happens the nuclei of two or more atoms join, or fuse, into one larger nucleus. This process is called **nuclear fusion.** In this type of fusion, hydrogen nuclei form helium. This gives off huge amounts of energy as radiation. We can see some of this energy as light.

Distances of Stars

Distances in space are too large to describe in units such as kilometers. Even the astronomical unit (AU) is too small to use. Scientists measure distances in space using light-years. A **light-year** is how far light can travel in one year. This is a distance of 9 trillion, 460 billion kilometers. At that speed, light can circle Earth seven times in just one second!

The Sun is the closest star to Earth. The next closest star is Proxima Centauri. It is 4.3 light-years away. Suppose that this star blew up tonight. You would have to wait more than four years to see the flash! Other galaxies and their stars are millions of light-years away. The light you see from them was given off millions of years ago.

By this model, Earth is 1 millimeter in diameter. This is very small. Even at this small size, it needs to be 11.7 meters from a model of the Sun. Now you can see why it is impossible to show the planets to scale in a book. This is true even when we shrink Earth to such a small size.

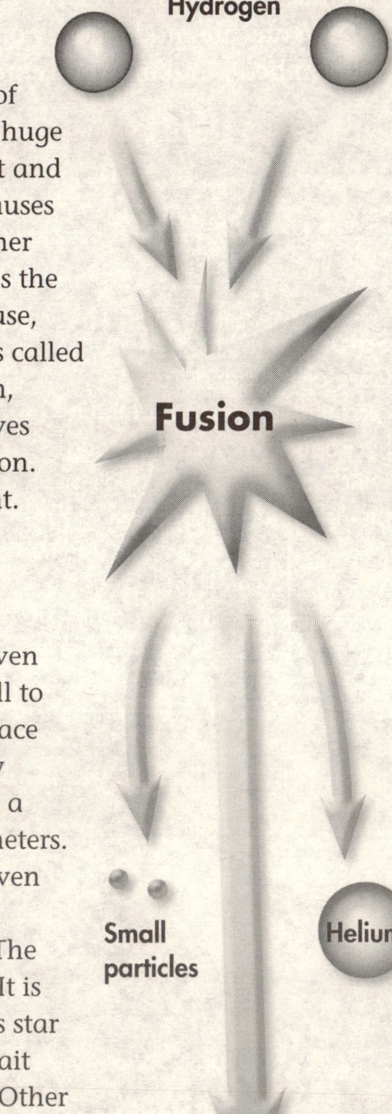

The Solar System: Relative Distances

	Planet	Size (mm)	Distance from Sun (m)
A	Mercury	0.4	4.5
B	Venus	1.0	8.5
C	Earth	1.0	11.7
D	Mars	0.5	17.9
E	Jupiter	11.2	61
F	Saturn	9.5	112
G	Uranus	4.0	225
H	Neptune	3.9	352
I	Pluto	0.2	459

Mars is actually about 4900 kilometers in diameter.

Venus is actually about 100 million kilometers from the Sun.

Why Planets Differ

A planet's distance from the Sun is not the only way in which planets differ. It is true that a planet nearer the Sun gets more sunlight than a planet that is farther away. Mars is about twice as far from the Sun as Venus, and this is one reason that Venus is warmer than Mars. But this is only one factor. Venus, Earth, and Mars were similar when they formed billions of years ago, but each has changed over time.

A planet's size affects how strong its gravity is. Larger planets have stronger forces of gravity than smaller ones. Stronger gravity holds more gases near to the planet, forming a thicker atmosphere. Mars has less gravity than either Venus or Earth, so its atmosphere is very thin. It holds in less heat, making Mars very cold.

People once thought that Venus might be very similar Earth. Both planets are about the same size and mass. Scientists have learned, however, that temperatures on Venus can get as high as 475°C. Its atmospheric pressure is about 100 times that of Earth.

Venus is very different from Earth because the thick clouds that cover Venus are made mostly of carbon dioxide. This gas traps and holds in heat, making Venus much hotter than Earth.

Venus
Mostly rock with craters. Atmosphere of carbon dioxide and sulfuric acid keeps it very hot.

Mars
Covered with red dust. White polar caps. Craters in southern part. Atmosphere mostly carbon dioxide.

Saturn
Core of rock and iron surrounded by ice and liquid hydrogen. Very cold. Strong winds and swirling clouds of ammonia in atmosphere.

Neptune
Possibly covered by liquid hydrogen and helium. Mostly hydrogen and helium gas in atmosphere. Appears pale blue.

Earth
Mostly water-covered. Only known planet with an atmosphere to support life.

Mercury
Rocky with craters. Extreme temperatures. Traces of hydrogen and helium in atmosphere.

Jupiter
Covered by liquid hydrogen. Very cold. Atmosphere mostly hydrogen with clouds of ammonia crystals.

Uranus
Composed mostly of hydrogen and helium gases. Very cold. Appears green.

Pluto
Frozen methane and ice. Small amounts of methane gas. Ice cap at north pole.

Space and Technology

Technology

by Martin E. Lee

233

Genre	Comprehension Skill	Text Features	Science Content
Nonfiction	Main Idea and Details	• Captions • Charts • Diagrams • Glossary	Technology

Scott Foresman Science 6.21

ISBN 0-328-14030-9

90000

9 780328 140305

What did you learn?

1. What two things must a machine be able to do in order to be called a robot?

2. How has computer technology led to advances in robotics?

3. What is nanotechnology?

4. **Writing** in Science Robots can do many jobs that people once did. Write to explain how robots are better at some kinds of jobs than human workers are. Include details from the book to support your answer.

5. **Main Idea and Details** Explain how an autonomous robot solves problems.

Illustrations: 14–15 Tony Randazzo
Photographs: Every effort has been made to secure permission and provide appropriate credit for photographic material. The publisher deeply regrets any omission and pledges to correct errors called to its attention in subsequent editions. Unless otherwise acknowledged, all photographs are the property of Scott Foresman, a division of Pearson Education. Photo locators denoted as follows: Top (T), Center (C), Bottom (B), Left (L), Right (R), Background (Bkgd).
Title Page: ©Toshiyuki Aizawa/Reuters/Corbis; 3 ©Wolfgang Rattay/Reuters/Corbis; 4 (T) ©Topical Press Agency/Getty Images, (C) ©Haruyoshi Yamaguchi/Corbis, (CR) Courtesy of Computer History Museum; 5 (TR) ©Bettmann/Corbis, (C, BR) ©JPL/NASA, (BL) ©Carnegie Mellon University; 6 (BL) ©Peter Menzel/ Stock Boston; 7 ©Peter Yates/Corbis; 8 ©ARC/NASA; 9 ©Mark Sykes/Photo Researchers, Inc.; 10 ©Issei Kato/Reuters/Landov, LLC; 11 ©Toshiyuki Aizawa/Reuters/Corbis; 12 Courtesy IBM Corporation

ISBN: 0-328-14030-9

Glossary

autonomous robot — a robot that acts without direct supervision

carbon nanotube — a carbon molecule whose atoms are in six-sided rings in the shape of a tube

industrial robot — a type of robot designed to handle several products or items at a time, or programmed to complete several different tasks

nanotechnology — the very small-scale technology of materials and processes measured in nanometers

robot — a machine that is able to get information from its surroundings and do physical work

robotics — the technology of the design, construction, and operation of robots

Technology

by Martin E. Lee

What is a robot?

Robots and Robotics

You probably know the figures on these pages as robots. But it is hard to define what a robot is. That's because there are so many different types of robots that do so many different tasks. Most scientists define **robot** as a machine that can get information from its surroundings and perform physical work.

Many robots do not look anything like these ones. Robots that do different tasks have different appearances. Robots can do jobs that are too dangerous or boring for humans. They can make very accurate and exact movements. And they will do them over and over!

Benefits and Risks

Nanotechnology may hold many benefits for the future. It may improve farming and manufacturing. It may help us fight diseases. But there could also be risks. Will the new molecules hurt the environment? Will they harm our health? Will they invade our privacy? Only time will tell whether gains from the new technology will be worth the risks.

Technology can improve our lives. Robots and robotic devices change how we work, play, and live. The new science of nanotechnology advances daily as scientists learn more about it.

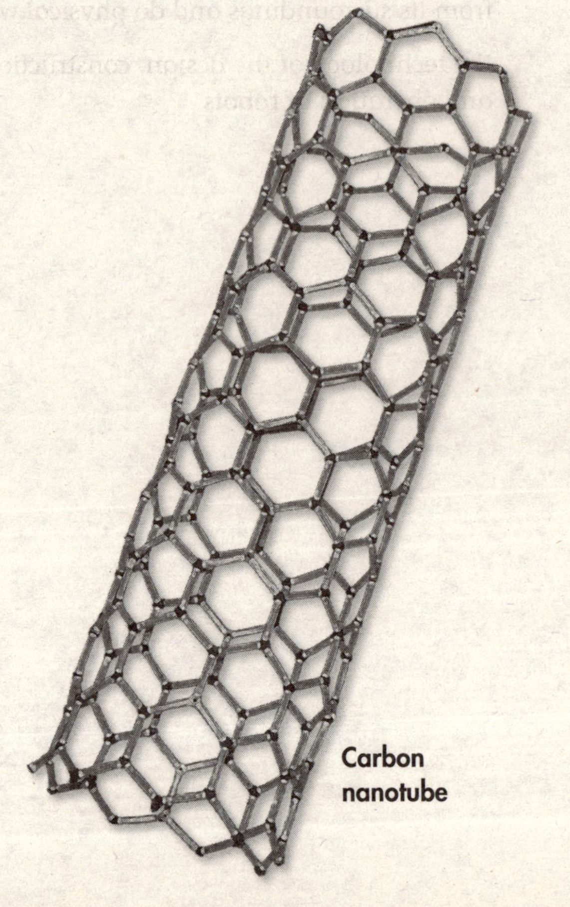

Carbon nanotube

Carbon Nanotubes

Scientists have long known that carbon comes in three forms. These forms are diamond, graphite, and "amorphous" carbon. In 1985 scientists found a fourth form. It is called a buckyball. Look at the diagram to see this special carbon molecule.

In 1991, scientists found a fifth type of carbon. A **carbon nanotube** molecule has atoms arranged in six-sided rings in the shape of a tube. This molecule is about one nanometer in size.

Diamonds have different properties than graphite has. The properties of carbon nanotubes are also different. Carbon nanotubes are very stiff. They can be one hundred times tougher than steel at only one-sixth the weight!

Carbon nanotubes have amazing electrical properties. They can conduct electricity as efficiently as copper. They can also be changed to conduct electricity less efficiently, like silicon. They can conduct heat better than silicon can. Silicon is used to make computers and transistors. We may one day be able to make very small electronic devices using carbon nanotubes.

Robots can work 24 hours a day, 7 days a week. Robots working in car factories can put parts together and weld them in place. Robots in bakeries can draw thin stripes of icing on cookies. They work in hospitals helping doctors perform operations. Robots can even work at home. Household robots can do jobs such as cleaning floors or mowing lawns.

Robots are part of a technological field called robotics. **Robotics** is the science of the design, construction, and operation of robots.

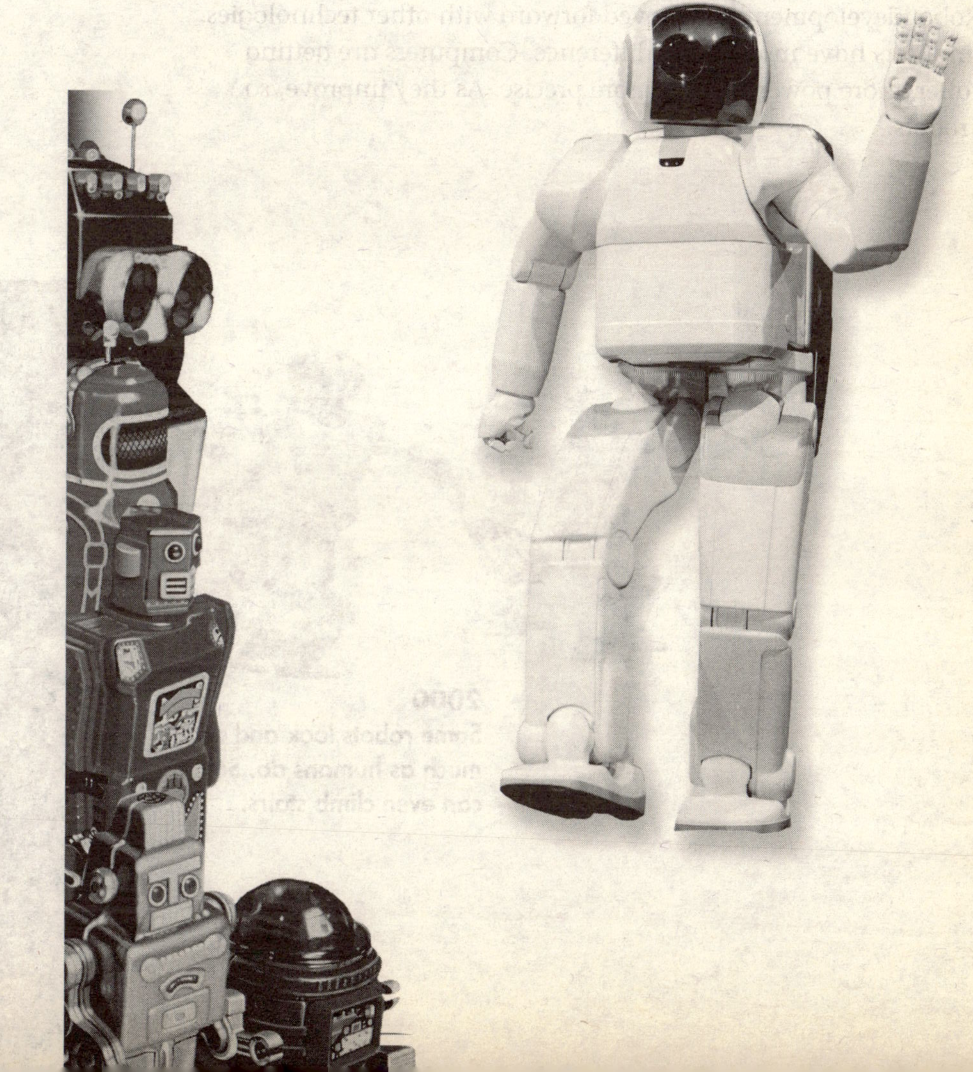

237

Robot Development

Many people remember robots they have seen in movies or on television. These made-up machines gave us ideas about how robots should look and what they could do. Fictional robots existed long before we built real ones. The desire to build real robots that could perform real tasks led to advances in science.

The term *robot* is less than one hundred years old. But people have thought about robots for thousands of years. In ancient Greece, Aristotle thought that one day machines might be able to do work for humans. Two thousand years later, that idea has become a reality. Robots work in nearly all areas of our lives.

Robot development has moved forward with other technologies. Computers have made a big difference. Computers are getting smaller, more powerful, and more precise. As they improve, so do robots.

2000
Some robots look and act much as humans do. Some can even climb stairs.

Nanotechnology Applications

Scientists have not yet built many things atom-by-atom. However, they have changed certain molecules called nanopores. Nanopores can act like sponges, soaking up mercury or lead from polluted water.

Nanoshells may help to fight cancer. Each is about 120 nanometers in size. That is 1,500 times smaller than a strand of hair! Nanoshells are put into a tumor in the body. They are then used to heat the tumor. Temperatures in the tumor are raised high enough to kill the cancer, but they do not harm the cells around it. Nanoshells may also be used to deliver strong cancer drugs to specific cells. These drugs can harm normal body cells as well as cancer cells. Using nanoshells would save more healthy cells.

Another medical use of nanotechnology involves nanocrystals. These crystals give off certain colors of light. Scientists can use nanocrystals to identify chromosomes. Then they shine light on a blood sample to see how the nanocrystals glow. They can use the results to tell how likely a person is to get lung cancer.

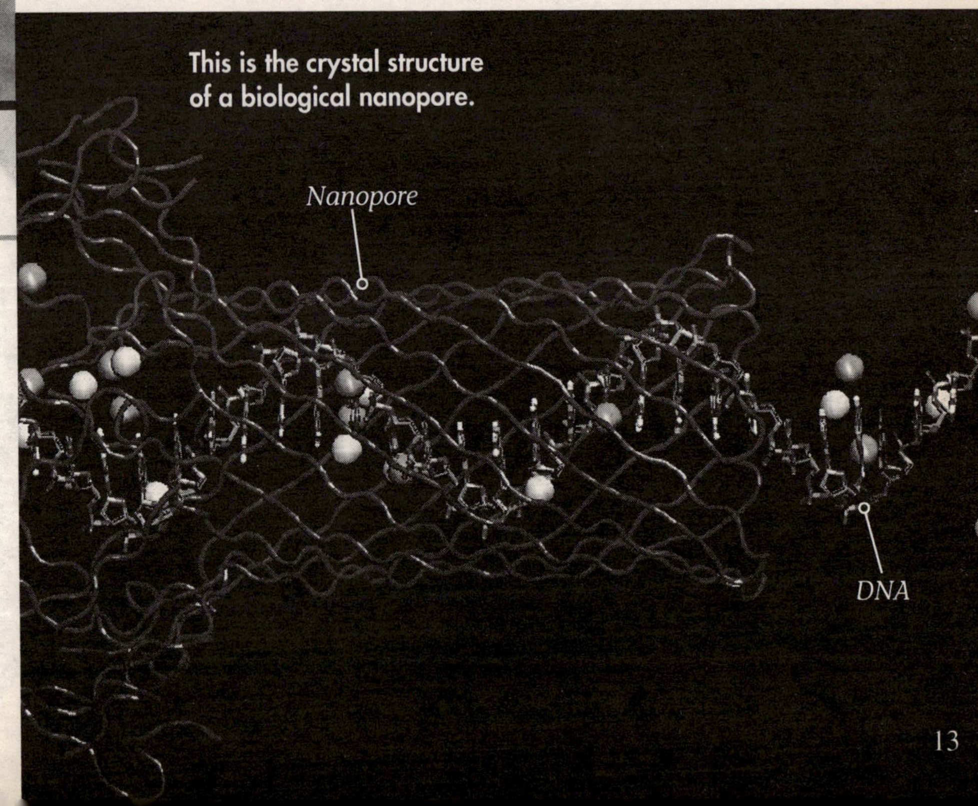

This is the crystal structure of a biological nanopore.

What is nanotechnology?

Very, Very Small Technology

Nanotechnology is very small-scale technology that deals with materials and processes on a scaled best measured in nanometers. A nanometer is a tiny unit of length. One nanometer equals one-billionth of a meter.

Researchers say that nanotechnology will let us build materials atom by atom. Scientists hope to line up atoms in a specific way to form certain shapes. Does this seem possible to you? Well, it has already been done! In 1990, researchers were able to move 35 xenon atoms, one at a time. They shaped them into three letters. Can you read them?

The cost of using nanotechnology to make new products should not be much more than the cost of the raw materials and energy used. This new technology is on its way. But scientists must find ways to move an atom to place it precisely, and to pick and position billions of atoms. Robots could help.

Engineers created these three letters with exactly 35 atoms.

1739
Jacques Vaucanson creates an automatic duck. It can drink, eat, and perform other functions.

1951
The Atomic Energy Commission uses the first automated arm that can bend. It handles dangerous radioactive materials.

1970
Shakey is the first moving robot that can "see." It can get around obstacles.

270 B.C.
Greek engineer Ctesibus builds organs and water clocks with movable figures.

1939–1940
A mechanical man and dog appear at the New York World's Fair.

1961
The first industrial robot begins work in an automobile factory.

1985
The first robot-aided surgery is performed.

2004
NASA's rovers *Spirit* and *Opportunity* land on Mars.

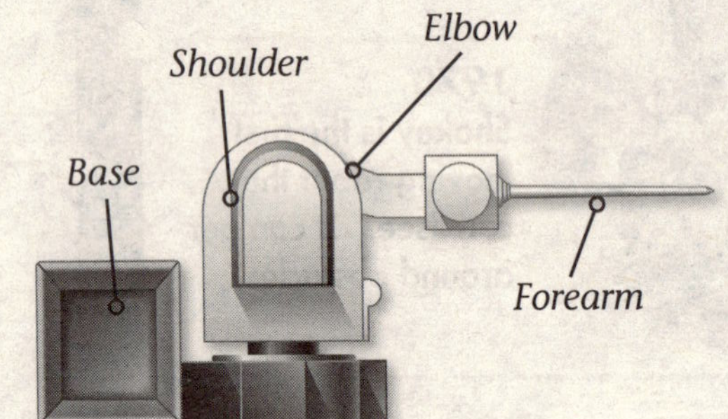

Robots in Industry

Almost 90 percent of robots today work in factories. More than half of them are found in car factories. Robot arms can weld, paint, put together, test, and pack parts. An **industrial robot** can handle several products or items at a time. It can be programmed to do several different tasks.

The robotic arm is the most common type of robot used in industry. Many industrial robots have joints that bend as a human arm does. A robotic arm may have a shoulder, an arm, and a wrist. A human arm can pivot in seven ways. Most robotic arms can pivot in six different ways.

Different parts attached to a robotic arm allow the arm to do specific tasks. The robotic hands below can be attached to a robotic arm to turn a bolt. Other devices, such as screwdrivers, drills, or spray painters can also be attached to a robotic arm.

A Mechanical Arm

Robots are here to stay. New robots will be able to perform new and more complex tasks. They will need less and less human control. They will be used by universities, research firms, and government agencies.

Today's robots do specific tasks. But a bigger goal is to make a universal robot. It would be able to do almost anything a person could do.

This robot is a remote controlled rover that plays games.

Robots at Home

You may not have to travel far to see robots at work. You can see robots compete on television. Toy makers sell kits that let people build different kinds of robots. You may have seen cute furry robots such as robotic cats. These are for enjoyment and fun. They have been so popular that researchers are trying to make doll-like robots. These robots will be able to do many things on their own.

Some companies have plans to make robots into household companions. One such robot would move around the house easily. It could help with daily tasks such as taking out the trash. Maybe a robot could be programmed to care for older or less able people. It could watch out for a person. If anything went wrong, the robot could call for help.

Many robots are used for welding. A welding robot has three arm movements and three wrist movements. It also has position sensors. The sensors make it possible to "teach" the robot how to weld. A worker leads the robot through the actions required to weld a specific spot. Sensors on the robot record the different movements it makes. The robot's computer saves this data. Then the robot arm can repeat the motions exactly.

This same process is used when robots make computers. Robots "learn" to attach silicon chips onto printed circuit boards. Robots can be "taught" to do other things too. They can learn to pick up a muffin from a conveyor belt. Then they can put that muffin into a box on another belt.

Can you see the elbow on this welding robot? It lets the robot use the welding torch almost as a person would.

A Robotic Pet

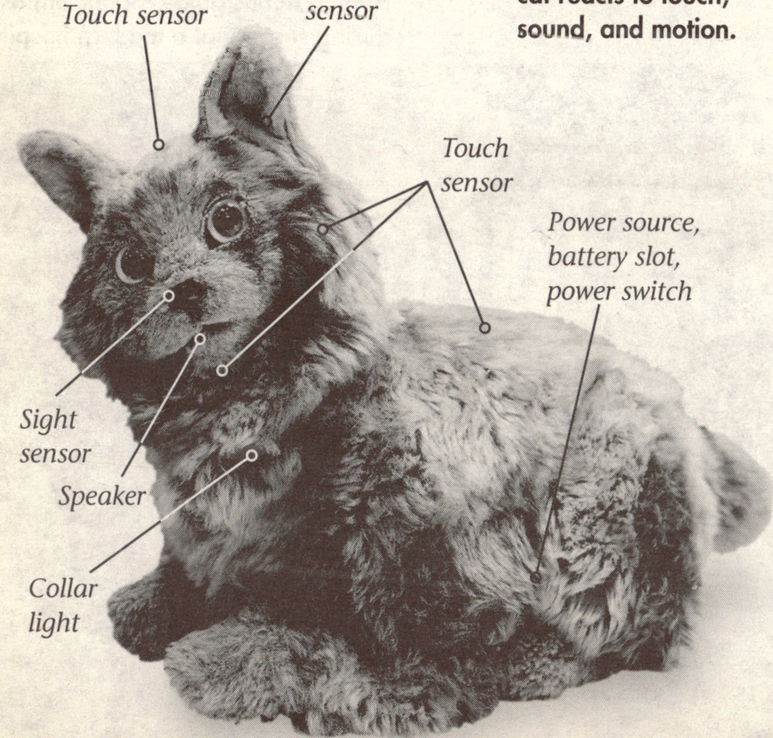

Exploring with Robots

Many robots are used in exploration. One type of robot is the remotely operated vehicle, also called the ROV or rover. NASA's Mars missions have used the rovers *Sojourner, Spirit,* and *Opportunity.* For these missions, an operator on Earth chose the speed and the direction of the rover. The operator also sent signals to the rover for each move it should make.

Rovers can do jobs and go places that are not safe for people. They can search sewers, heating pipes, and collapsed mines. They can defuse bombs and go into areas polluted by radioactive waste.

Another type of robot runs itself. An **autonomous robot** acts without direct command. It can "decide" what to do. NASA is developing an autonomous robot called the Personal Satellite Assistant, or PSA. It is about the size of a softball. It has sensors to gather data. The PSA will be able to move through a spacecraft on its own. It will be extra "eyes, ears, and nose" for the human crew.

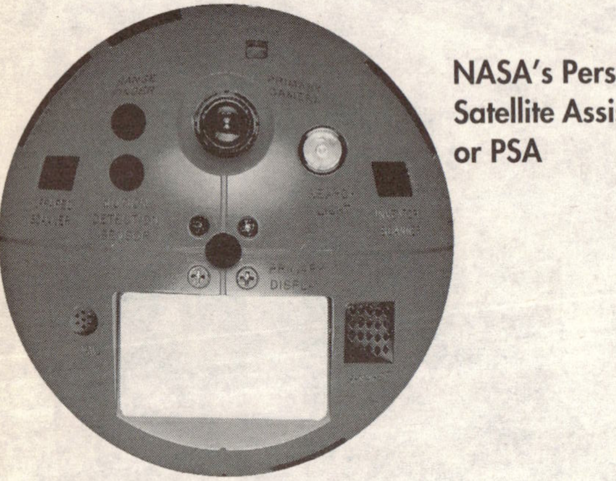

NASA's Personal Satellite Assistant, or PSA

Robots in Medicine

Robots are good at going back and forth between locations. This helps in hospitals. They can carry supplies and medicine. They can also carry equipment.

Many hospitals around the world use robotic surgeons. These are robotic hands moved by a human surgeon. Human hands cannot always be as exact as robotic hands. Robotic surgery has led to smaller scars, less pain, and shorter hospital stays.

One robotic system has the doctor sitting at a control center. The patient lies nearby. A tiny camera put inside the patient sends pictures of the operation site. The doctor uses tools to move the surgical equipment.

Robots can be used as teaching tools too! They act as patients for medical students. The robots are programmed to show different symptoms. Then they respond to treatment given by the students. Some robots "die" if they get the wrong treatment or care.

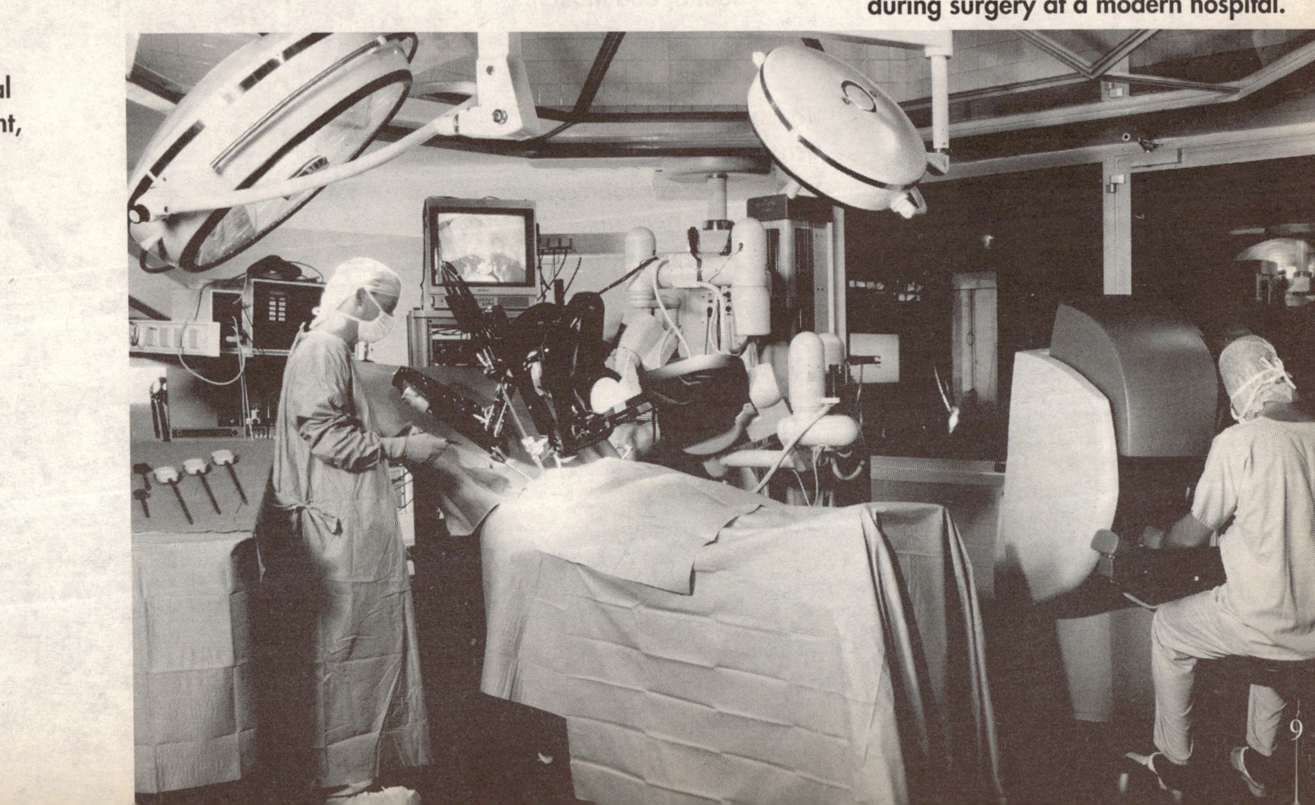

Human hands guide robotic hands during surgery at a modern hospital.